IMAGES
of America

AROUND PUNXSUTAWNEY

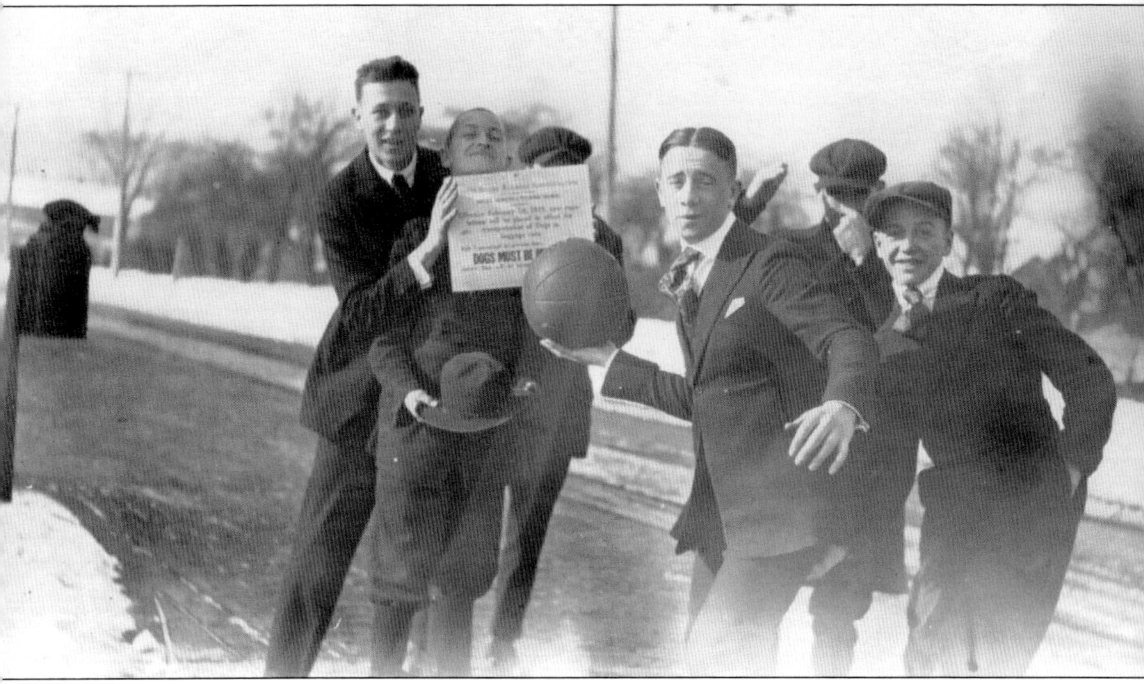

A group of lads enjoys a trek along the road, *c.* 1919. They apparently derive much merriment from being together. A basketball game is in the works. The newspaper date is February 1, and the headlines mention curbing dogs. Note the dress code. Knicker trousers were common early in the century.

IMAGES
of America

AROUND PUNXSUTAWNEY

Sr. Anne Frances Pulling

ARCADIA
PUBLISHING

ISBN 978-0-7385-0530-5

Published by Arcadia Publishing
Charleston, South Carolina

Printed in the United States of America

Library of Congress Catalog Card Number: 00-110237

For all general information contact Arcadia Publishing at:
Telephone 843-853-2070
Fax 843-853-0044
E-mail sales@arcadiapublishing.com
For customer service and orders:
Toll-Free 1-888-313-2665

Visit us on the Internet at www.arcadiapublishing.com

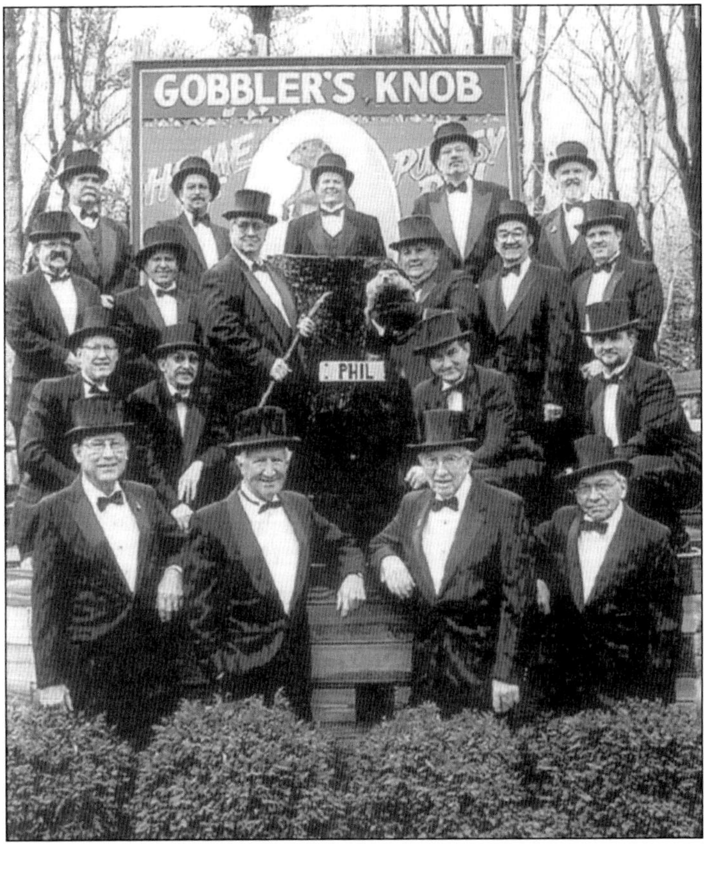

Burrowing through time brings us to the members of the Groundhog Club's Inner Circle. These include, from left to right, the following: (first row) Rusty Johnson, Bud Dunkel, Bob Chambers, and Jim Means; (second row) Bill Anderson, Ron Ploucha, Jeff Lundy, and John Griffiths; (third row) Butch Philliber, Bob Roberts, Bill Cooper, Bill Deeley (holding Phil), Bill Roberts, and Keith Shields; (fourth row) Barney Stockdale, Chris Lash, Steve Means, Ed Jekielek, and Mike Johnson.

Contents

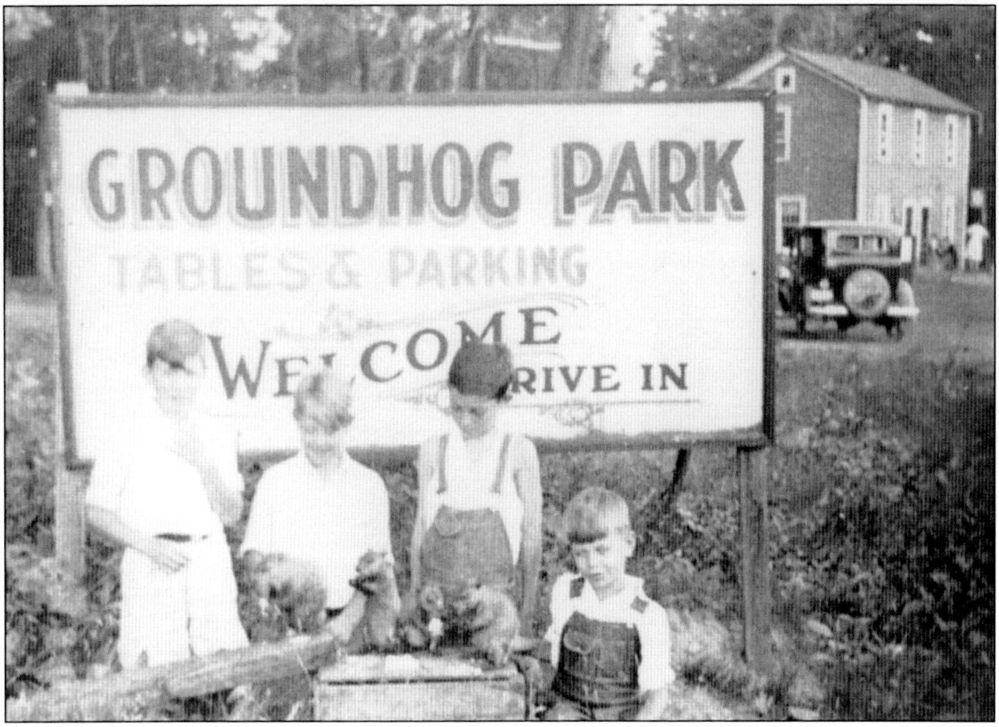

Four future members of the Groundhog Club's Inner Circle observe baby woodchucks at Groundhog Park. This site has long been an attraction for young and old alike. The park, located on the Indiana Road, gave children hands-on experience with young groundhogs.

Acknowledgments

This publication is based on research, records, documents, newspapers, and interviews with townsfolk, many of whom generously supplied information and offered constructive suggestions. A special thank-you goes to the Punxsutawney Historical and Genealogical Society for sharing so many images along with their wealth of knowledge and to the White Studios for the role they played in preserving many scenes of yesteryear. A word of gratitude to the Punxsutawney Public Library, the *Spirit* newspaper, William Scott, the Punxsutawney Borough Office, William and Jessie Anderson of *Hometown Punxsutawney*, Saints Cosmas and Damian Parish, Indiana University at Punxsutawney, Peg Ragley, Kathleen Nikolishen, and Naomi Brennan, without whose help this work could not have been accomplished. A special thanks to William and Jean Deeley for their generous help and encouragement and to Mary Molinare and Paul Farcus for their valuable information and assistance in this project.

A prayerful gratitude goes to all who assisted in any way by supplying photographs, constructive suggestions, proofreading, and so forth. It is because of your gracious preservation of Punxsutawney history that we bridge a gap between past and future. I am especially grateful to my own religious community, the Sisters of Mercy of the Dallas Regional Community for their support and encouragement in this project.

INTRODUCTION

Punxsutawney, a picturesque little settlement nestled in the Mahoning Valley of western Pennsylvania, gained worldwide prominence as the weather capital of the world. The tradition began when German settlers brought a legendary custom from the Old World that was absorbed into our American culture.

The groundhog idea took root gradually. Over the years, crowds became larger as publicity became more extensive. A few members of the Groundhog Club immortalized the saga. *Punxsutawney Spirit* editor Clymer Freas set the stage through his newspaper articles. Dr. Francis Lorenzo arranged transportation to bring dignitaries from Pittsburgh and other cities to witness Groundhog Day. Lorenzo spread the word through gatherings at his spacious mansion and generated interest in the news media and general public.

Gobbler's Knob was designated as the site where Punxsutawney Phil would make his annual prognostications. Samuel Light introduced the Inner Circle with its specific dress code befitting nobility. The Inner Circle is a group of 15 dedicated businessmen with a keen interest in promoting and maintaining the tradition of the groundhog. They form the executive branch of the Groundhog Club. The entire town is geared toward its most famous resident. While all the townsfolk are celebrating, the furry celebrant is usually snoozing in his burrow in Groundhog Zoo. However, Punxsutawney had a life before Phil the groundhog made the town internationally known.

Mahoning Creek meanders through the area, creating a charming village. Fed by streams east of Big Run, the creek flows through Punxsutawney and on down to the Allegheny River in Pittsburgh. It was in this setting that Native Americans first realized the area was invaded by annoying "ponks," or sand flies. The town derived its name from this phrase.

The earliest white settlers recognized potential in a town with a flowing creek. In 1790, the Holland Land Company purchased most of the land. In 1814, Jacob Hoover settled in Punxsutawney. David Barclay built a log cabin here in 1818. Gristmills and sawmills sprang up, and agriculture became the economic base of the early settlers. Rev. Daniel Barclay laid the town out in squares and designated a site in the center as the Public Square. That location continues to hold its original status. Rafting and lumbering businesses were established, and the little town in the valley was well on its way to becoming a hub of activity.

Punxsutawney is surrounded by coal fields. Big Run, Adrain, Walston Rossiter, Valier, Anita, and Frostburg were all local coal mining settlements that were serviced by the rising industrial trade center. Immigrants from many countries found employment in the coal fields bordering

Punxsutawney as it grew into the largest industrial center in Jefferson County. The ironworks sprang up early in the 19th century, followed by wool, silk, and hoop mills. The brick works, planing mills, breweries, and a host of hotels populated the town.

A foundry, various markets, and specialty stores lined the old Chinklamoose Trail, later known as Mahoning Street. Punxsutawney flourished as a trade and service center for mining communities. Industry continued to expand. Jean White Studios, the firm responsible for many of the images in this book, was established in 1897. Jefferson Theatre introduced talking motion pictures after it replaced the old opera house. This drew crowds from nearby settlements. Bridges were forged across Mahoning Creek, and the earliest hospitals were established to serve the miners.

Nearby Walston boasted a nightly glow in the sky from its 700 coke ovens. These formed the largest string of such ovens in the world. Punxsutawney was long the hub of commercial activity. It was the shopping center, the financial center, and the business center. Industry was prevalent and the town grew. The economy was good, and commerce was excellent. The townsfolk developed a sense of neighborliness and cordiality among themselves. They were very amicable even before their little town took on a prestigious and notable place in history. It was this amiable manner that created the clannish spirit they would exhibit later with the Groundhog Festivals, Old Home Weeks, and parades. Punxsutawneyites love to celebrate. They love good times and know how to create them. They love working together. The spirit of camaraderie is strong among the people.

Punxsutawney was a quiet, close-knit community, bustling with trade and commerce when a legend was initiated that would give it an unique place in history. The town became an illustrious and notable site as the weather capital of the world. The custom derived from the Roman legions of old who brought this practice to the Germans. They concluded that if the hedgehog cast a shadow on February 2, Candlemas Day, there would be six more weeks of winter. Our early settlers chose the groundhog in the absence of the hedgehog. The groundhog was considered intelligent, sensible, and wise. The first official weather forecasting took place in Punxsutawney in 1887.

Punxsutawneyites have nurtured and defended the groundhog legend. They are firm in their assertions that the tradition belongs specifically to them. It sets the town apart and makes it unique. It is a legend that transcends centuries and cultures. Traditions such as this tie our present to our distant past, when nature more readily influenced our lives.

Groundhog Day is designed to be a pause in midwinter for fun, diversion, and festivity. Gobbler's Knob sets the stage for an intermingling of drama, myth, and reality. For more than a century, the groundhog has given Punxsutawney more publicity for fun than any other community of its size in the nation.

Every year on February 2, thousands of people from all over the world and from all walks of life gather at Gobbler's Knob. Frigid air and zero temperatures cannot chill the enthusiastic crowds. The pageantry and festivities compensate for any trace of cold weather. The crowds cheer as they watch Phil emerge from his burrow. This event is a dramatic production starring Punxsutawney's perennial prognosticator.

One

LAND OF A LEGEND

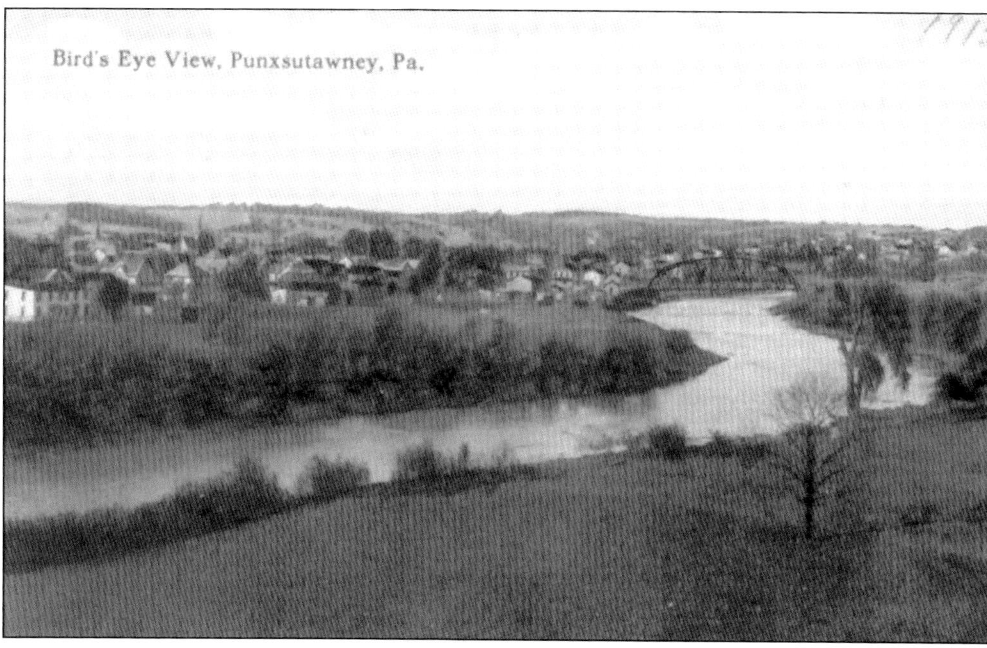

Punxsutawney was founded by Native Americans. The word means "sand fly," or in their language, *ponk*. They called it Ponksutenink, the place of ponks, because these pesky flies were a source of annoyance. Mobachun Creek made its way through the settlement and was responsible for the flies; however, many industries capitalized on the creek. Later named Mahoning Creek, it provided a waterway for the early industries, beginning with the logging and rafting businesses.

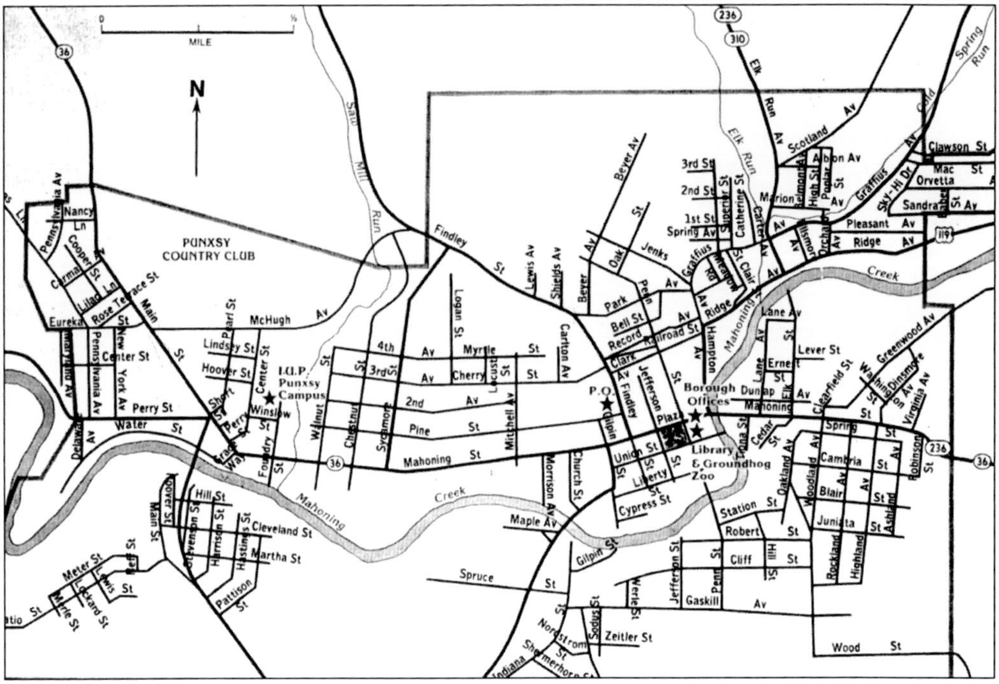

In the 1790s, the Holland Land Company, formed by a group of Dutchmen, bought land in what is now Punxsutawney. The first white settler was Elijah Graham, who arrived in 1797. In 1814, Jacob Hoover settled in Clayville, now the west end. He constructed a gristmill and built a dam across Saw Mill Run in order to obtain power. This action began industry in Punxsutawney. The town had not yet become a legend.

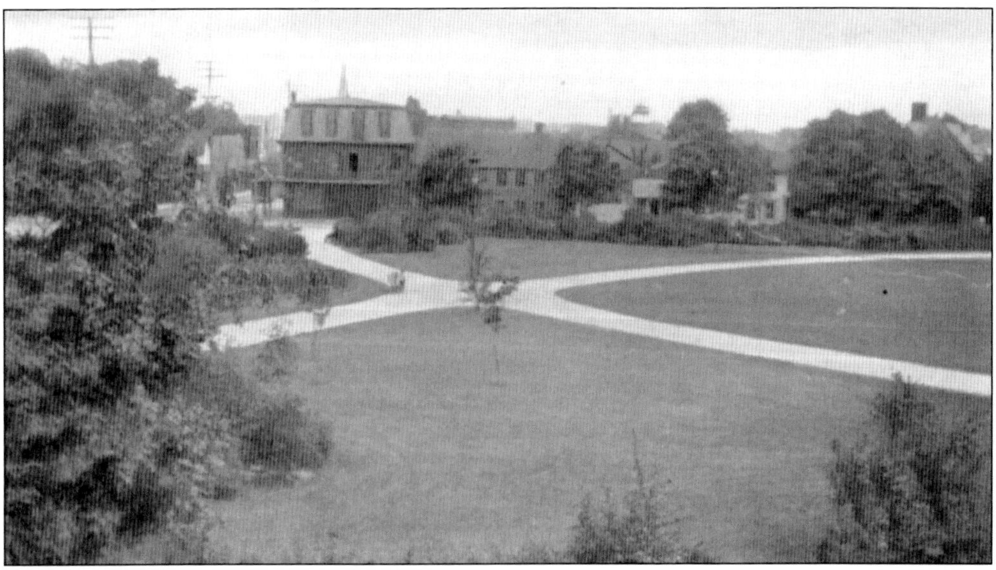

In 1816, Rev. Daniel Barclay and Abraham Weaver built log cabins and established farms. This began the economic basis of the town. Barclay constructed a gristmill on Elk Run, north of town. He, with Dr. John Jenks, owned most of the land that now comprises Punxsutawney. Barclay laid out 327 acres of the original site into eight squares. One square in the center of town was designated for public use. It was long known as the Public Square.

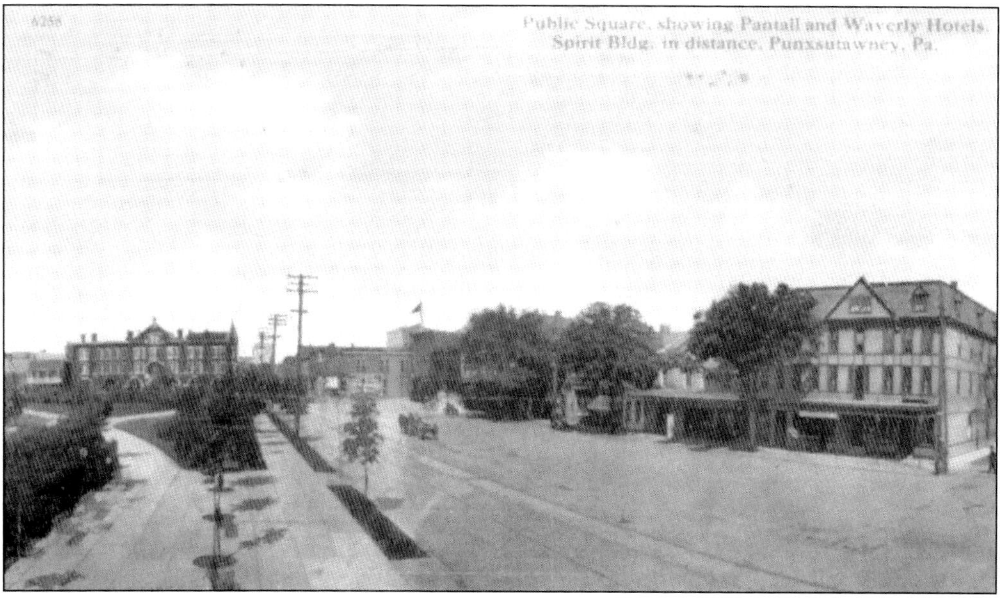

The Pantall Hotel, on the left, was established on Mahoning Street in 1888. Theo Pantall created a charming building complete with an authentic Victorian bar. The brick building was constructed from 1,200 perch stones and 1 million bricks. There was provision to accommodate the horses of the guests. Legend says that in the hotel's early days, area merchants and New York dealers bought and sold diamonds at the bar. The Waverly Hotel is on the right.

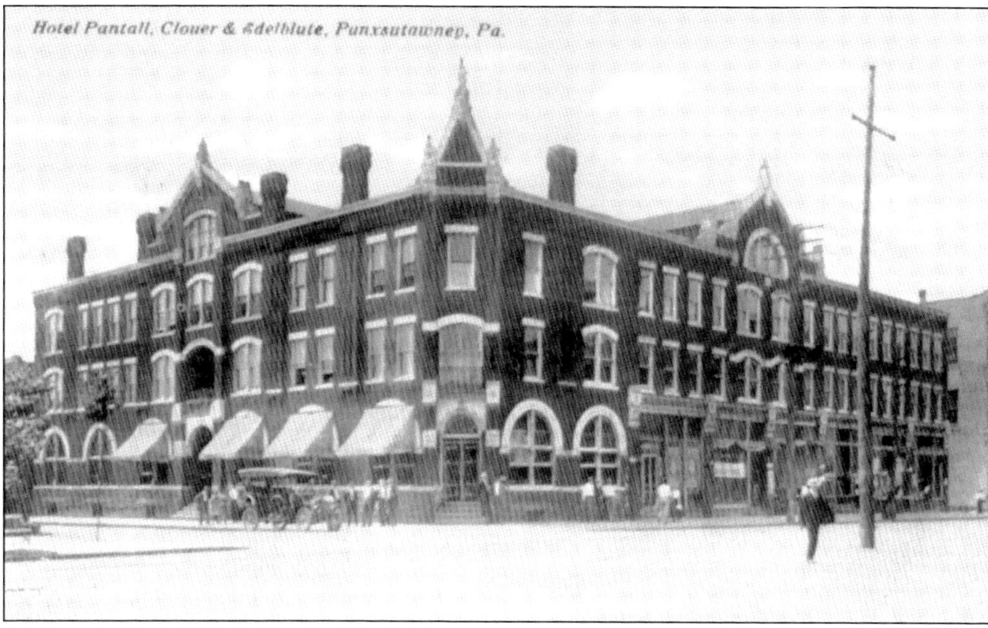

The Pantall Hotel is the showplace of the town. The site was originally occupied by the home of Charles R. Barclay in 1820. It passed through several hands before becoming a hotel. It was the Mahoning House and later the Jenning House. In 1868, the original building was destroyed by fire. Theo Pantall then bought the property and erected the three-story, red-brick edifice on the corner of Mahoning and Jefferson Streets. Mahoning Street is to the right. The historic hotel remains a Punxsutawney landmark.

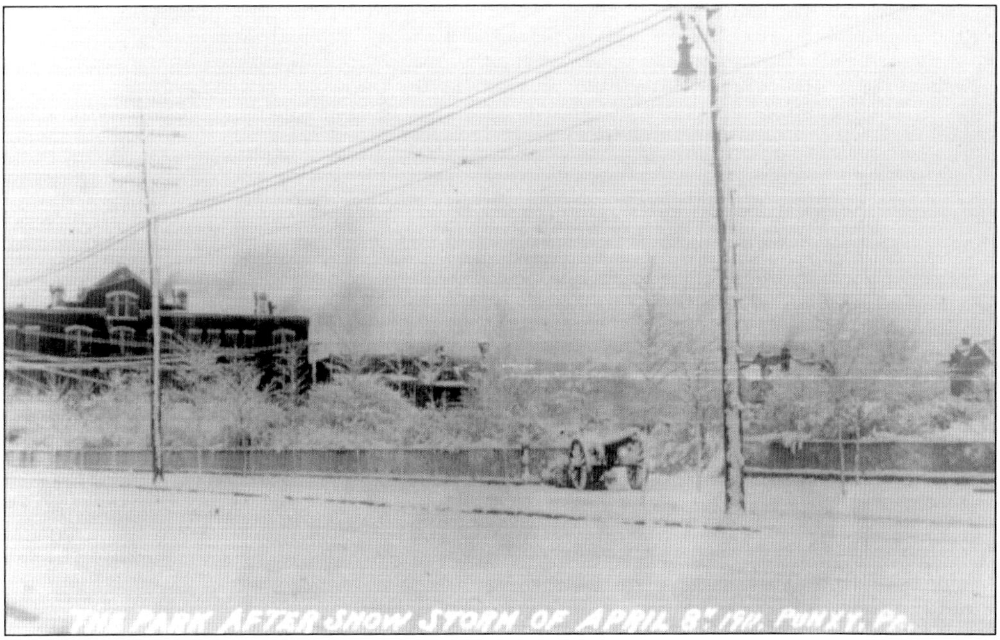

The Public Square, later Barclay Square, is cloaked in snow after the blizzard of April 8, 1911. The Pantall Hotel rises on the left. Note the cannon in the foreground. Daniel Barclay, a Presbyterian minister, relocated here in 1819 and built a log cabin on the northeast corner of Mahoning and Front Streets. He and his son-in-law, John Jenks, went into the mercantile business. Barclay was instrumental in establishing schools in Punxsutawney.

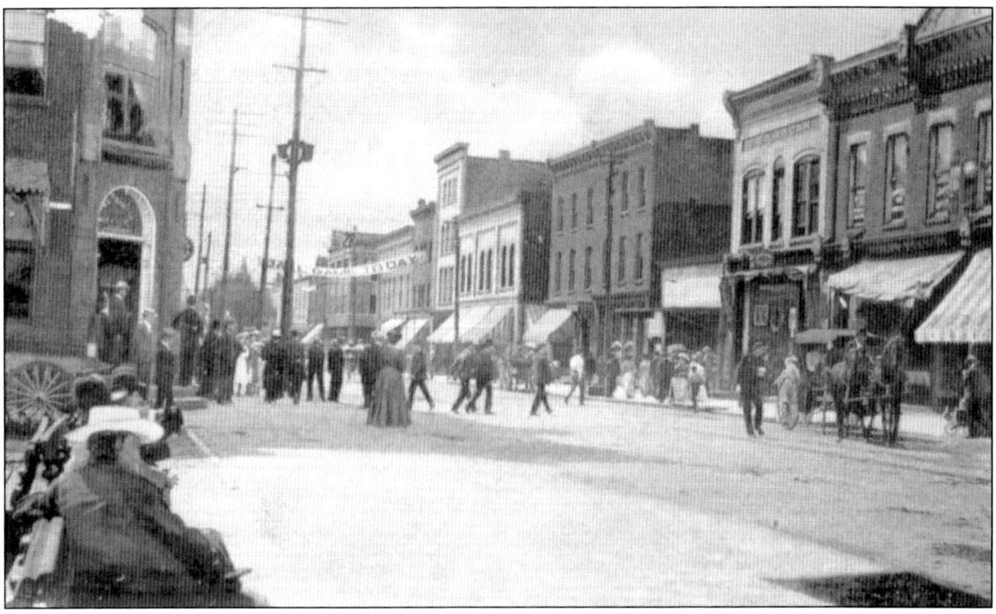

Looking west along Mahoning Street affords a glimpse of industry on the rise. From his vantage point on the bench, a gentleman watches the shoppers hustle about. The patrons of the Pantall Hotel read the sign strung across the street: "Ballgame Today." This game would be played in nearby Barclay Square. The J.E. Langan Building is the second from the right.

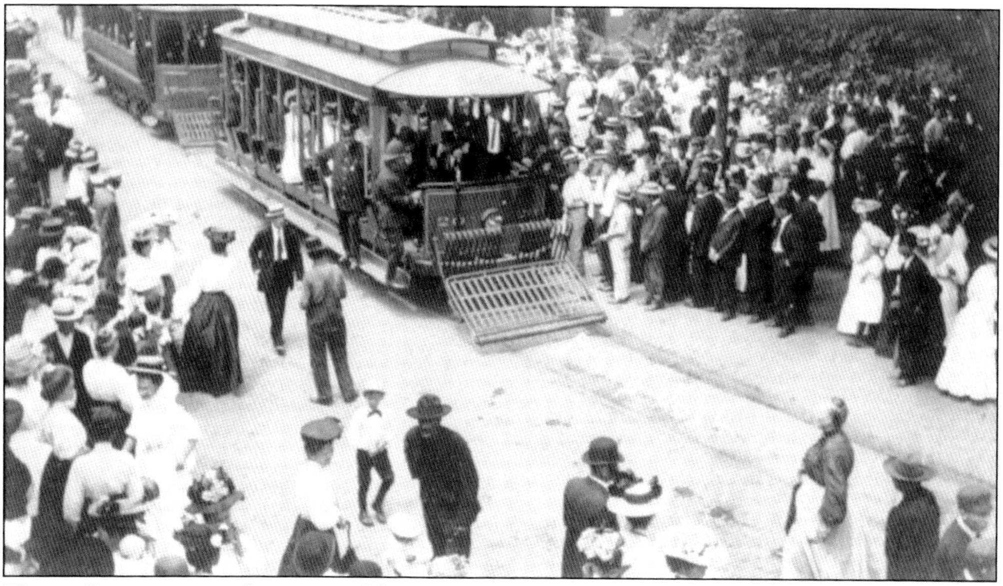

The trolley arrives at the scene of festive activity. It brings crowds to the annual Groundhog Festival, which lasts for one week each summer. Special events have been featured through the years. Streetcars began operation in 1892. Local businessmen chartered the Punxsutawney Passenger and Railway Company to run a 1.6-mile trolley line to Claysville, which is now the western end of town. In the first year of operation, 497 passengers availed themselves the opportunity to ride the trolley at 5¢ each.

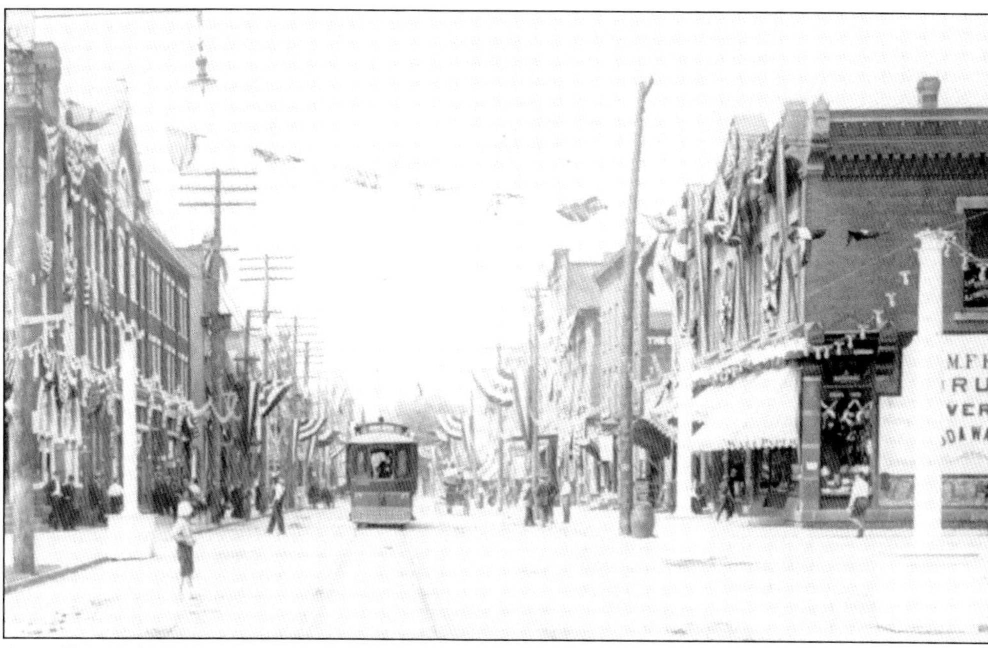

A trolley makes its way east on Mahoning Street amid an array of decorative shops. Bunting, banners, and flags beautify Mahoning Street, the route of the trolley and the parade. Note the streetlight in the upper left. Streetlights were installed when electricity came to Punxsutawney, making the former gaslights look pale. By 1890, an electrical plant was in operation.

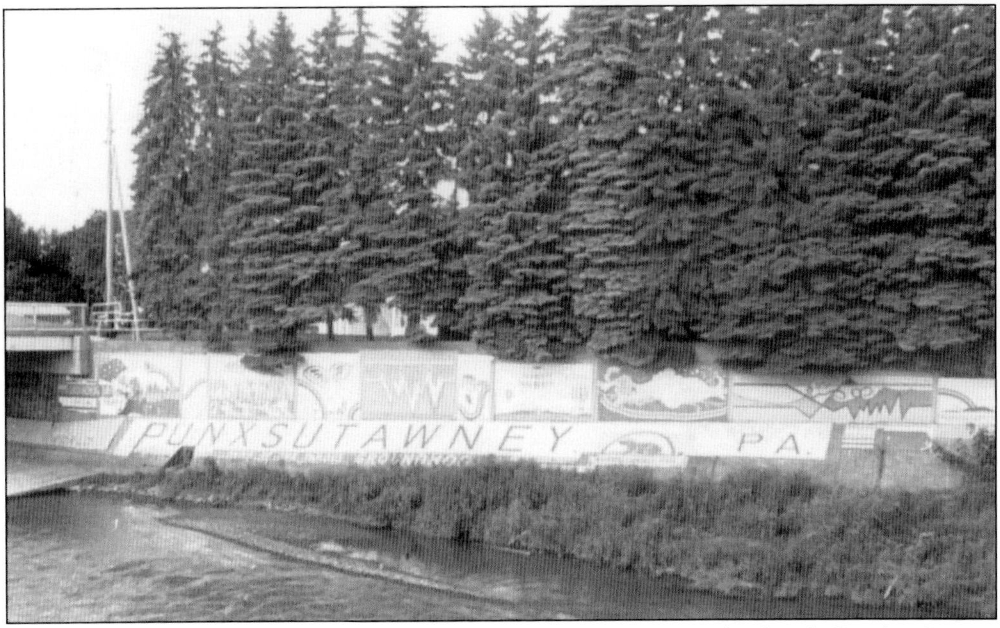

Punxsutawney Creek ripples beneath the East Mahoning Street Bridge beside Barclay Square. The dike displays the artwork of the high school students of 1990. The printing on the side of the creek affirms the town as the home of the famous groundhog. The narrow, 30-mile-long creek that winds its way through Punxsutawney has made an outstanding impact on the area. The creek is formed from several streams above Big Run and flows into the Allegheny River beyond Kittanning, Pennsylvania.

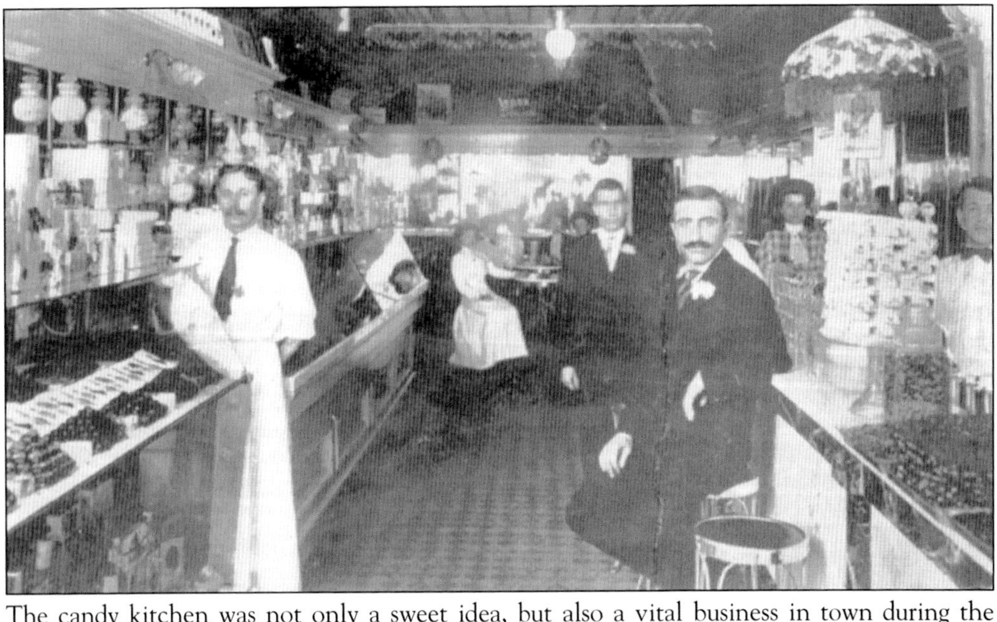

The candy kitchen was not only a sweet idea, but also a vital business in town during the post-Depression era. Barletta's Palace of Sweets was founded in 1920 by Peter Barletta. Sweets initially included candy and ice cream. It was an era just before wrapped penny candy became common. Most candy was homemade at that time. Barletta's of Punxsutawney was also in the grocery business.

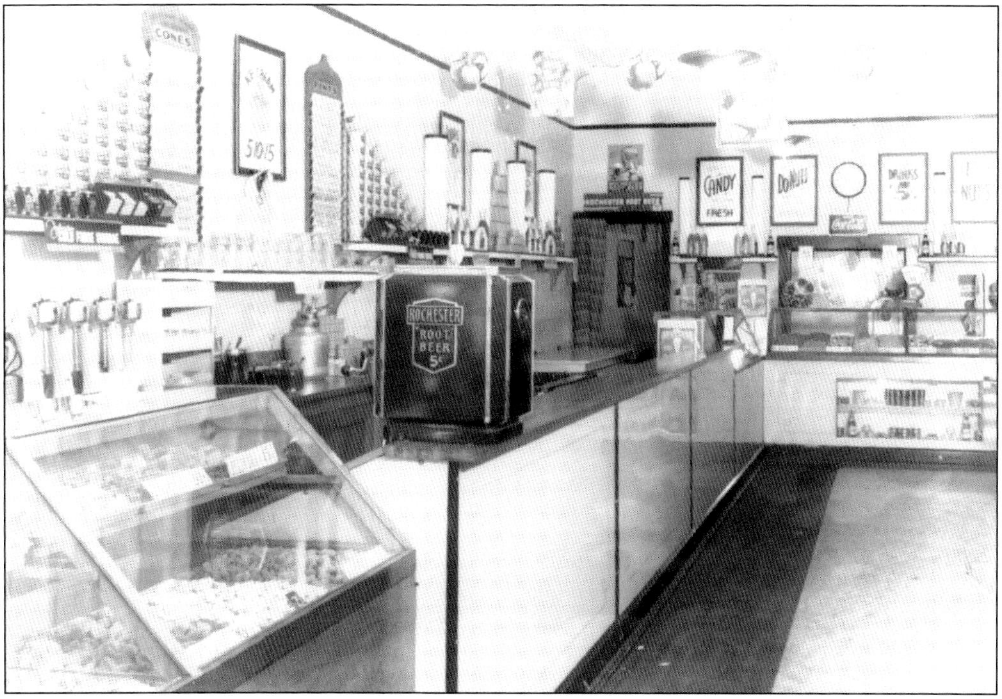

The Nut Shop was opened on Mahoning Street in May 1936. Its founders were T.A. Zimmerman, A.H. Anderson, C.A. Langhearst, and H.B. Johnson. The former Fort Pitt Market had been vacated when the four friends conceived the idea of such an enterprise. Does anyone remember root beer at 5¢ per glass, ice-cream cones at 5¢ per scoop, or jelly-filled doughnuts at 15¢ apiece?

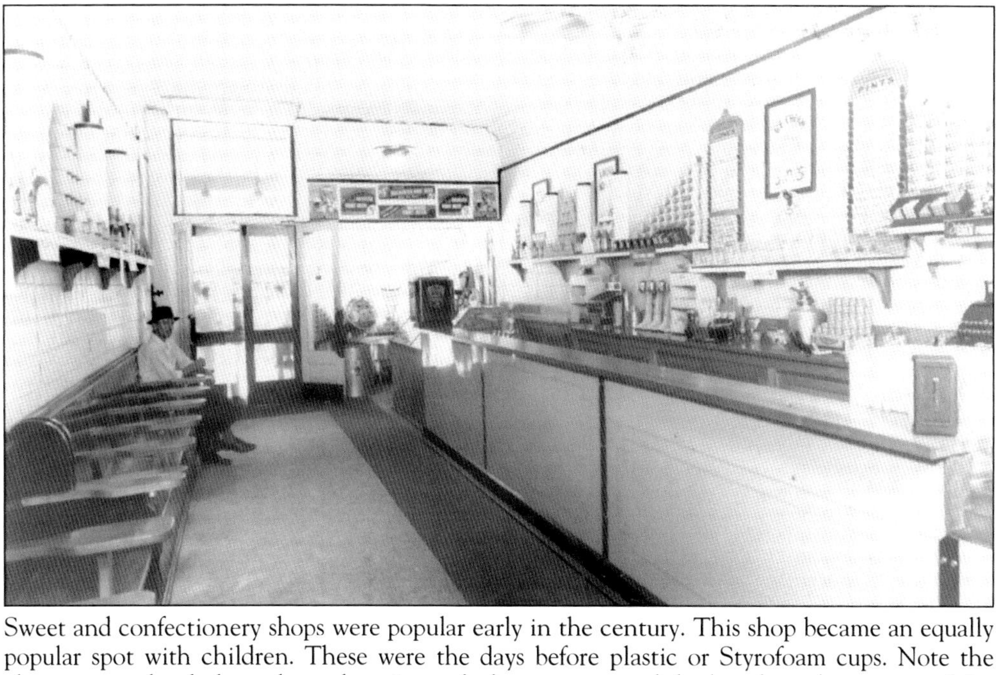

Sweet and confectionery shops were popular early in the century. This shop became an equally popular spot with children. These were the days before plastic or Styrofoam cups. Note the glassware on the shelves, the cash register of a bygone age, and the benches where treats of the day could be enjoyed. A trip to the shop was a treat for everyone in the post-Depression era.

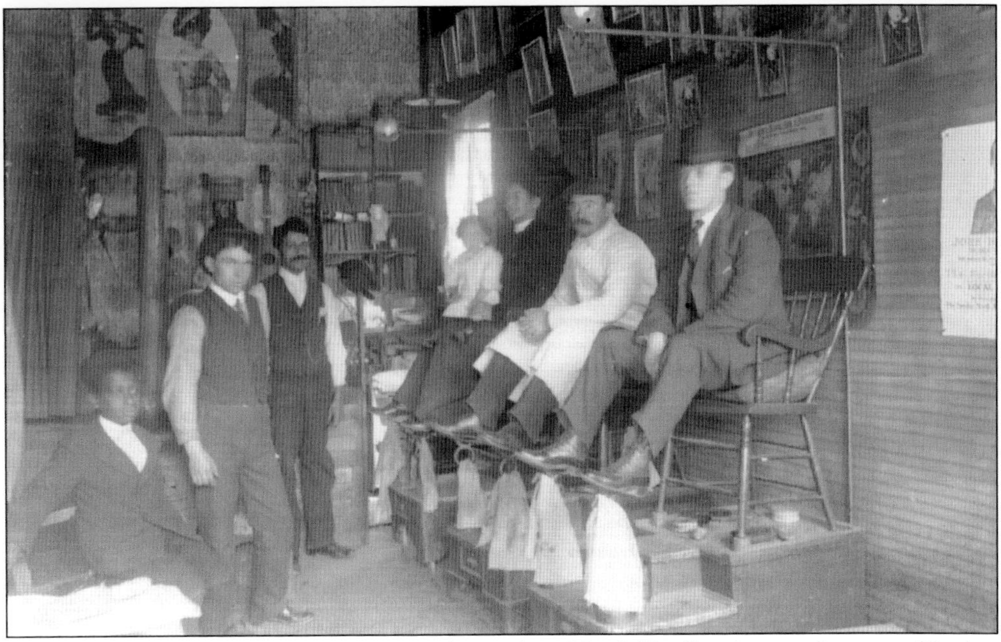

This shoeshine shop, shown in 1908, was located on North Findley Avenue between Glecker Hotel and Weaver's Meat Market. It was the time when John Mitchell was prominent in the news as a labor leader, according to the sign on the right. Note the stovepipe in the background. This site later became the home of a Punxsutawney Hotel and municipal parking. The caption above the world map on the wall reads, "The Farmers National Bank of Punxsutawney."

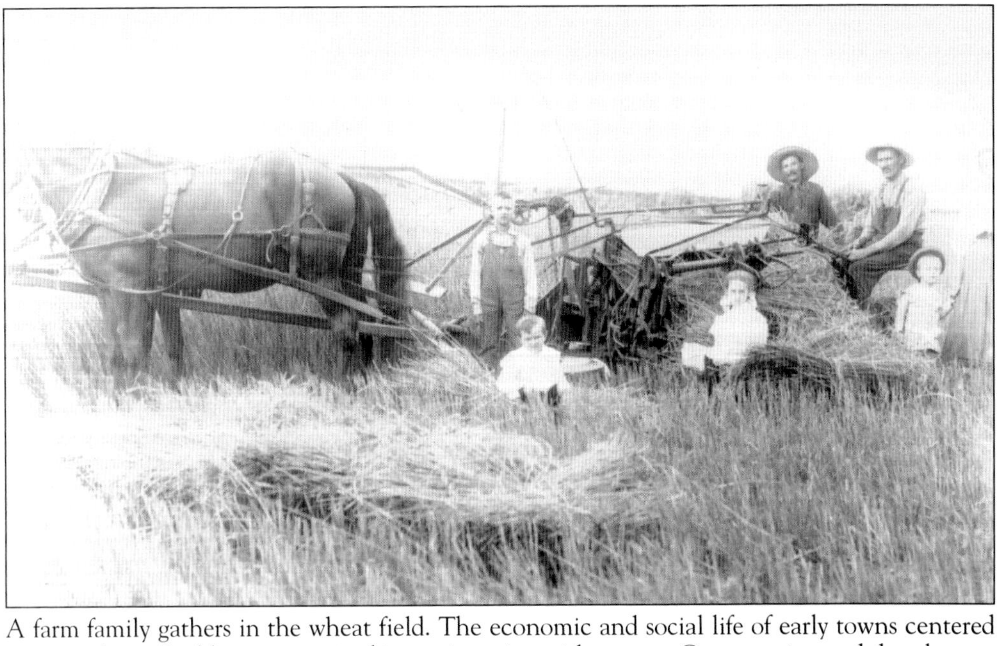

A farm family gathers in the wheat field. The economic and social life of early towns centered on agriculture. Buildings were raised in conjunction with a party. Conversation and the pleasure of visiting neighbors made up the social aspects of one's life, and commercial amusements were unknown. On rare occasions, parties were held where the settlers danced, sang, played games, and told tales, even when buildings were not going up.

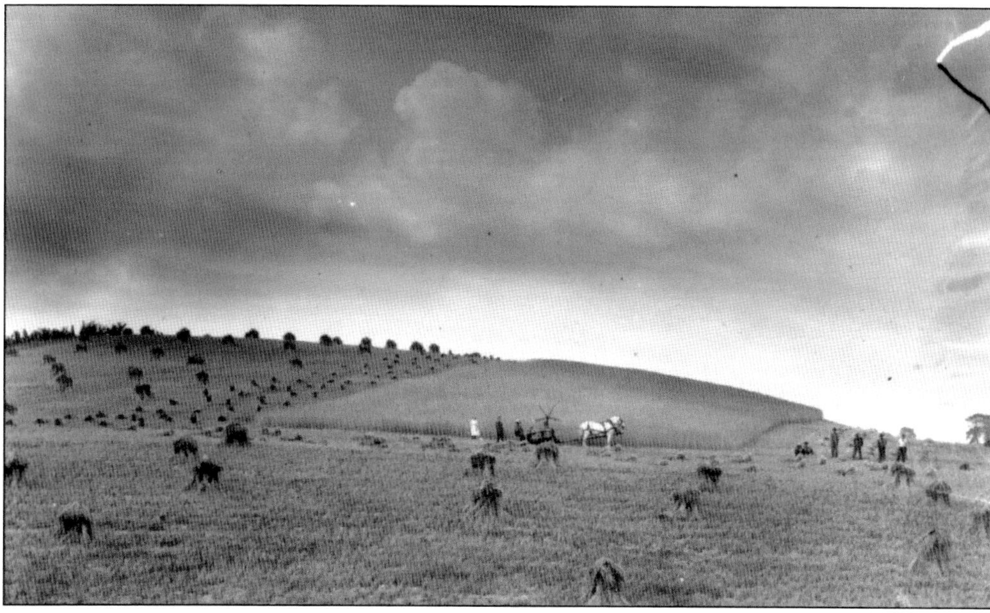

Harvesting wheat on a large farm was a common chore every autumn. Wheat was gathered into bundles, collected, and taken to the mill to be ground into flour. The mill gave rise to many expressions, including "run of the mill," "same old grind," "put through the mill," "go with the flow," and "rule of thumb." A trained miller would test the consistency of flour by rubbing some between the index finger and thumb.

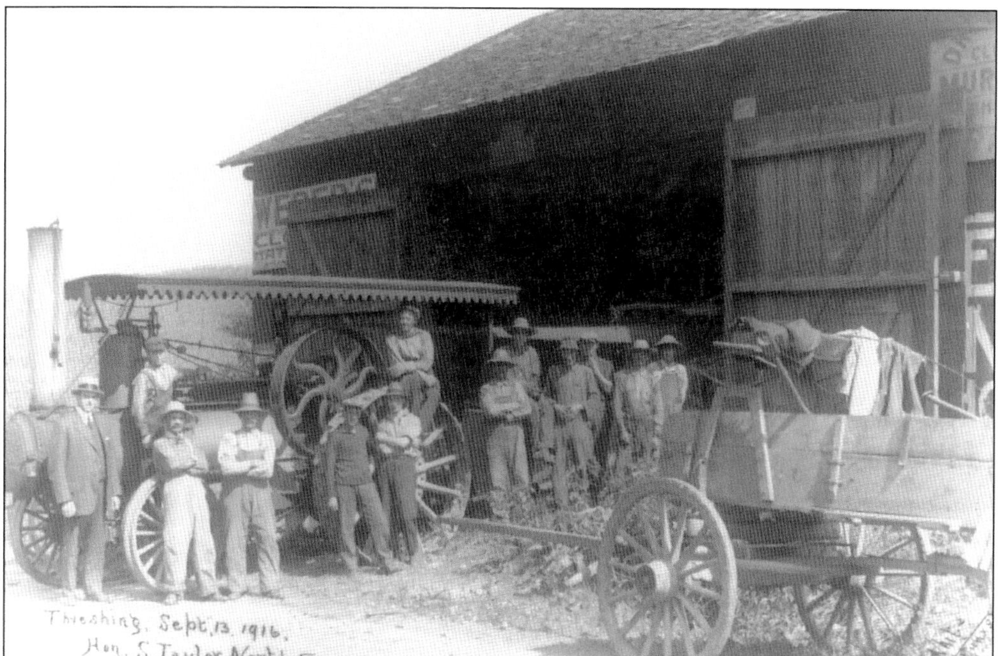

Threshing and agriculture were vital industries to the early settlers. On September 13, 1916, these farmers are gathered on the North Farm of the Honorable S. Taylor with the machinery of their trade. Note the advertisements on the upper left and lower right for Weber's Clothing Store, a prominent men's clothing business in town.

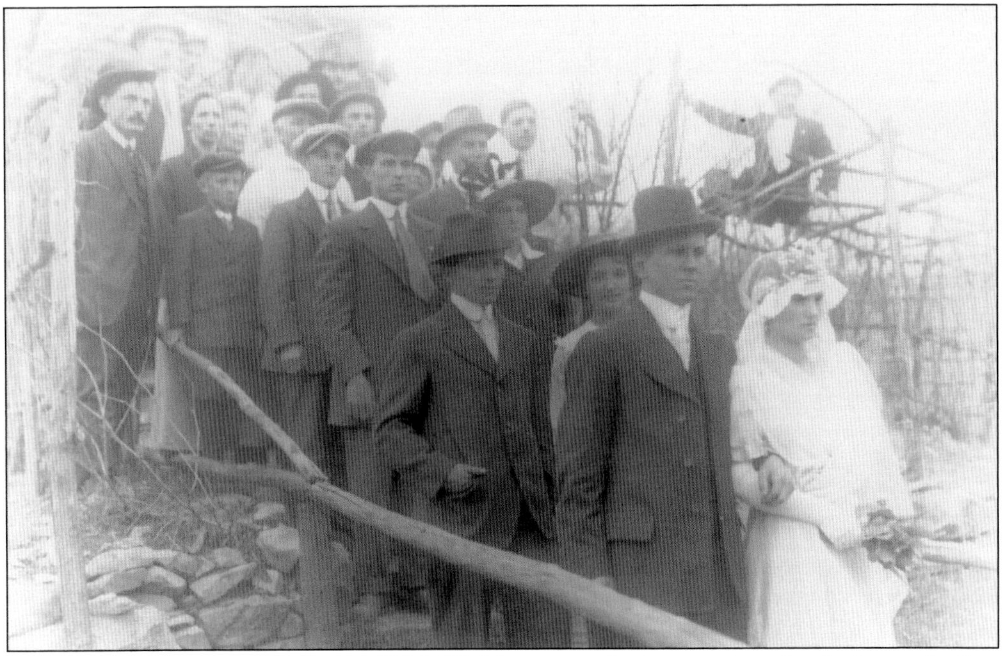

The Delvitto wedding took place in 1915. Weddings were festive occasions for the intermingling of pioneer relatives. Early in the century, social life was locally centered. Weddings provided companionship, exchange of ideas, and news from the outside world.

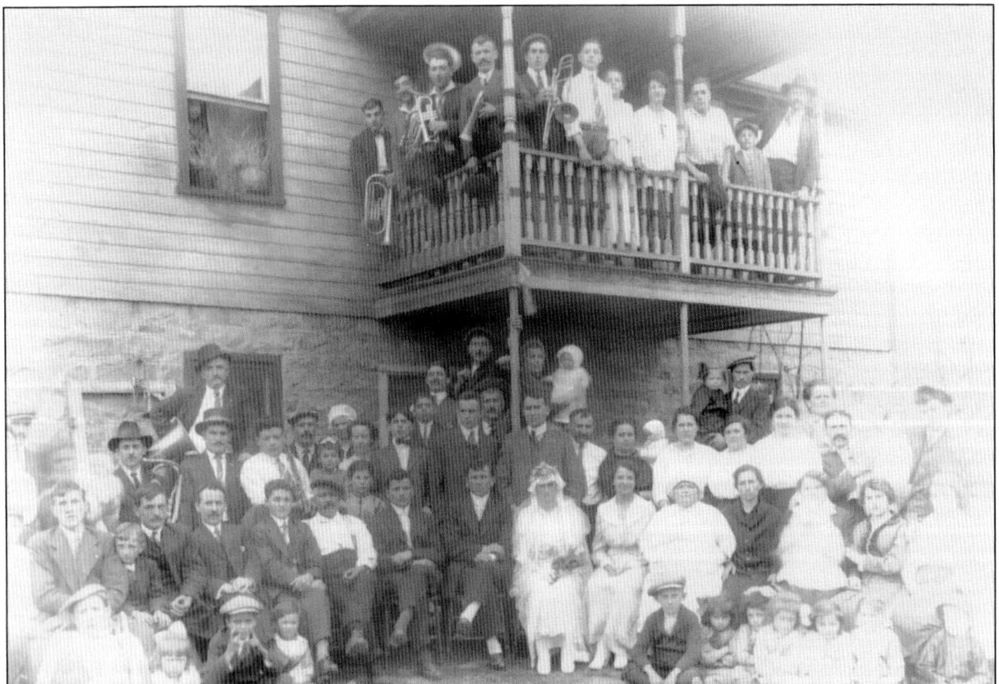

The wedding reception has brought neighbors, relatives, the wedding party, and even the band around the celebrants for this historic scene. The band will supply the music when the merriment begins. Dining, singing, and dancing will follow.

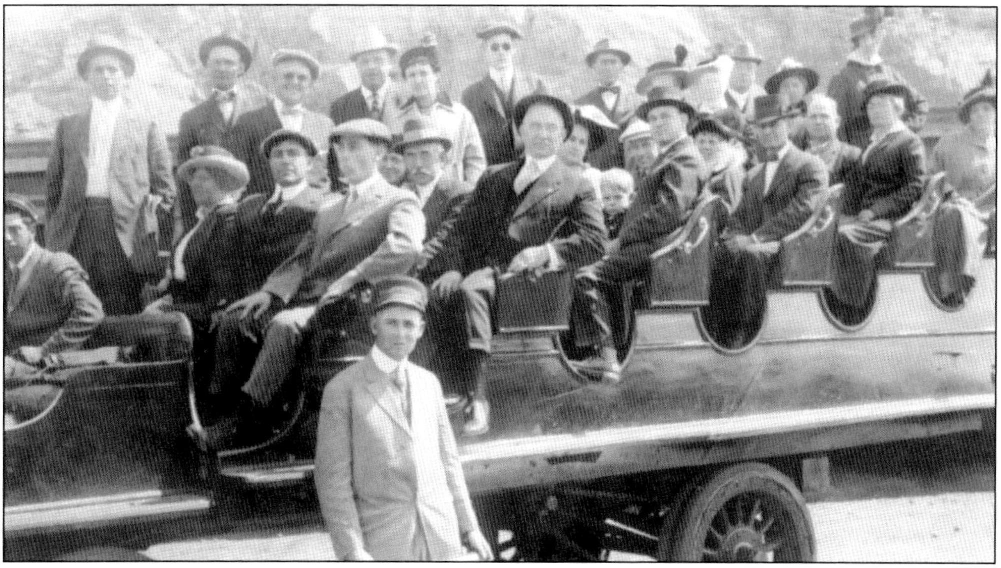

This sightseeing bus is of an early vintage. The tour guide explained the sites to his passengers through a megaphone. Recreation of 1900 was just beginning to emerge from the Victorian era and it was coming out of the home. These folks are out to enjoy the new open-air bus that would give them a guided tour.

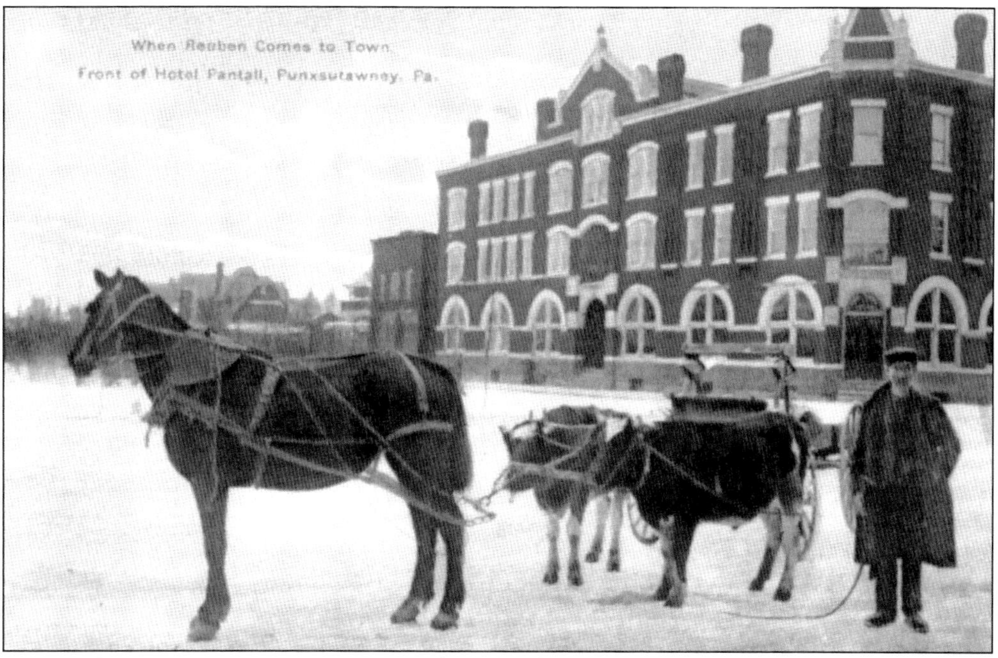

Ben Rueben came to town in 1918 and established an auto repair shop. Here, the locals swapped news and argued politics. In 1930, 1934, and 1937, he acquired the franchises for Oldsmobile, General Motors, and Cadillac, which was the largest selling automobile at that time. He added a sales department to the growing business. In 1947, he completed a new tile building with a spacious showroom.

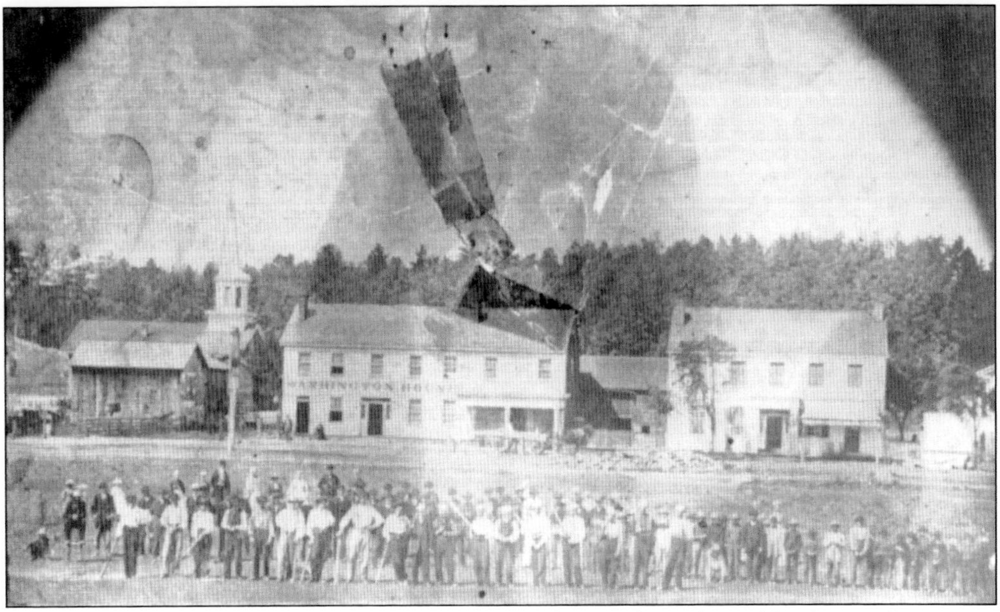

The Washington House, shown in 1865, was located across from the Public Square. It was one of the earliest hostelries in the town. On the left is the First Baptist church, located on Jefferson Avenue. The men are prepared for work with picks and shovels.

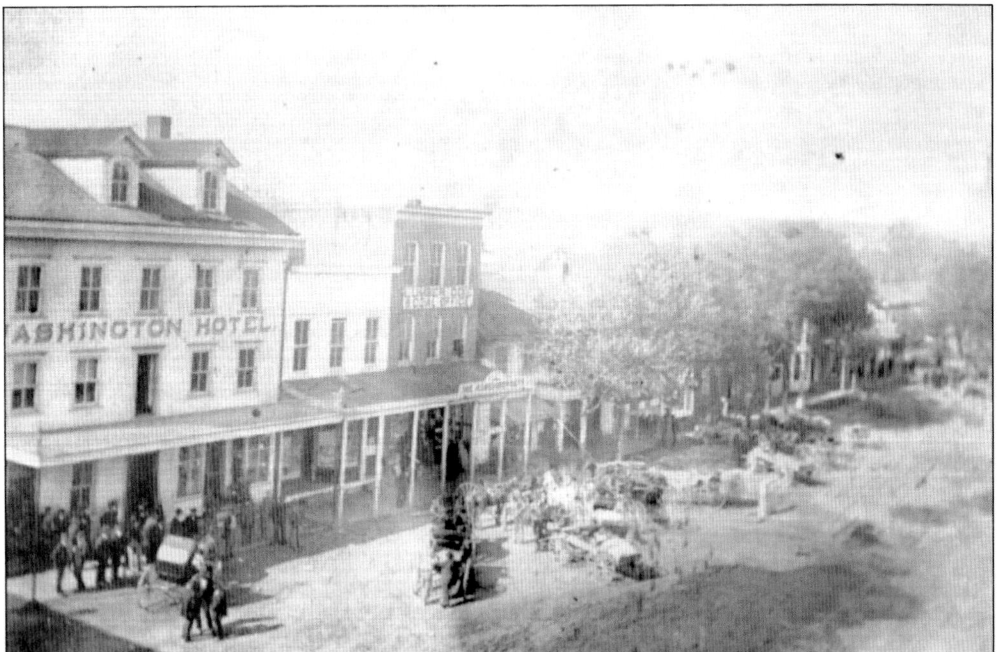

The Washington Hotel, along with the Lumber and Coke Company, is bustling with activity in 1888. The hotel was initially owned by F. Hummel and stood on the corner later occupied by Kroger's. It was in the area facing Barclay Square. It served a thriving business community and accommodated patrons prior to 1880. Like other phases of economic life, the hotel industry flourished with many changes in ownership and name. In 1818, Abraham Weaver opened a hotel and included entertainment; a restaurant was part of the hotel business.

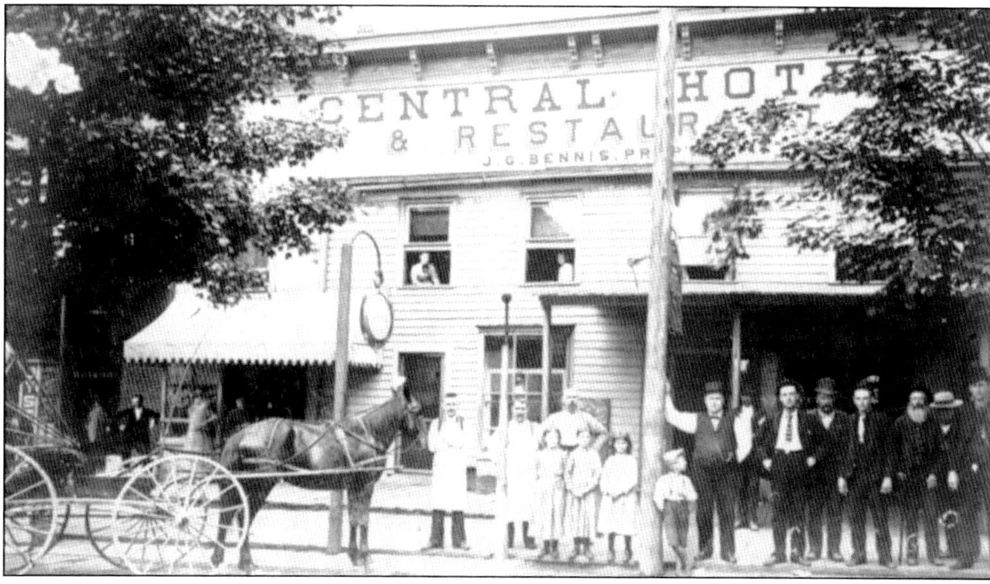

The Central Hotel was established by J.G. Bennis before the turn of the century. Hotels were vital in the early days of Punxsutawney. Even short trips were a chore. Unpaved roads and travel by horse or foot contributed to very slow and uncomfortable travel. Hotels solved the problem for many families who would reside in them while waiting to move into their newly constructed homes.

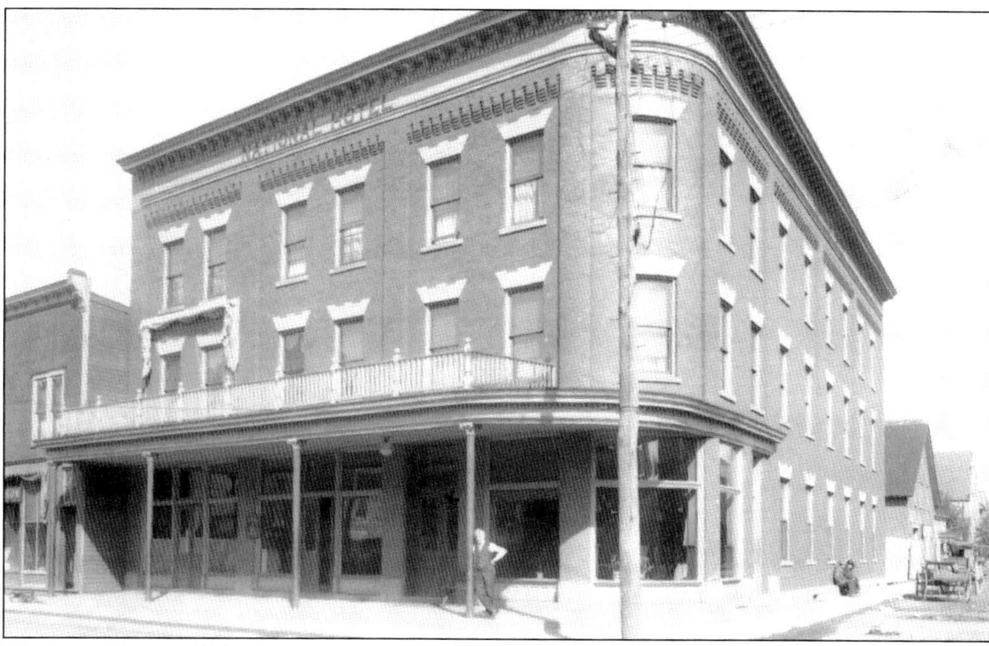

The New National Hotel was located on the corner of south Gilpin Street and Union Avenue. It was owned and operated by Joseph Baumgartner on the site of the old National Hotel. Built in 1905, it was leased to David Naylon until 1964, when Edward Baumgartner became proprietor. He remodeled the building with updated electricity and installed new heating, plumbing, and lighting systems. All rooms were equipped with running water and heat. The rooms were also refurbished and redecorated.

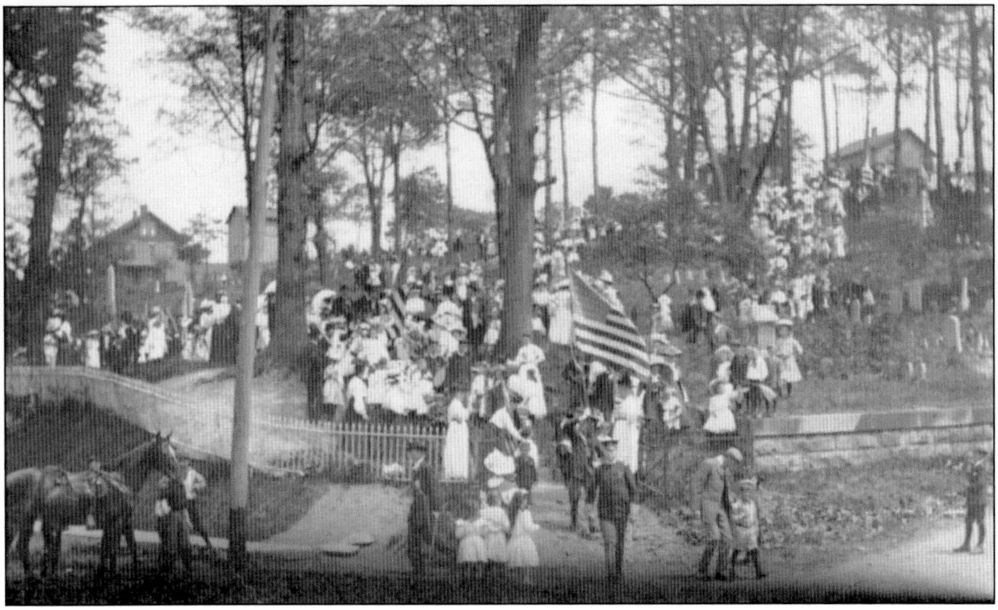

The North Finley Street cemetery is the oldest one in the vicinity. The earliest burial was Hugh McKee in 1821. He was a Revolutionary War veteran and was followed by veterans of the War of 1812, the Civil War, and World Wars I and II. They are all interred here with their families. Services were held in the cemetery every Memorial Day and Armstice Day for many years.

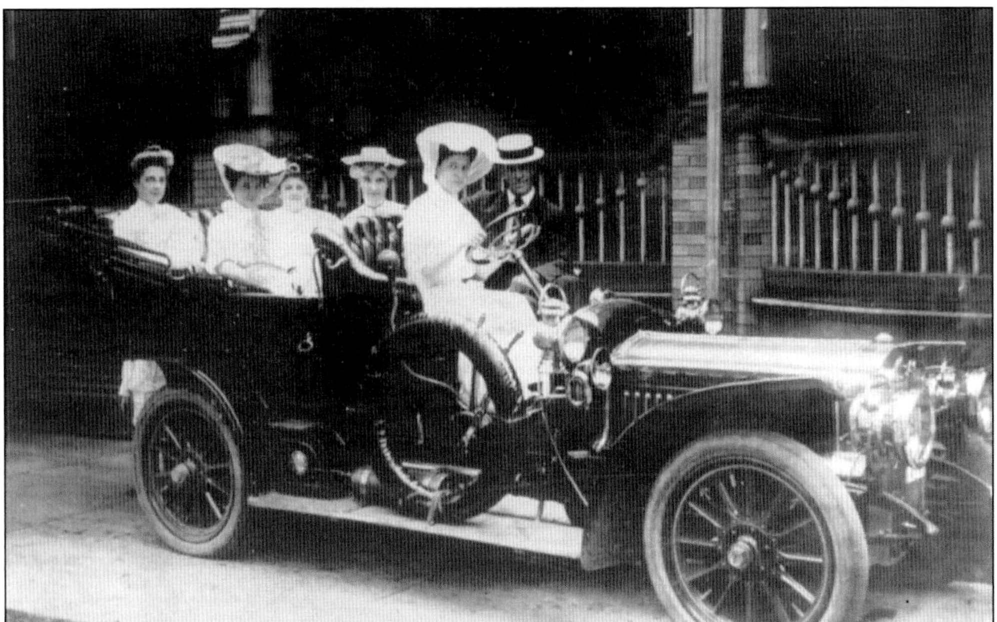

The Sarnin Thomas Flyer car made its appearance in 1904. It was the most modern vehicle of its time. Notice the steering wheel on the right side of the car. When this noisy novelty chugged into town, it attracted the attention of citizens curious to see the new innovative contraption that could attain such high speeds as 10 mph. Older people frowned upon the new clamorous fad. Men envisioned themselves in such a fascinating style of travel. Whoever thought women would drive back in 1904?

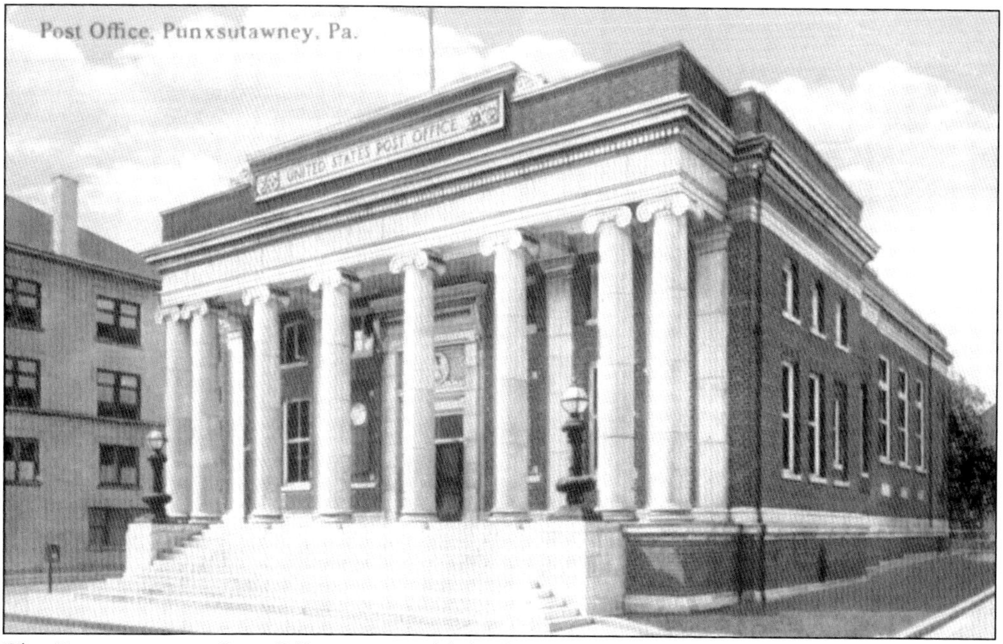

The Punxsutawney Post Office was established in 1862 with Charles A. Barclay as the first postmaster. It was originally located in the general store on the corner of Front and Main Streets. Later, it was relocated to the William Davis Store on the northeast corner of Mahoning and Gilpin Streets. In 1914, this building was erected on North Findley Street to house the post office. In 1935, it reached first-class status. A heavy volume of mail and parcel post is handled here daily.

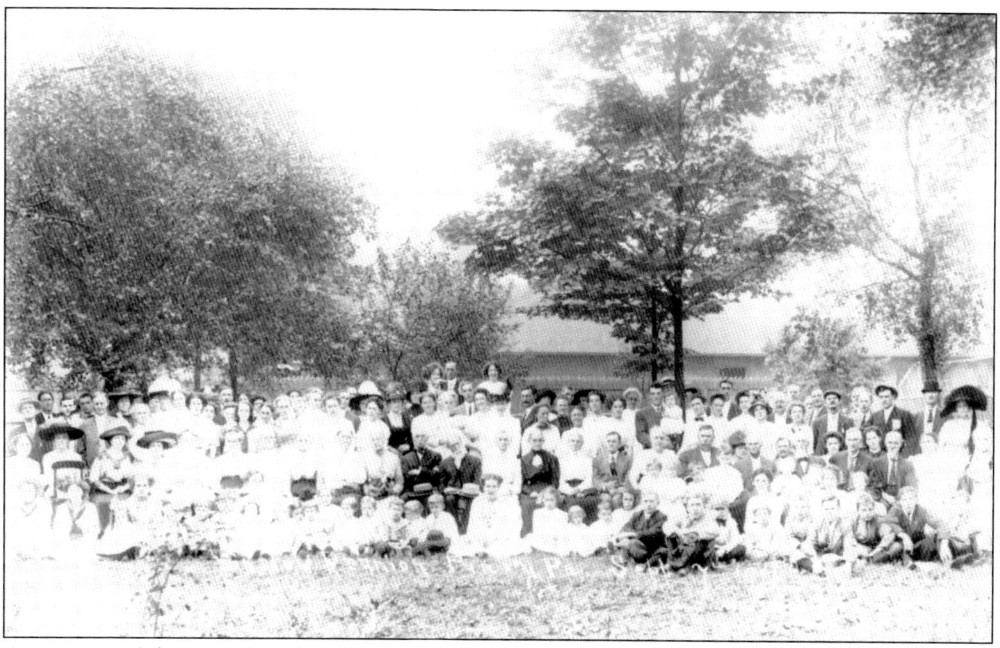

A reunion of the Winslow family took place in Jefferson Park on September 7, 1911. Reuben C. Winslow was admitted to the practice of law in 1860. He became a leading attorney and was later elected state senator from the district. He served a long, useful life in the community.

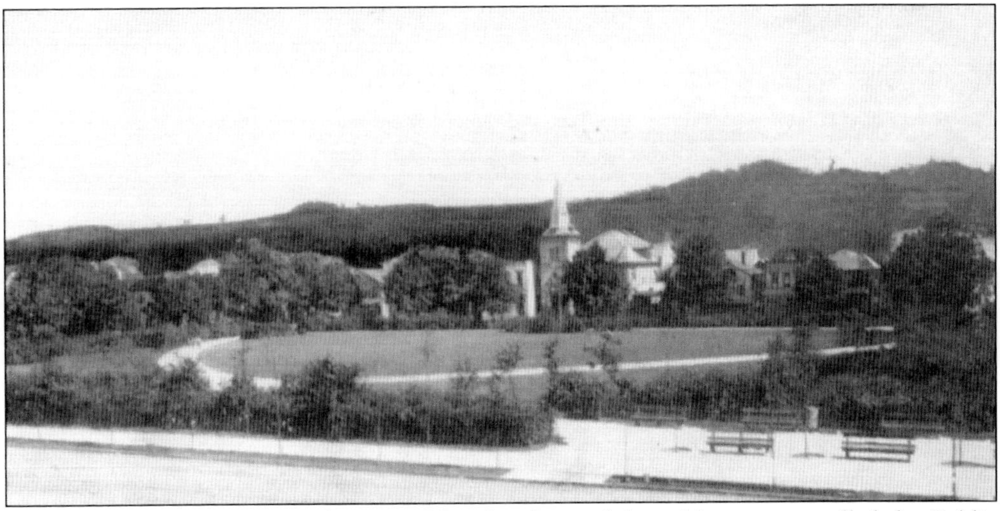

Originally, the center square that David Barclay donated for public use was called the Public Square. It was in the center of eight squares of his original plan. It was later renamed Barclay Square as a tribute to him. Barclay's name was placed on a plaque in recognition for his place in history. This site is now occupied by the civic center.

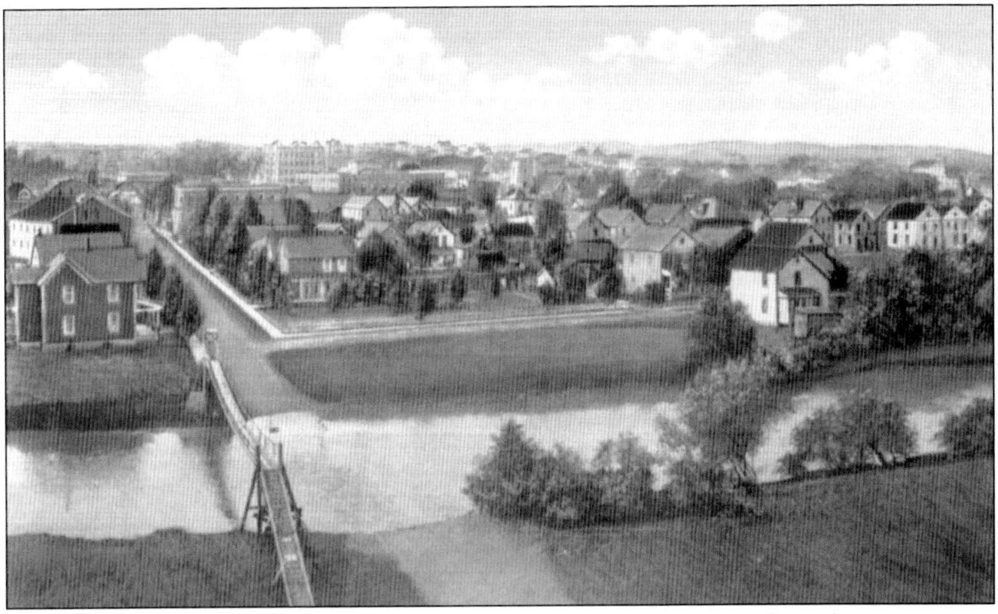

This bird's-eye view of Punxsutawney affords a glimpse of the largest industrial community in Jefferson County. It served as the hub of commercial activity since its inception. It gained in industrial employment and became a small, diversified commercial center. Located 1,226 feet above sea level, it occupies 2,206 acres, or approximately 3.4 square miles of land. Punxsutawney is dotted on all sides by bridges spanning the creek.

Two

Industry Comes to Punxsutawney

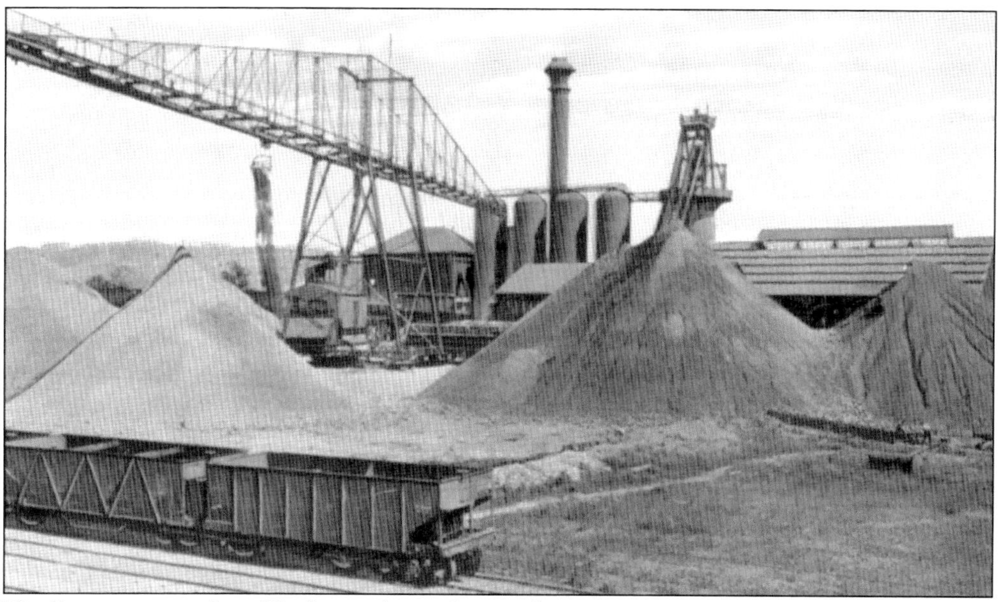

The Punxsutawney Iron Works was located on Mahoning Street. Founded by Jacob Hoover in 1850, it was the oldest establishment of its kind in the area. Operated by an overshot wheel, manpower was sometimes necessary to tread the wheel and maintain power. Plows, threshing machines, windmills, and agricultural implements were manufactured here. In later years, G.W. Porter established a machine shop business on the former ironworks site. This is where the blacksmith was located.

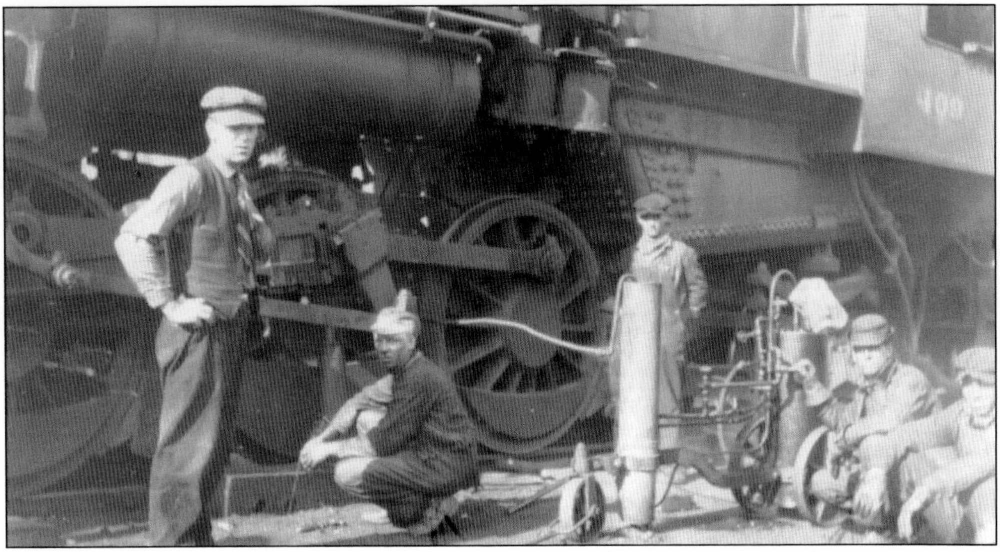

This *c.* 1900 image shows George Keeler, second from right, and August Keeler, extreme right, with coworkers. They are repairing a railroad engine used in the Punxsutawney Iron Works. Four years after Jacob Hoover established the ironworks, D. Mundorf became proprietor, followed by W. Gillespie. The railroad was vital to the iron industry. It transported coal, coke, and iron to various markets around the country.

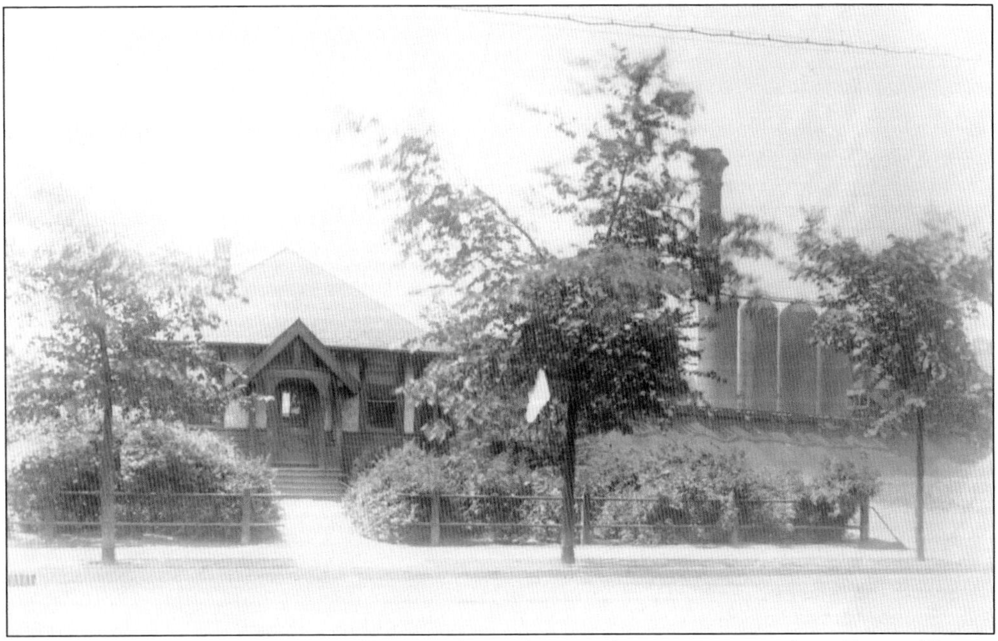

The Punxsutawney Iron Works office was located on Mahoning Street, where Punxy Plaza is today. The project was lit for the first time on September 29, 1897, with a capacity of 250 tons of iron rolling from the furnace. For many years, the steady, warm, night glow of the furnaces radiated stability, peace, and prosperity throughout the town. The glow guaranteed consistent and dependable work for the 150 employees.

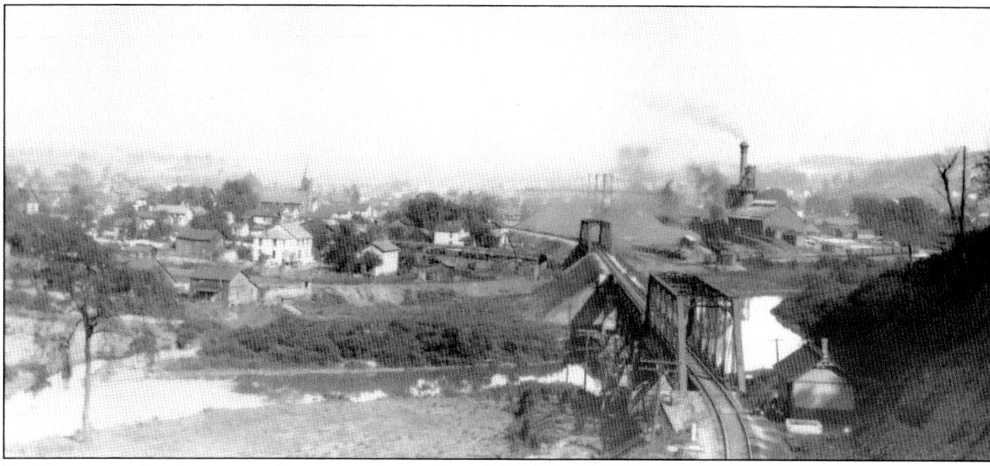

In this view, looking south across the railroad bridge, the Punxsutawney Iron Works presents an imposing scene. The works included a sizable plant with a massive factory and a towering smokestack. E.C. McKibbon, who also built the Bennis house, managed the works. This company was the center of commerce in Punxsutawney for many years. The ironworks prospered, and the Walston coke ovens kept it in operation.

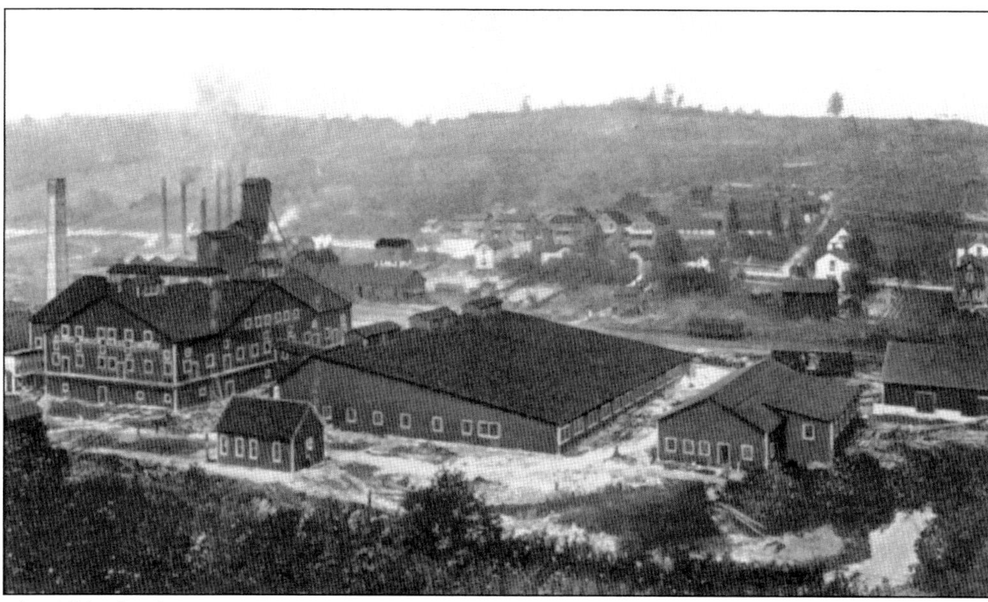

The Eldred Glass Company was established in Eldred, Pennsylvania. A branch had been planned for Punxsutawney when a disastrous fire leveled the Eldred plant. The company relocated, and by June 20, 1908, the new site was in operation. It employed 150 men, most of whom were from Belgium and France. They were skilled in glass making. Molton glass was refined in a tank where raw materials were melted. The manager was Jules Wery.

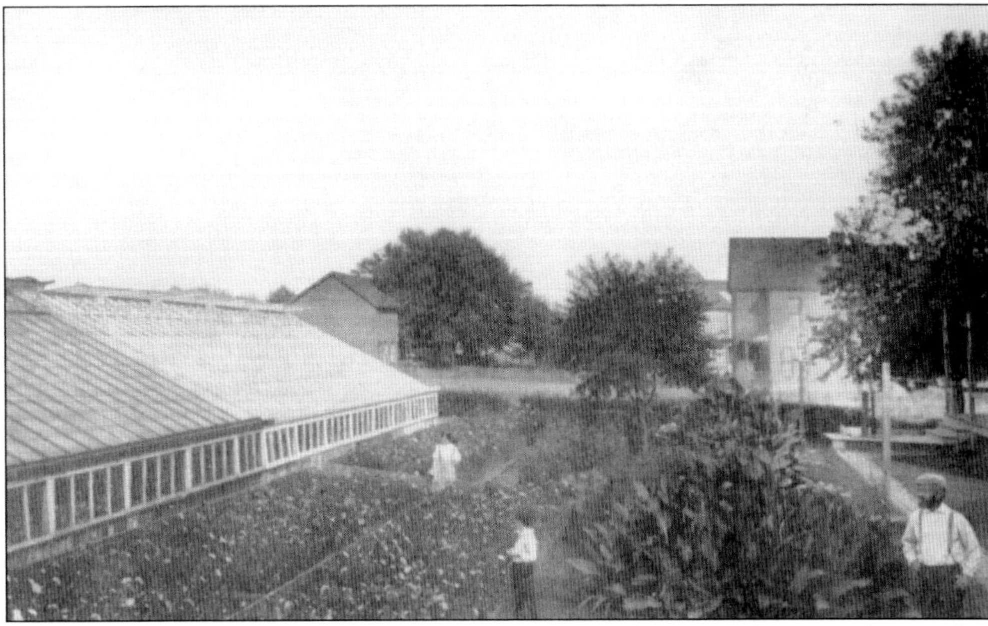

In 1891, Oliver Crissman began his greenhouse project with tomato plants in a bay window. These were later transplanted to a wooden frame from the old Cumberland Presbyterian Church. His first greenhouse, built in 1892, was heated by two brick ovens. These ovens extended the length of the building and contained tile chimneys. The warm smoke heated the greenhouse. In 1900, George Crissman became an associate of his father in the greenhouse business.

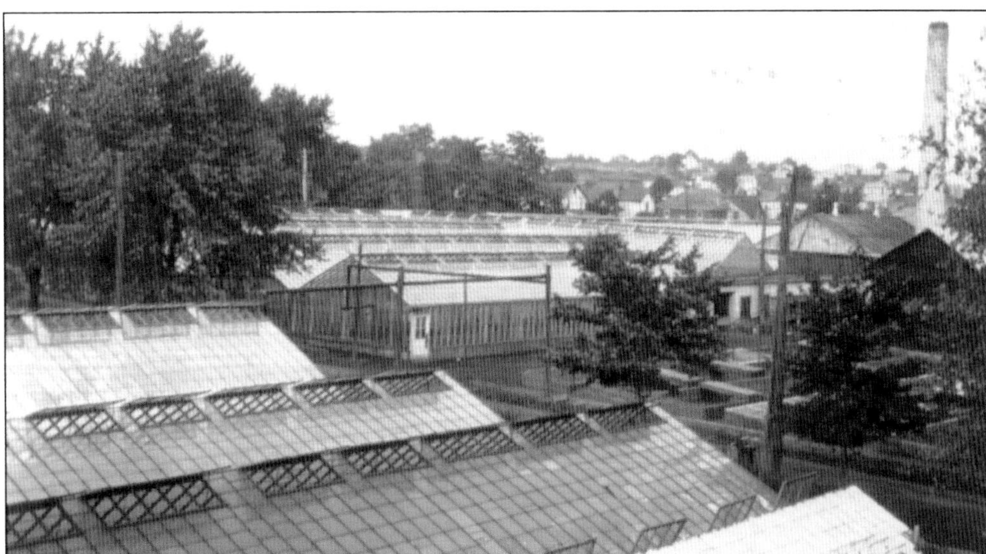

The Crissman Greenhouse Company was established in 1911. George Crissman and his sisters became partners in the business. In 1908, the firm became a floristry. The Crissman greenhouses covered 75,000 square feet, and the family owned 2 acres of growing fields. They were located where the new Punxsutawney Spirit building now stands.

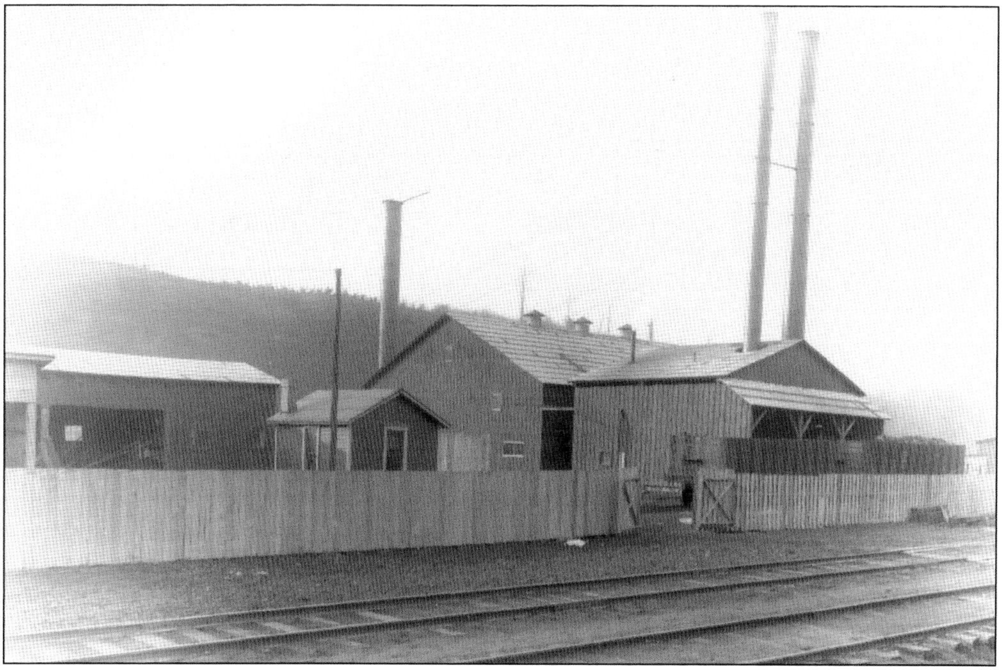

The Clark Steel Hoop Mill manufactured hoops for barrels. The mill was completed and opened in November 1908. The officers were F.L. Clark, president and manager; E.C. Mc Kibbin, secretary; and J.A.Weber, treasurer. Big wooden barrels, bound by steel hoops, were widely used early in the century.

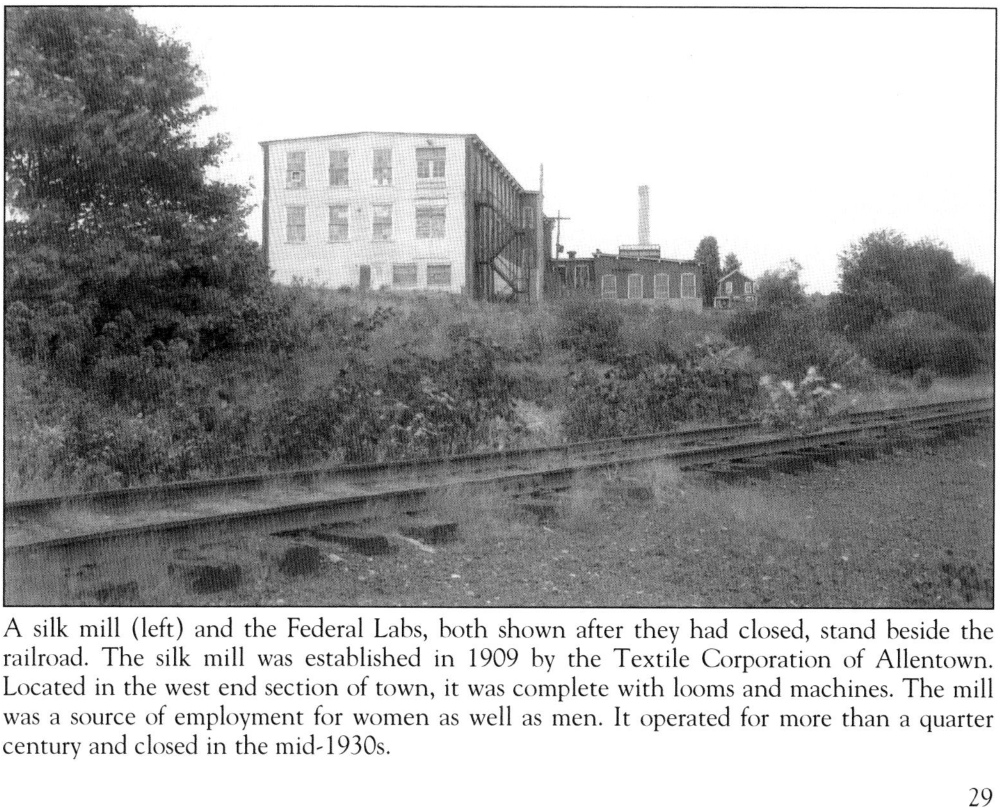

A silk mill (left) and the Federal Labs, both shown after they had closed, stand beside the railroad. The silk mill was established in 1909 by the Textile Corporation of Allentown. Located in the west end section of town, it was complete with looms and machines. The mill was a source of employment for women as well as men. It operated for more than a quarter century and closed in the mid-1930s.

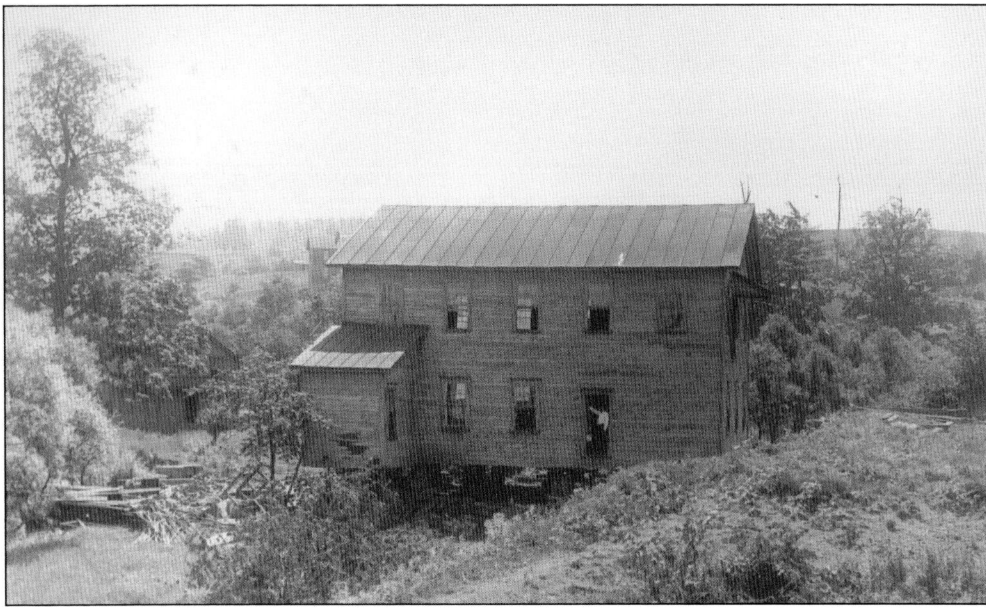

Obediah Nordstrom opened a woolen mill in 1909. Born in 1821, he moved to the area from Maine at age 21. He was one of the town's most prominent and influential citizens. His woolen mill, the only one of its kind in Punxsutawney, was in operation for many years. It turned out many yards of wool and fabric needed by early settlers. This later became the site of the Mahoney Valley Milling Company plant.

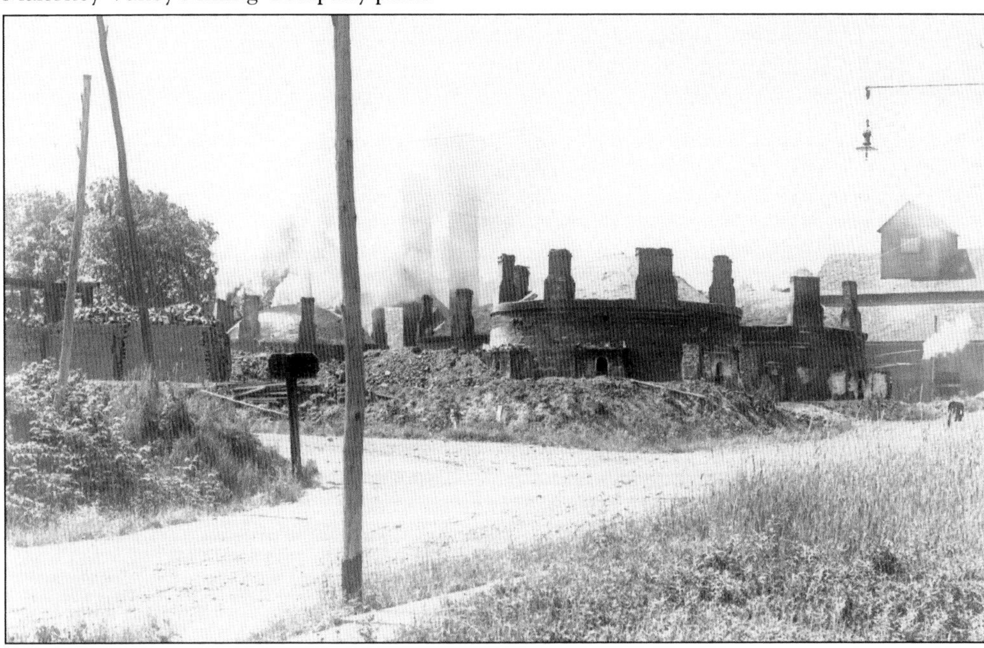

Indiana Hill was transformed when Obediah Nordstrom converted the site into Brick Hill. He set up a brick quarry and turned out substantial, strong bricks that have endured for years. Many buildings in Punxsutawney are constructed of these Nordstrom bricks, and many streets have been paved with them. Nordstrom established this business near his woolen mill, on the corner of Gaskill Avenue and Indiana Street, in 1909.

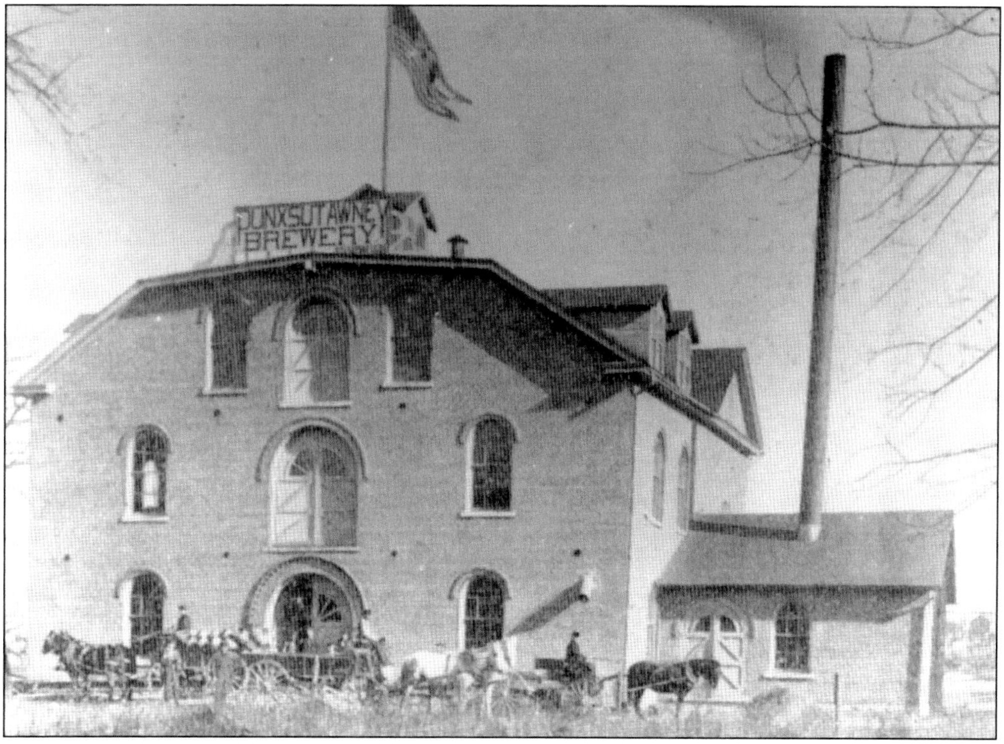

The Punxsutawney Brewery was established in 1900. It was located near the Mahoning Valley Milling Company across Mahoning Creek from the Elk Run Brewery (below). The earliest proprietors were Baumgartner and Schneider. It operated for many years until Prohibition forced the brewery to close.

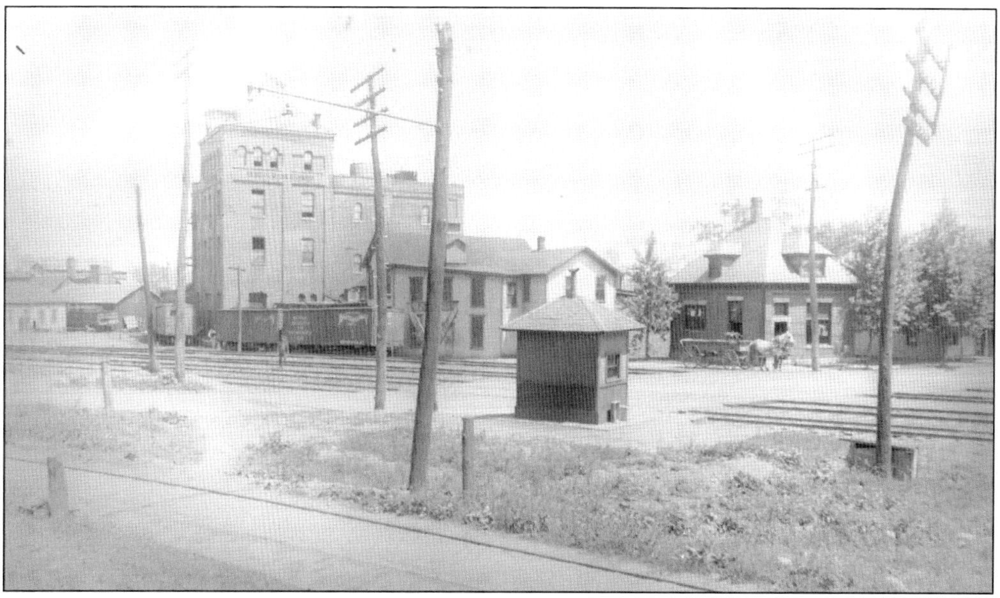

The Elk Run Brewery, established in 1909, rises in the background. The little railroad gatehouse provided shelter for the gatekeeper, who would warn drivers and pedestrians of approaching trains.

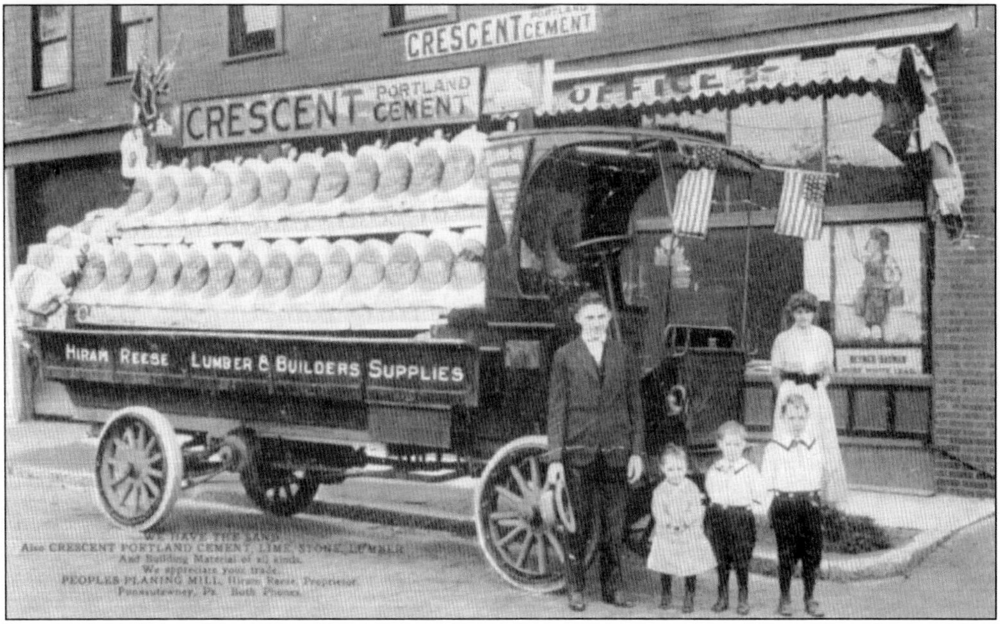

The Peoples Planing Mill was established in 1886 by Hiram Reese of Lancaster, Pennsylvania. Organized originally as Reese & Rodgers Company, it was located on the corner of Jefferson and Union Streets. In 1895, Reese became the sole owner; he poses here with his wife and family. Many of the buildings in town were constructed by Reese. The advertisement in the window reads, "Beymer & Bauman, Pure White Lead." The mill had a capacity of turning out 10,000 bricks per day.

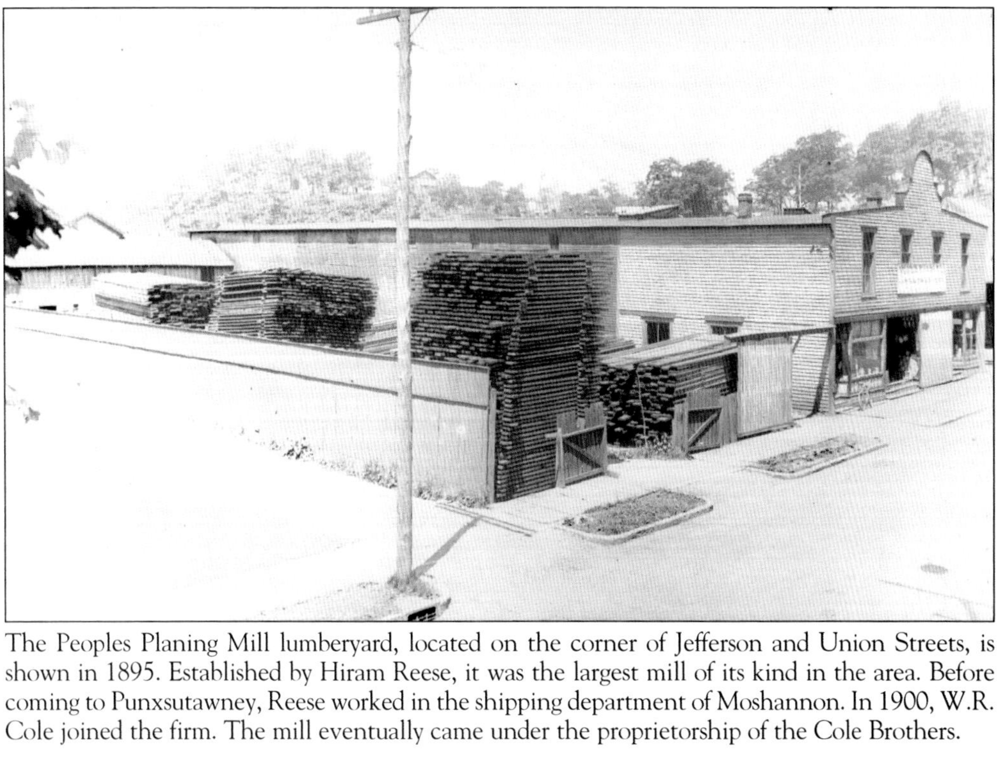

The Peoples Planing Mill lumberyard, located on the corner of Jefferson and Union Streets, is shown in 1895. Established by Hiram Reese, it was the largest mill of its kind in the area. Before coming to Punxsutawney, Reese worked in the shipping department of Moshannon. In 1900, W.R. Cole joined the firm. The mill eventually came under the proprietorship of the Cole Brothers.

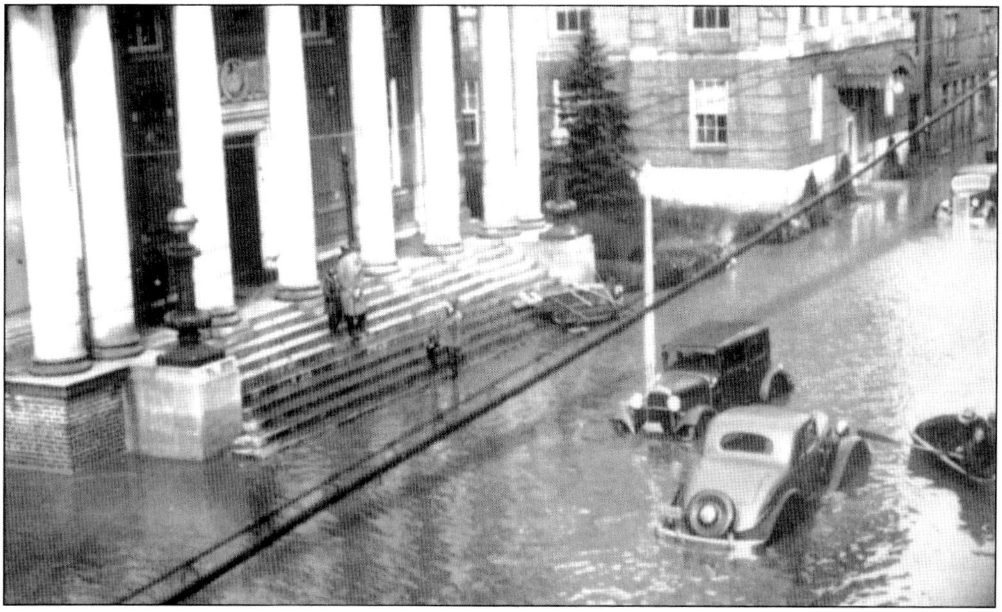

Rescue by boat has occurred four significant times in Punxsutawney's long history. The placid, calm Mahoning Creek has been known to overflow its banks and become a raging torrent, devastating everything in its wake. This watery wrath of nature occurred in 1861, 1911, 1936, and 1996. The 1936 flood, shown here, made rescue by boat a necessity. This scene happened in front of the post office on North Findley Street.

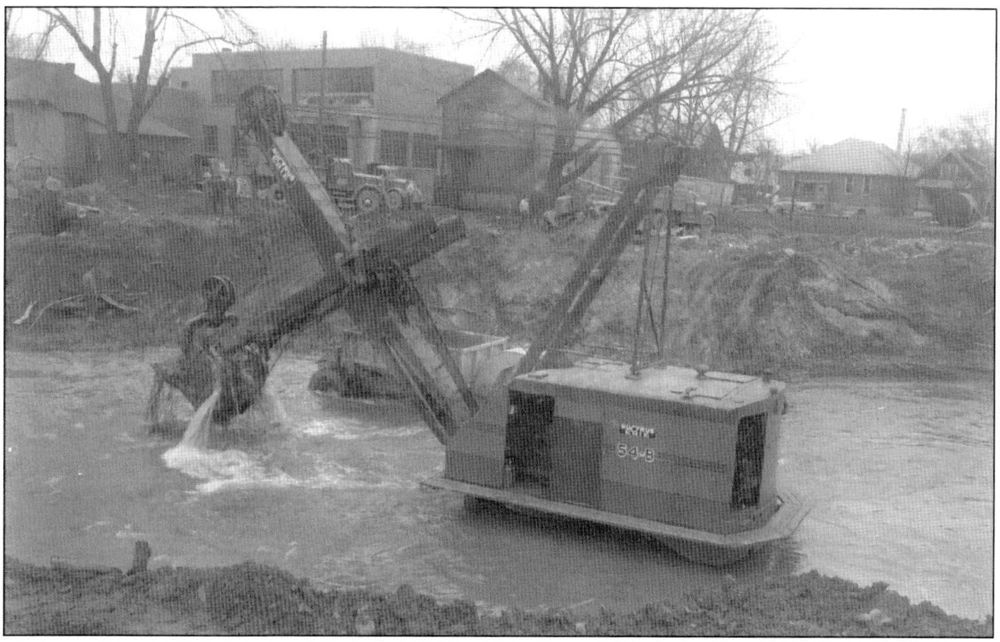

A flood control project was installed following the devastating flood of March 17, 1936, which inundated the business section of the town. Civic leaders began efforts to implement flood control, but it would be another decade before they received a grant to proceed with the project. The grant was awarded in parts, all of which were most beneficial to the area. It provided for the widening, deepening, and realigning of the channel.

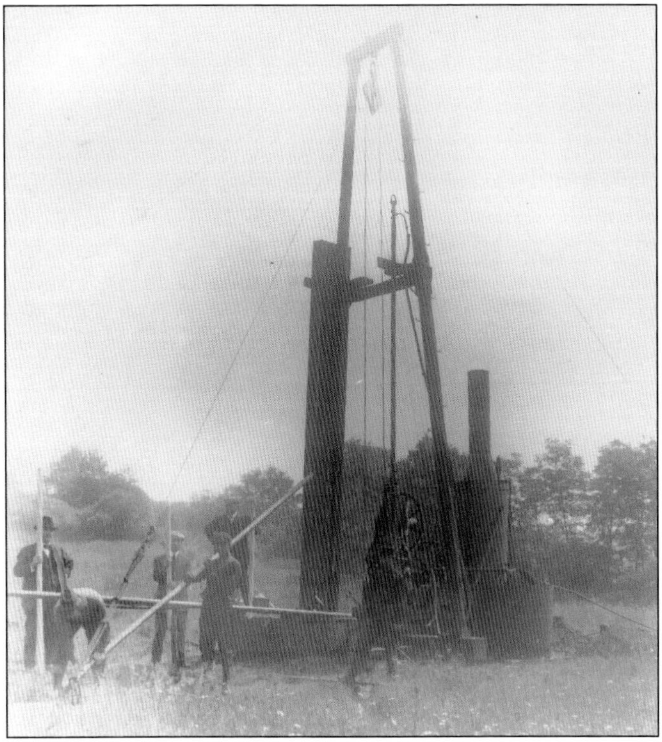

German immigrant Philip Hoffman was a skilled driller and passed the art on to his sons, Orvis and Leon. He established the Hoffman Brothers Drilling Company, the first offices of which were in the Zeithler building on the corner of Penn and Mahoning Streets. The first equipment used by the company was a single Keystone drilling machine. The firm later purchased a double beam machine and enjoyed business with individual contracts. By 1903, the company turned to diamond core drilling as well as water.

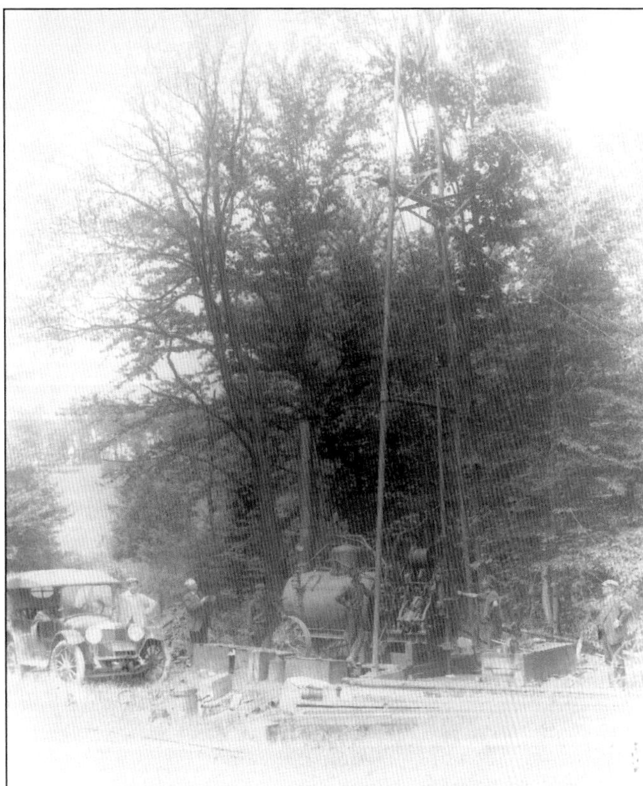

Diamond drilling was very specialized. Travel was limited and the Hoffman rigs were cumbersome. The brothers secured accommodations for their rigs, drillers, and equipment with a reliable farmer near the drilling sites. Steam-driven drills came into play later. These were followed by motor-driven drills, and the brothers modernized each machine to work off electricity.

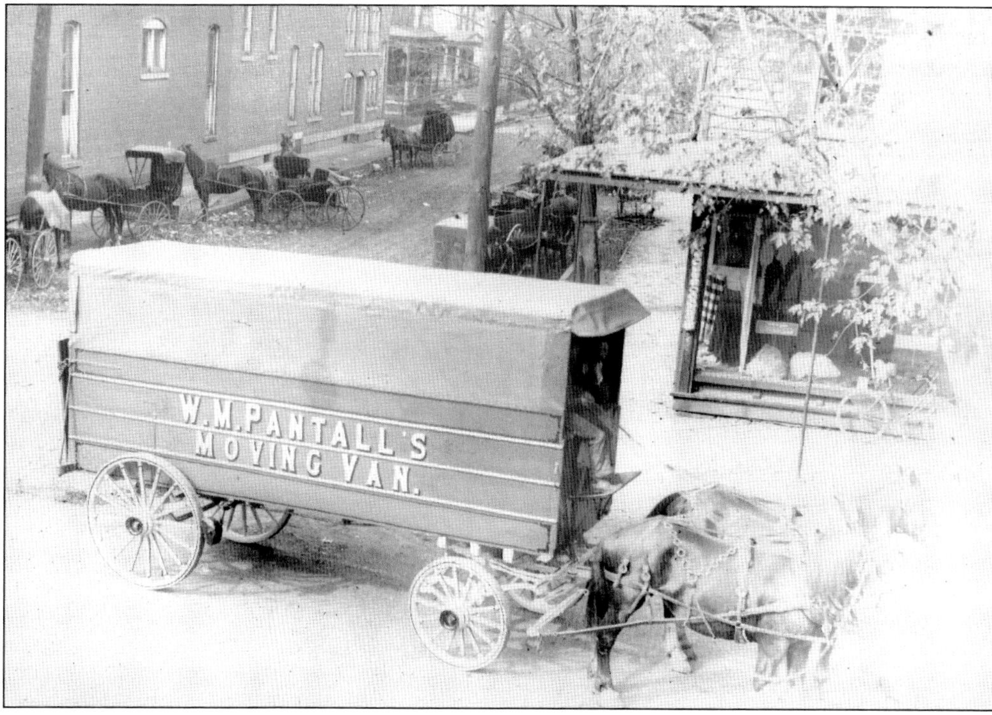

Pantall's had a moving van very early in the century. Families resided in hotels, especially when coal mines opened. Many early miners came seeking employment, and the hotel was their home until housing became available. They sometimes waited many months for a house to be built because population grew faster than housing. Moving vans were available to people staying at the hotel, and the Pantall moving van served its purpose well.

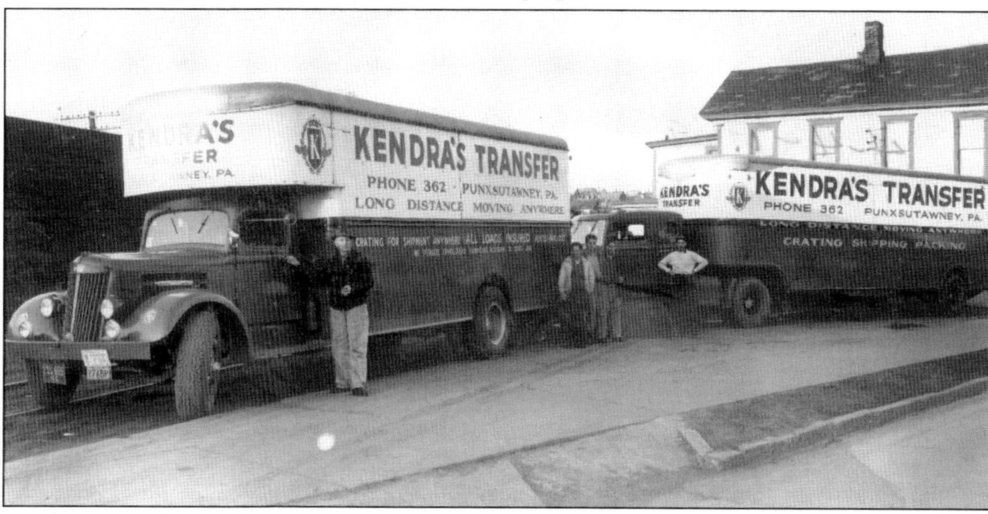

Kendra's Transfer Company was founded on July 5, 1911, by John Kendra. He had come from Austria in 1900 with the idea of going into business for himself. Not only did he found this transfer company, but he also founded the Jefferson Bottling Company. Here, John stands beside one of his trucks while two of his sons, John Philip and Gerald, join two drivers. It is interesting to note that the desk used by this distinguished gentleman is preserved at the Punxsutawney Historical Society.

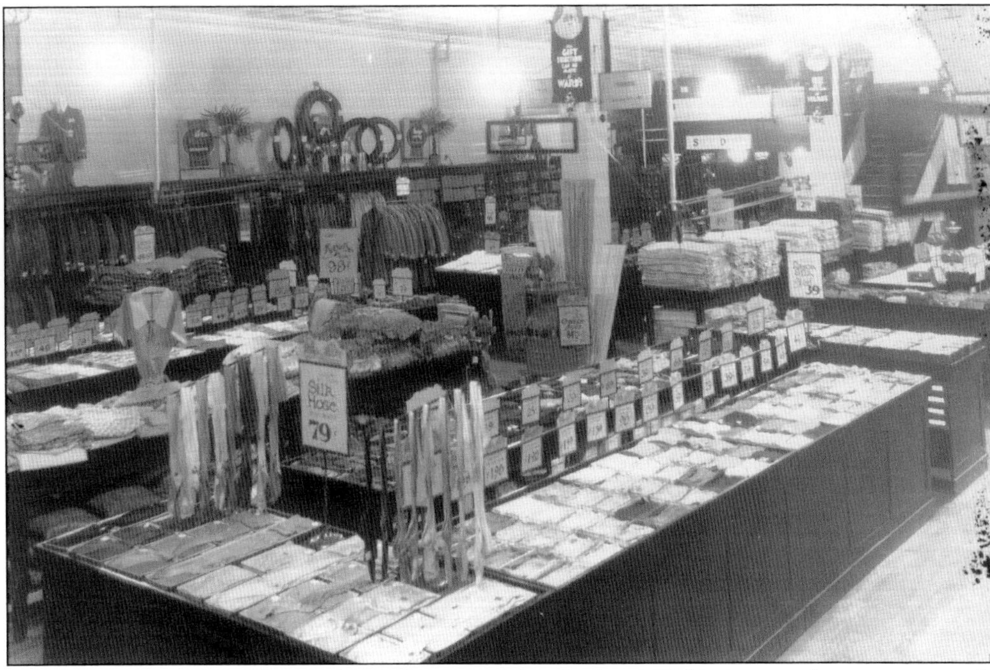

Montgomery Ward was founded in 1872 as a mail order house. The first catalogue was a single sheet sent to a list of prospective customers. In 1926, an experimental display store was opened. Customers could see the merchandise and order what they wanted, but they insisted on buying across the counter. The store in Punxsutawney was opened in 1928 on the southeast corner of Mahoning and Findley Streets. It prospered for 20 years.

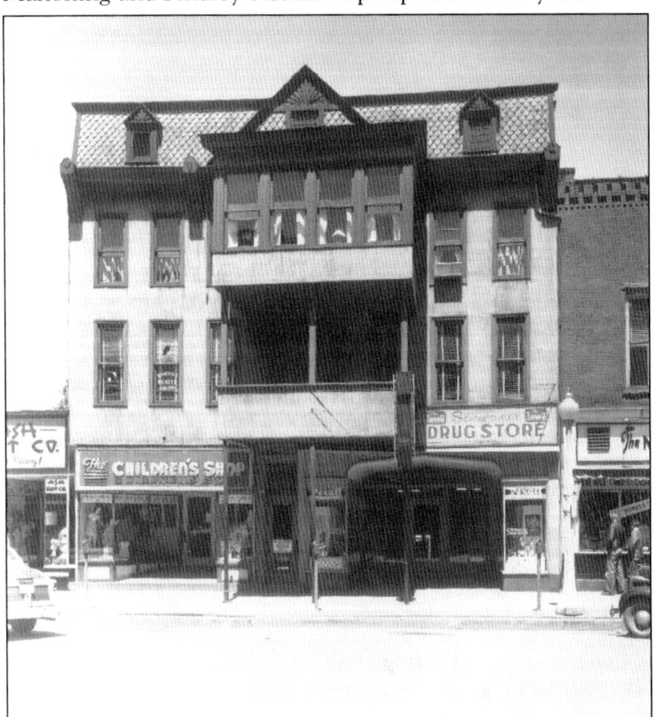

The Whitney Hotel building was constructed on West Mahoning Street between 1874 and 1878. James Dean was the first known owner. In 1892, Elmer Schaffer purchased the building from Dr. and Margaret E. Beyer. Shaffer converted it into a hotel that functioned for 24 years. In 1916, the structure was sold and converted into two storerooms with offices. Geraldine Bley and Anna Clark Benson bought the building in later years.

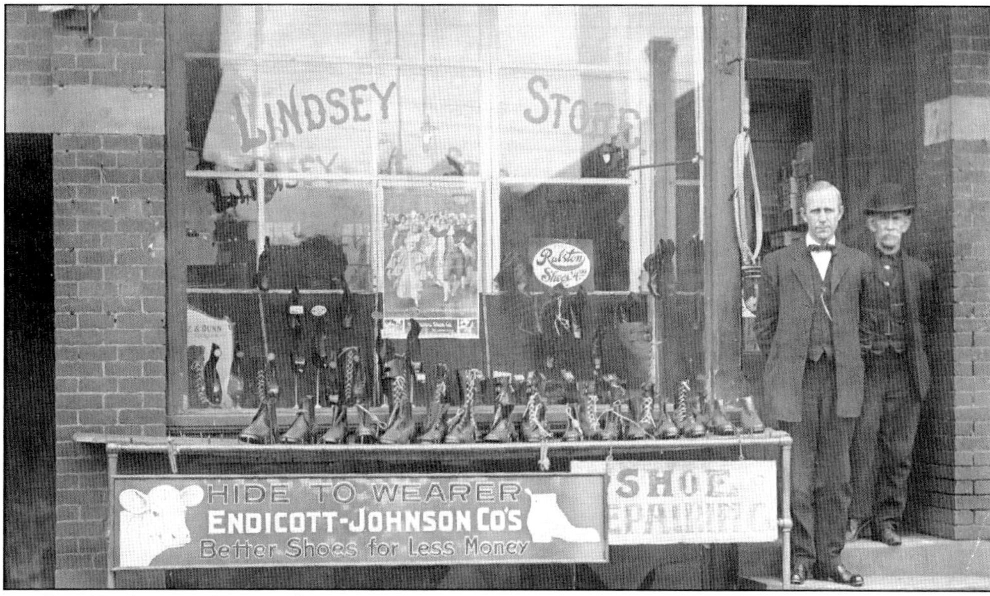

Lindsey Endicott-Johnson shoes were a specialty at the Lindsey Store. They were prominent early in the century. Advertised as "hide to wearer," they were dubbed "better shoes for less money." The Endicott-Johnson Company originated in upstate New York. Note the very high shoes considered healthy for the feet. There were special shoes for dancing as well. Ralston shoes cost $4 per pair. The hamlet of Lindsey was once known as Clayville.

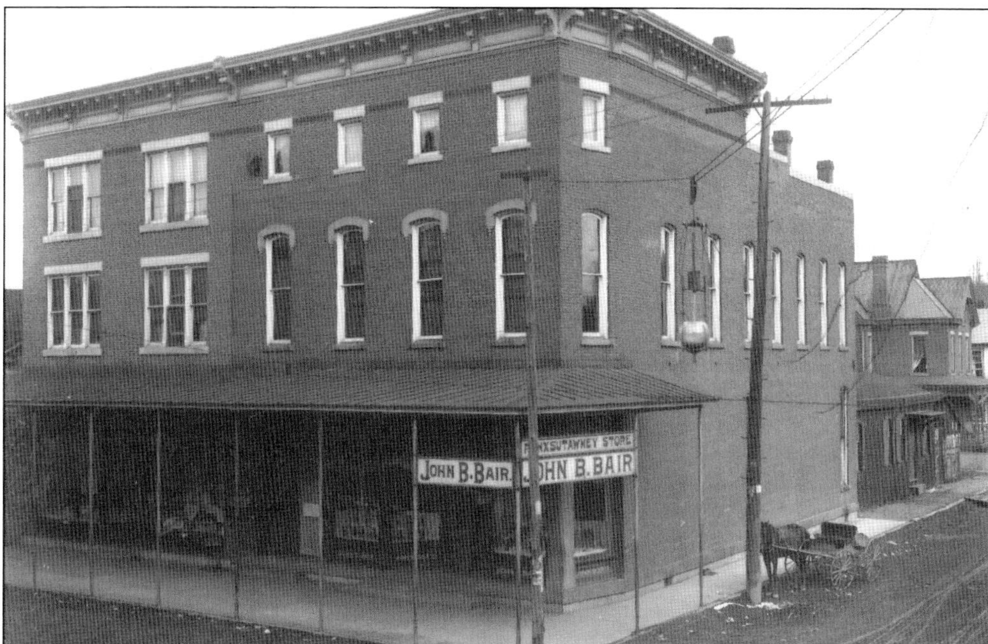

John Bair's general store was established on the corner of West Mahoning and North Gilpin Streets. His father, Ephriam, was a carpenter by trade and came to Punxsutawney in 1832. He became a property owner of considerable status and gave his son the land on which to build the huge store, which prospered for many years.

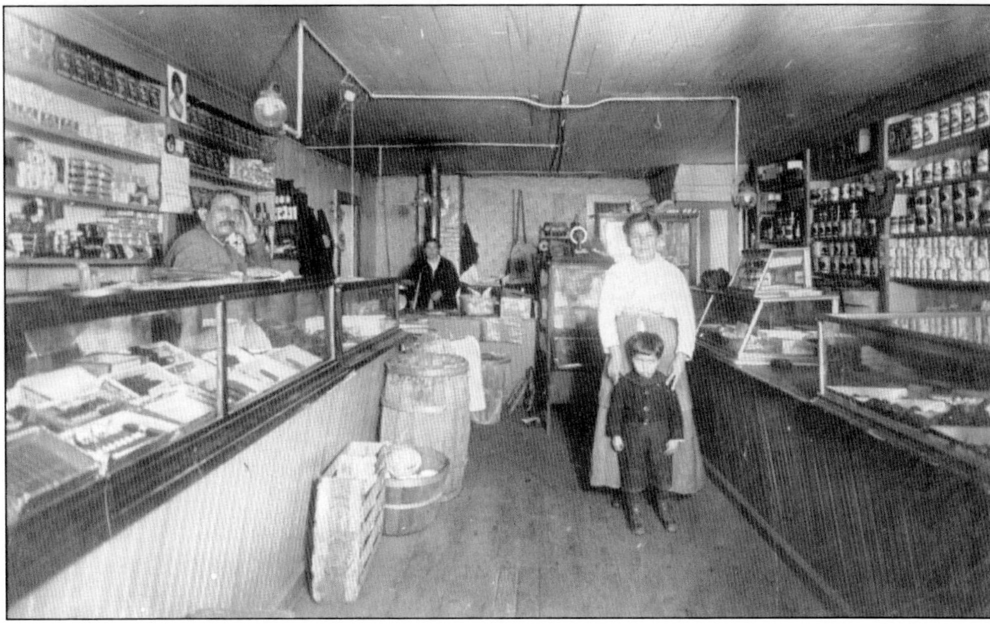

Mayo's Market was established on Gilpin Street in 1915. John Mayo, seen here behind the counter, was the proprietor. He and Rose Mayo were the parents of little Nicholas, standing with his mother. His grandmother, Pauline Schalliei, is in the background. This small grocery store was typical of those early in the century. Note the stovepipe in the background and the very early electric lights over the counters.

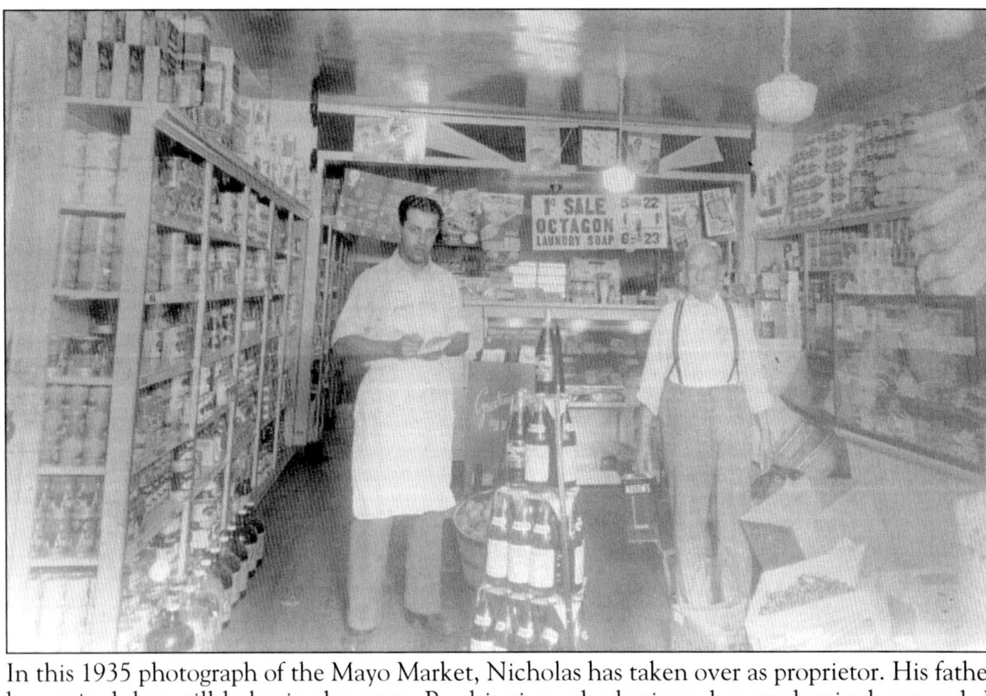

In this 1935 photograph of the Mayo Market, Nicholas has taken over as proprietor. His father has retired, but still helps in the store. By this time, the business has modernized, expanded, and relocated to the corner of Ridge and Elk Run Avenues. Expansion was necessary to serve an ever increasing population.

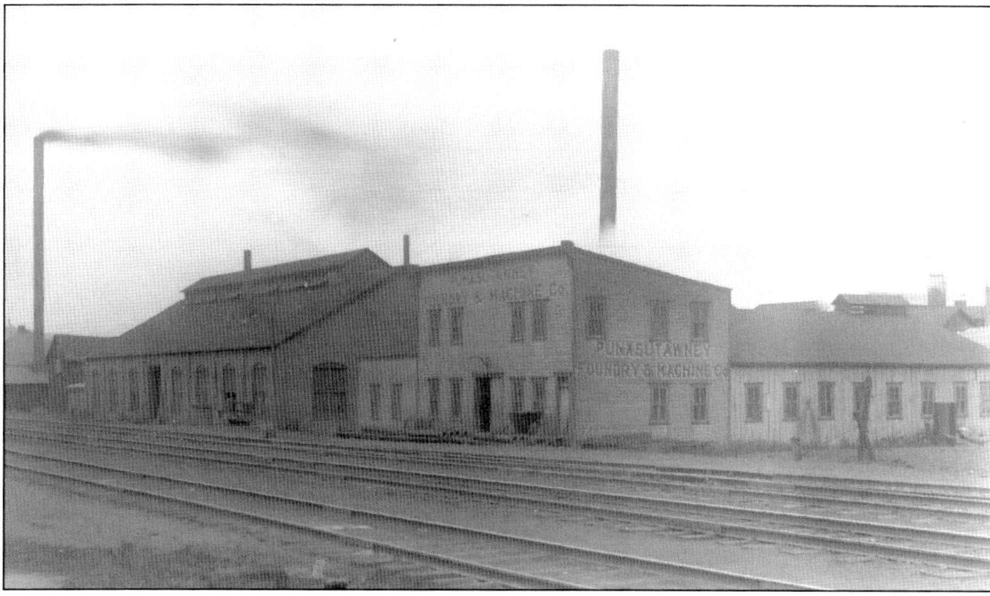

In 1850, Jacob Hoover established this foundry, operated by an overshot wheel. On occasion, the water ran out, and men would tread the wheel to regain power. The foundry was a manufacturing center for plows, threshing machines, windmills, and agricultural implements. In 1890, it was destroyed by fire. A year later, G.W. Porter established a Star Iron Works on the site of the former foundry. The Star Iron Works included a blacksmith, a boiler room, and a machine shop.

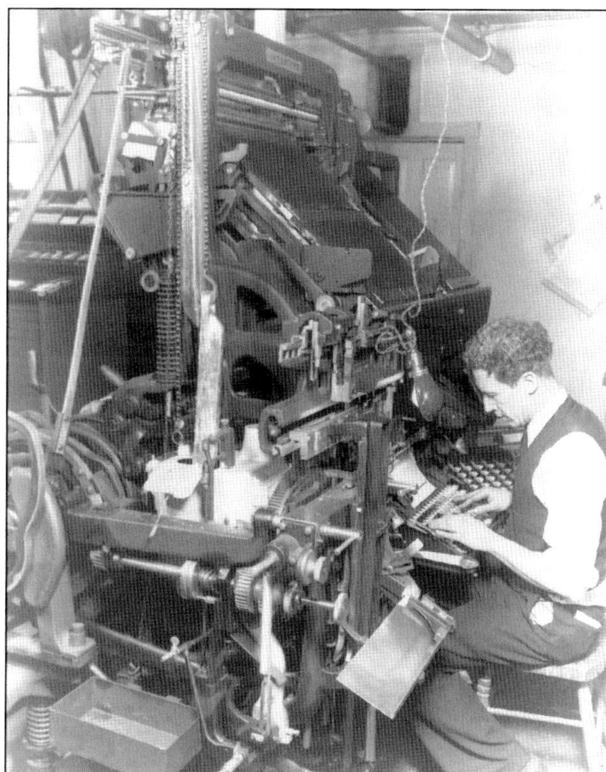

Newspapers came upon the Punxsutawney scene early in its history. Horace G. Miller is busy at his *Punxy News* linotype machine. The news publishing company was located at 230 West Mahoning Street. Horace G. Miller and Frank P. Tipton established the *Punxy News* in October 1885, and remained on as sole proprietors. They had several assistants through the years.

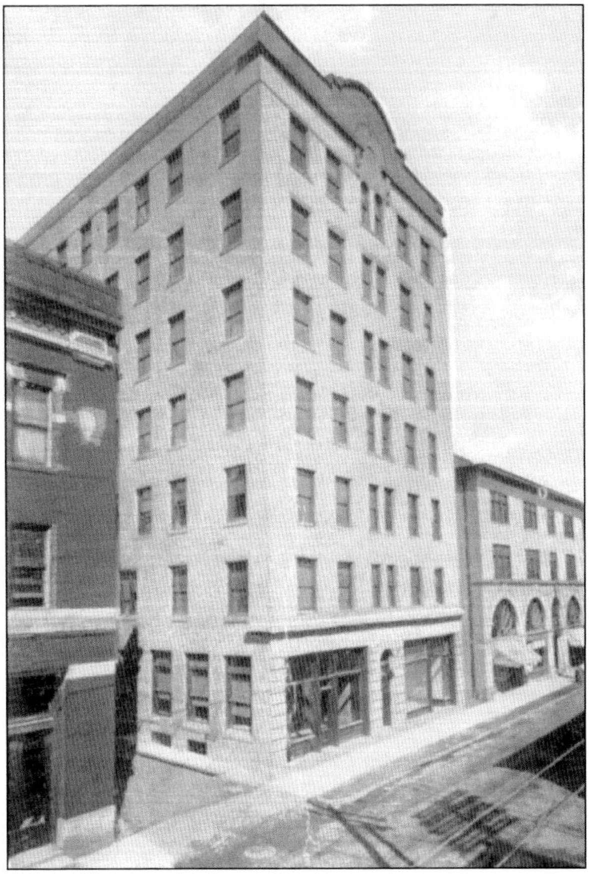

The Punxsutawney Spirit newspaper used several locations prior to 1906, when the skyscraper of the town was constructed on North Findley Street. The publication dates back to 1874, when the paper was called the *Mahoning Valley Spirit*. Clymer Freas was the first city editor. In 1906, the paper became a daily publication. It occupied three floors of the new building, including executive offices, a news plant, job printing, a bindery, an office machine department, and a retail store.

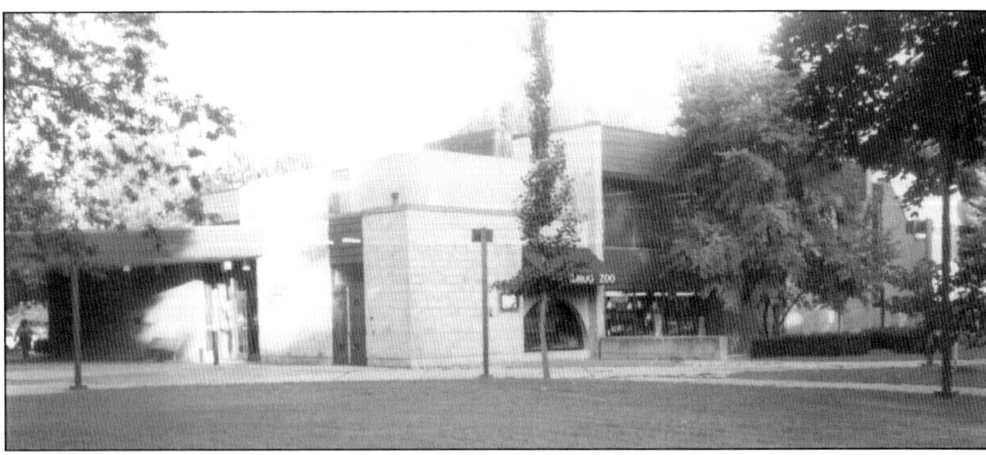

A literary society was formed in Punxsutawney. The first library was opened in Punxsutawney in 1916 at the home of Mrs. F.D. Pringle. A few years later, it relocated to South Mahoning Street. The John Jacob Fisher Post of the American Legion donated the John J. Fisher residence on West Mahoning Street for a library. It was a building of three stories and 27 rooms. The library functioned here until the new civic center complex included a library in its network of buildings.

Three

A Thriving Settlement

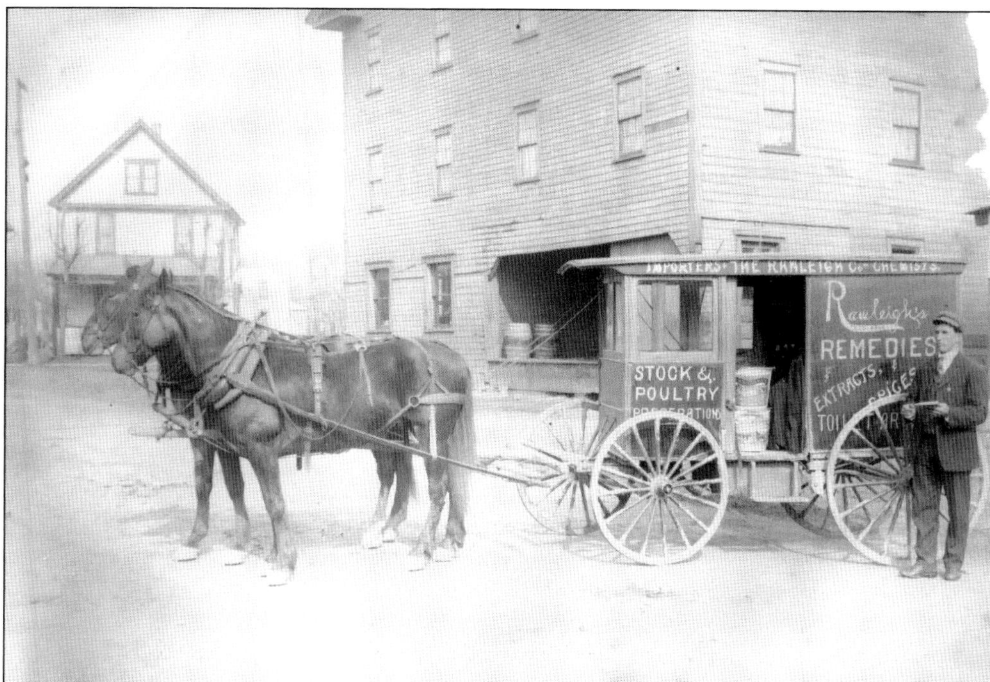

P.C. Heilbrun was a successful businessman. His first Rawleigh wagon in 1911 assisted him in serving all of Jefferson County. He boarded with regular customers and traded goods for lodging and meals, as well as for stable room and feed for his horses. People were glad to see him come because he not only supplied their needs, but often brought news of happenings elsewhere. His travels were particularly difficult during the influenza epidemic. He owned a 51-acre farm in Punxsutawney.

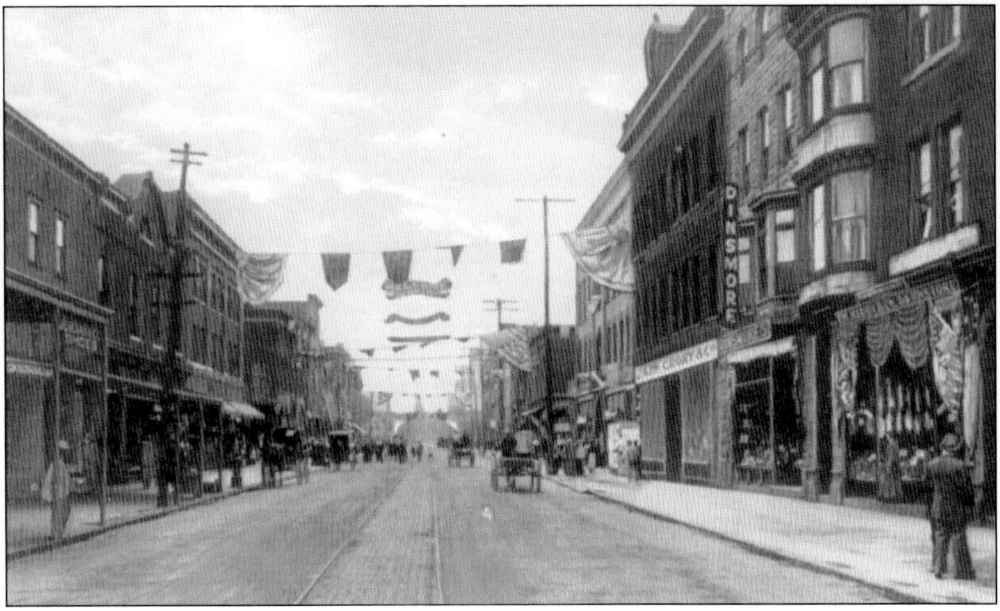

Mahoning Street of the 1800s was already flourishing with business, both retail and wholesale. The companies establishing themselves in town served all the surrounding hamlets and villages. Punxsutawney had become an industrialized community rooted in quality and service. This created a genuine asset toward maintaining the integrity of the town. In this view, banners fly over the area, and the Dinsmore store is on the left.

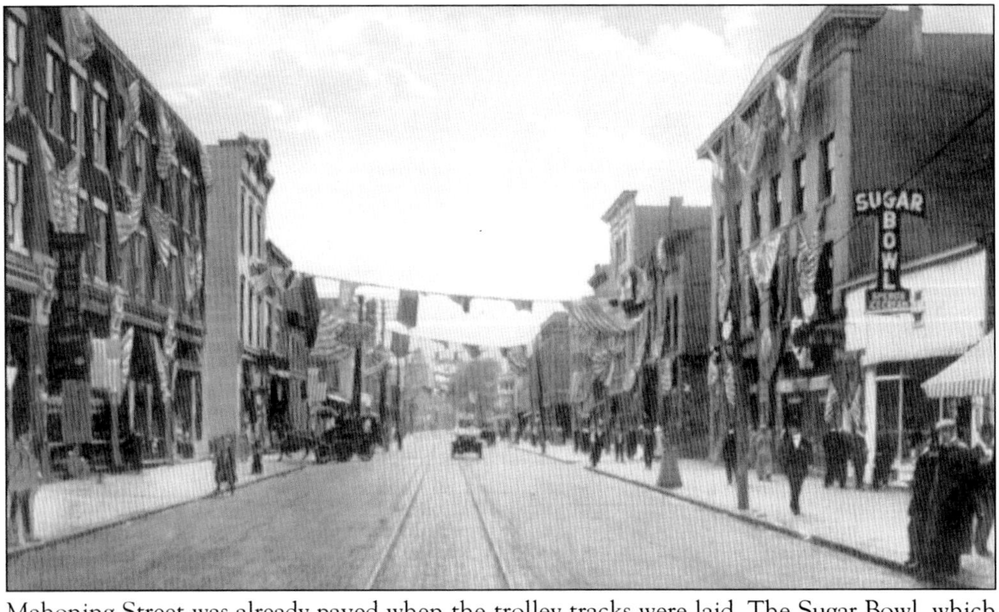

Mahoning Street was already paved when the trolley tracks were laid. The Sugar Bowl, which also advertised ice cream, was an early attraction. In many instances, ice cream could be procured only between Memorial Day and Labor Day. The flags and bunting indicate a festive occasion such as Old Home Week or the Groundhog Festival.

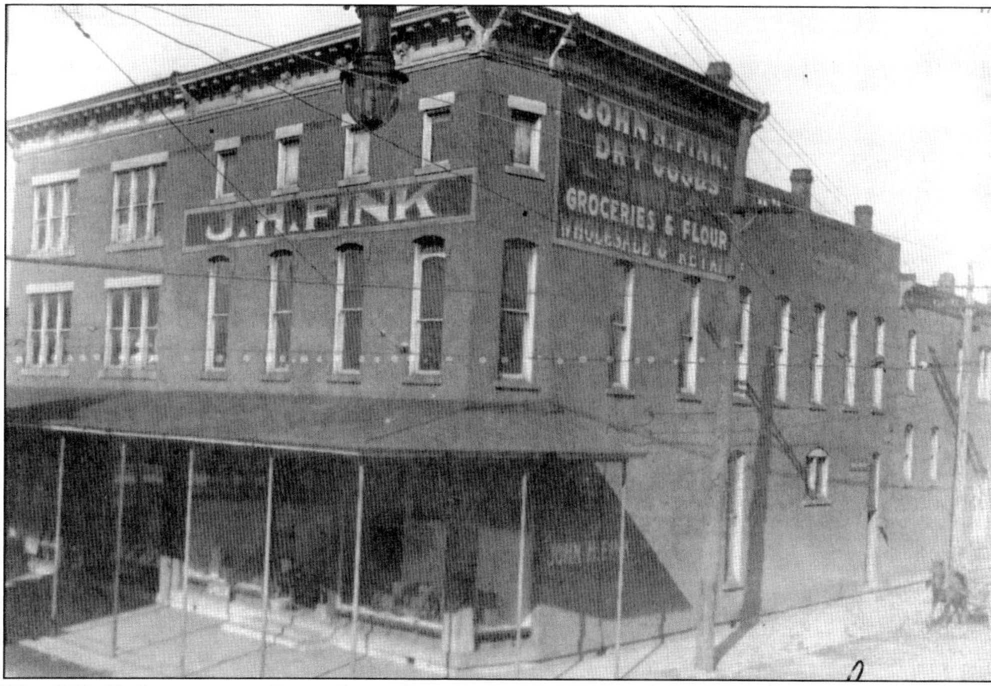

The J.H. Fink store was located on the corner of Main and Gilpin Streets. This prestigious establishment bordered on the general store. It was all part of the industrial expansion that swept Punxsutawney in the last quarter of the 19th century. The front roof of this building was often featured in parades, Old Home Week, the Groundhog Festival, and other Main Street activities since it afforded a grandstand for spectators.

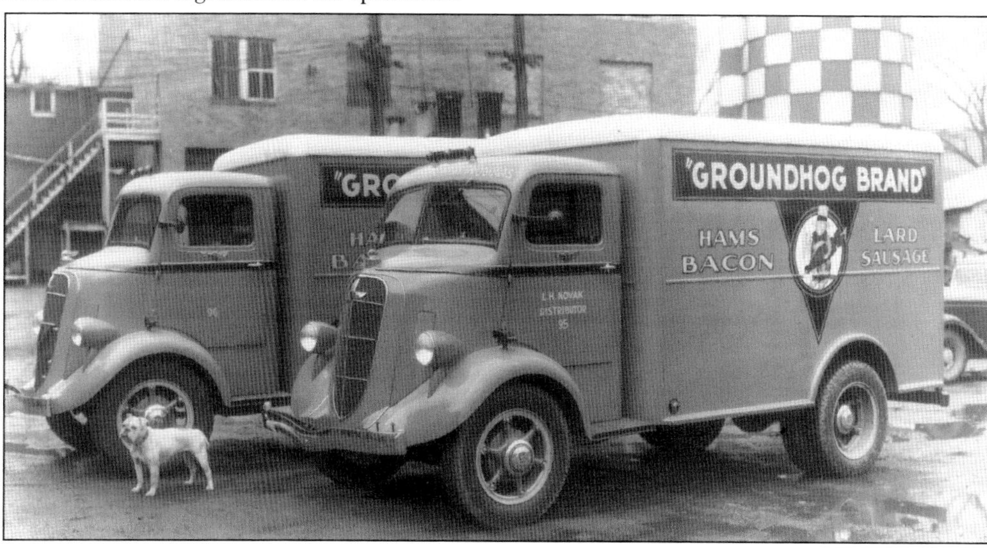

Groundhog Brand was an appropriate name for an industry founded and operated in Punxsutawney. This company was established in 1905 by John A. Philliber and was known for its beef and provisions. Philliber's sons, Jack and Harry, later took over the business. Their outstanding brand of cured meats was known and esteemed throughout the area. Originally, they established a store on South Indiana Street known as the Star Market and delivered via horse and buggy. These 1932 trucks were an asset to the business.

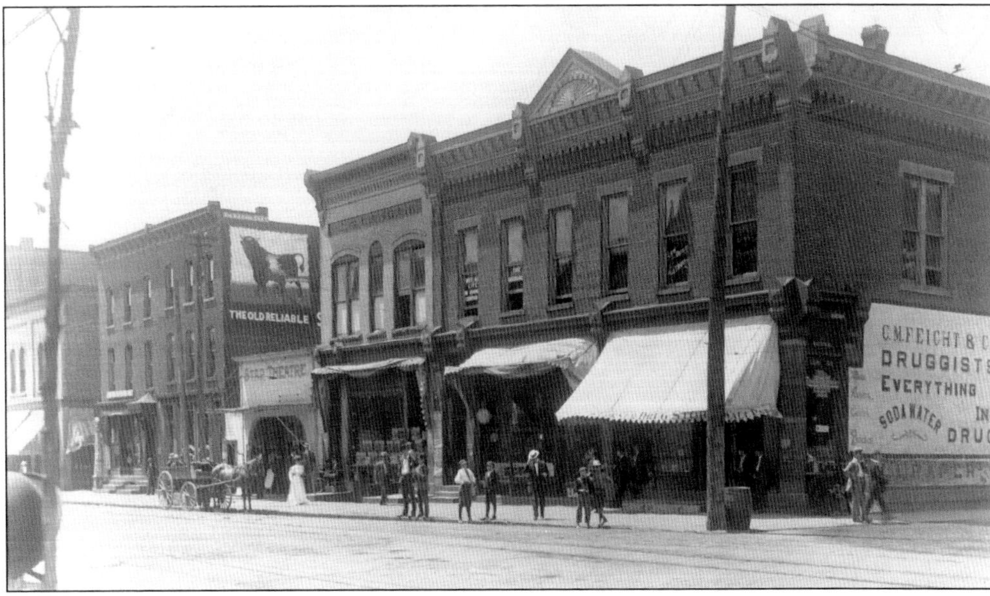

The Charles M. Feicht Pharmacy was established in 1910 on the northwest corner of Mahoning and Jefferson Streets. Feicht's wife assumed ownership in 1922 after his death. Nine years later, she sold the building to Peter Johnson, who opened Johnson's Grill. In 1937, a nephew of Feicht returned to Punxsutawney to manage the Means and Laut Pharmacy, which he eventually bought. The Feicht name was returned to a local drugstore after an 18-year absence. Note the law office of A.J. Trulett above the store.

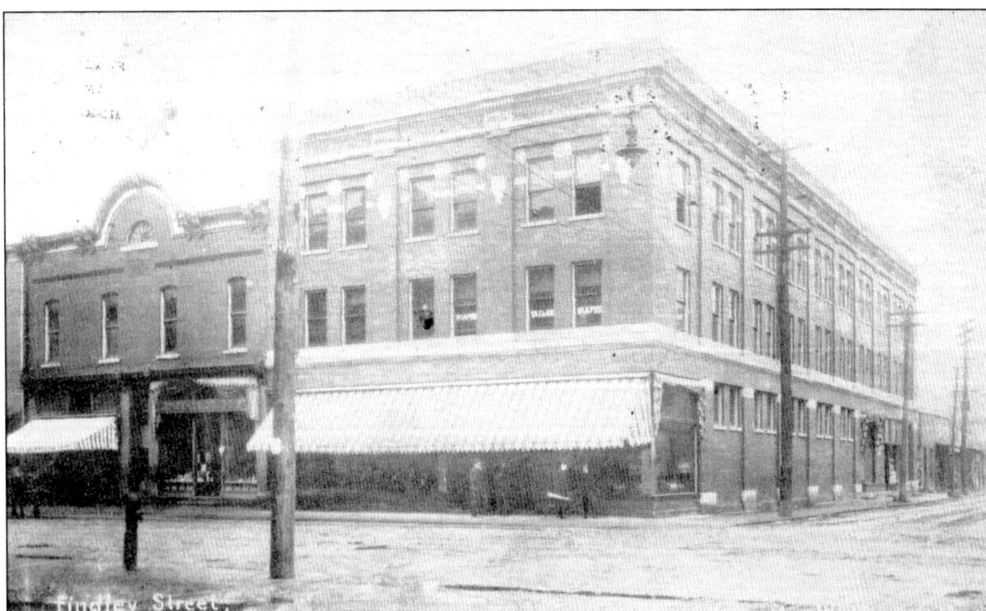

John A. Weber was a successful businessman in the late 1800s. Owner of the Weber Men's Clothing Store on Mahoning Street and president of several other enterprises, he amassed a small fortune. He and his wife, Emma, had two children. His desire after his death (1910) was to be remembered for doing something for the community. He donated his fortune to the construction and maintenance of a manual training and domestic science school for Punxsutawney children.

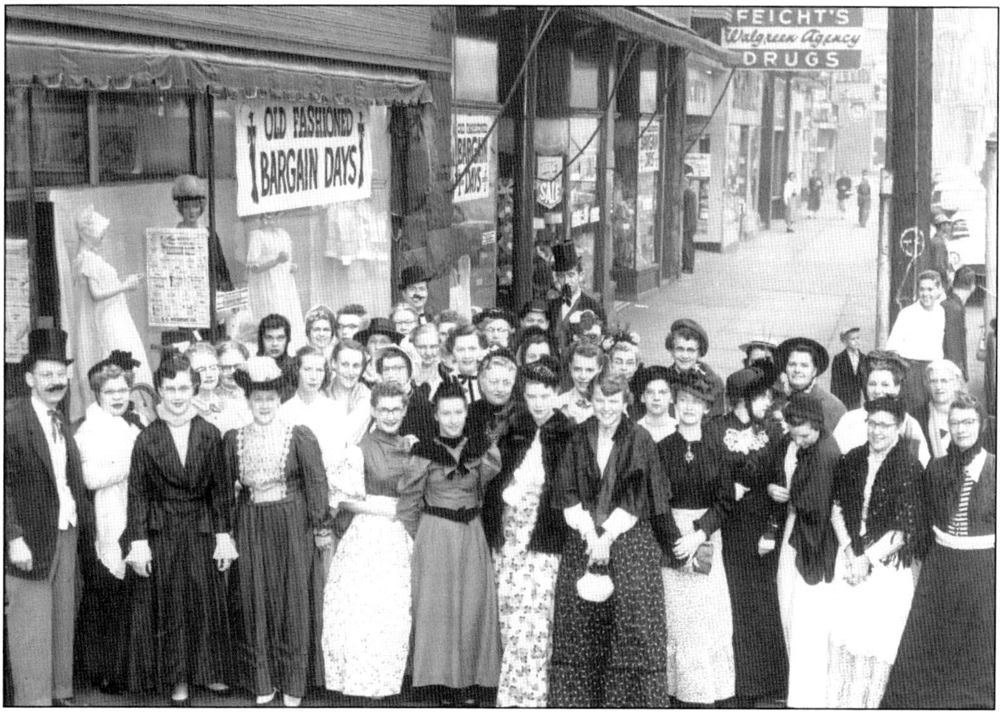

The G. Murphy Five & Ten employees were numerous in the mid-20th century. Located on West Mahoning Street, the chain store was especially popular during bargain days. The building was later purchased by J.B. Eberhart, who envisioned a department store there. The first variety store in town was established in 1820 and was followed by a long line of prosperous businesses.

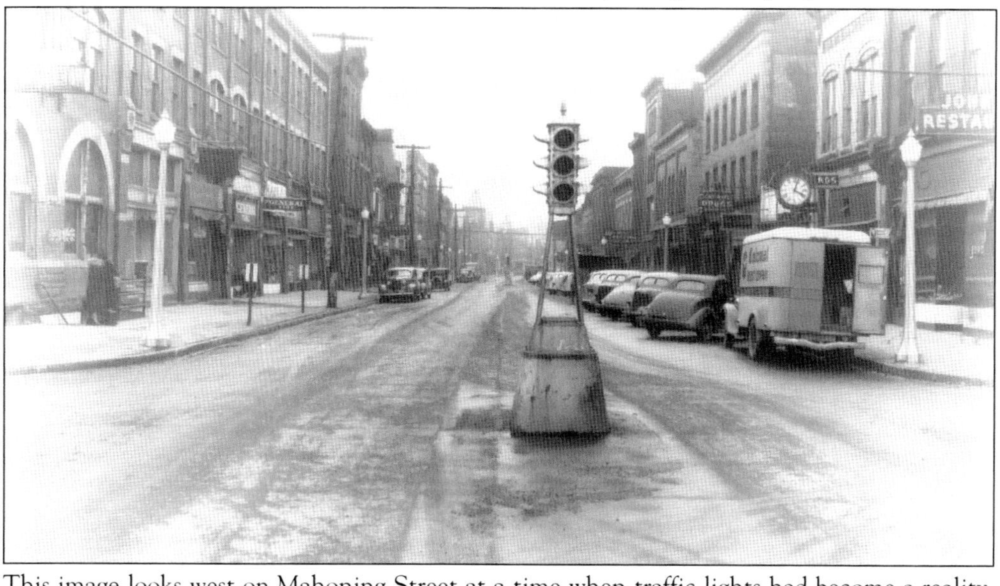

This image looks west on Mahoning Street at a time when traffic lights had become a reality. The concept of incandescent traffic lights at the town's major crossroads created a fascination that drew crowds from far and wide. This strange modern curiosity was not to be missed. Extraordinary little glowing sparkles lit the night sky and presented an innovative peculiar spectacle to early pioneers.

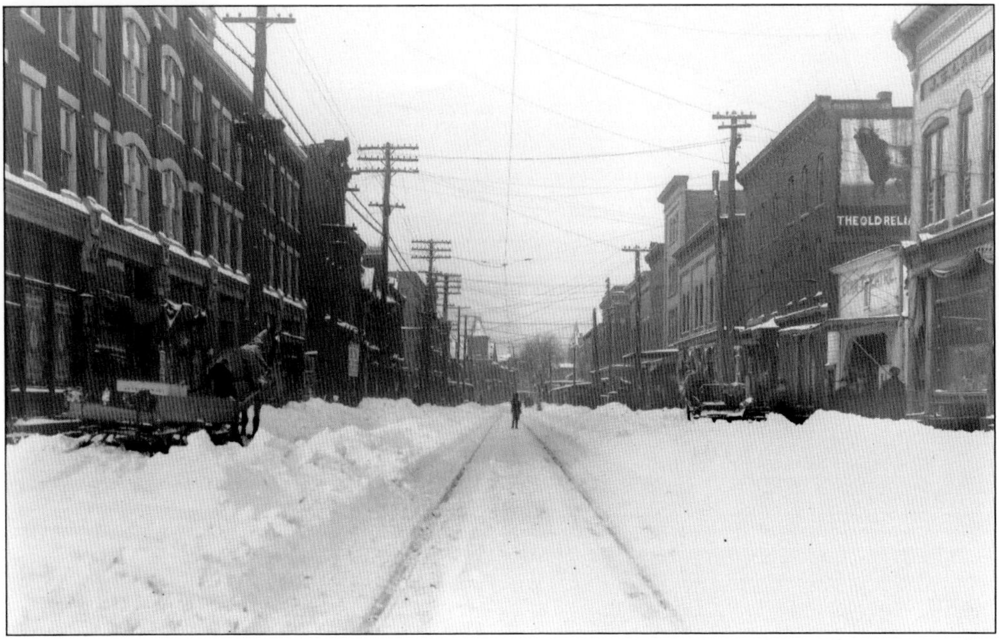

Mahoning Street presented a challenge to the winter traveler early in the 20th century. This abundant natural resource, snow, is a very common phenomenon in western Pennsylvania. High snowdrifts were part of the seasonal scene. Winters were very long and often extremely cold. Note the delivery sleigh on the left and the carriage on the right. The horses are ready to brave the elements.

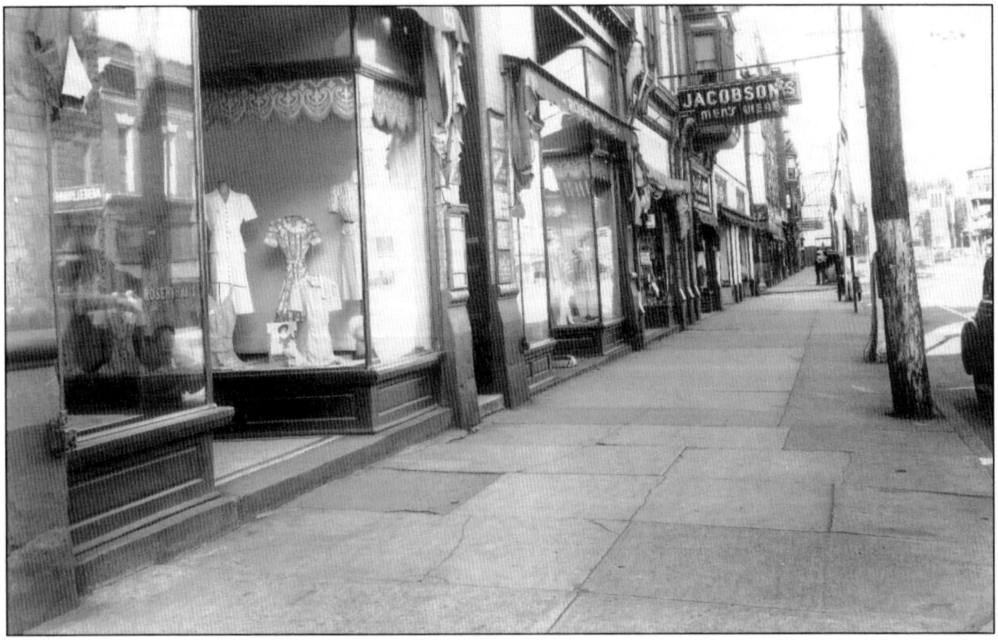

Jacobson's Men's Wear was established in 1911 by Louis Jacobson. Initially situated on Findley Street, it prospered in an era of specialty shops. These were a forerunner of our department stores today. The little shop quickly outgrew its space. In 1921, Jacobson relocated the business to the center of town on East Mahoning Street.

Stanton Ragley established the Maytag Company in 1932. He opened initially in the old Glecker building on Findley Avenue. During the war years, his business was curtailed and he closed the store temporarily, but kept the service of appliances open in his warehouse. In 1944, he relocated to Mahoning Street across from Barclay Square and resumed business. Appliances and furniture were added later. Ragley's descendants keep the tradition alive with Ragley's Hardware on Findley Street.

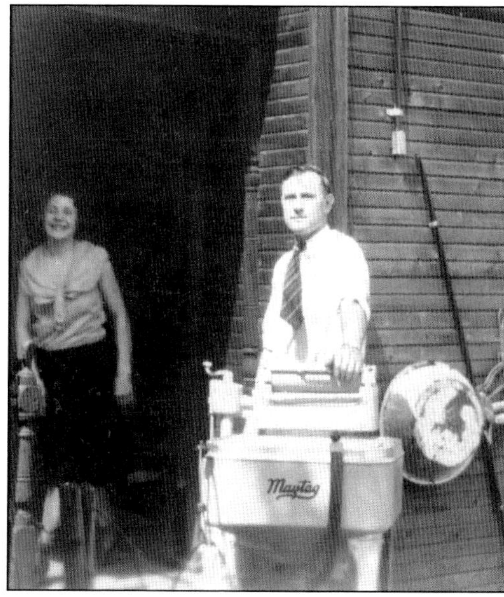

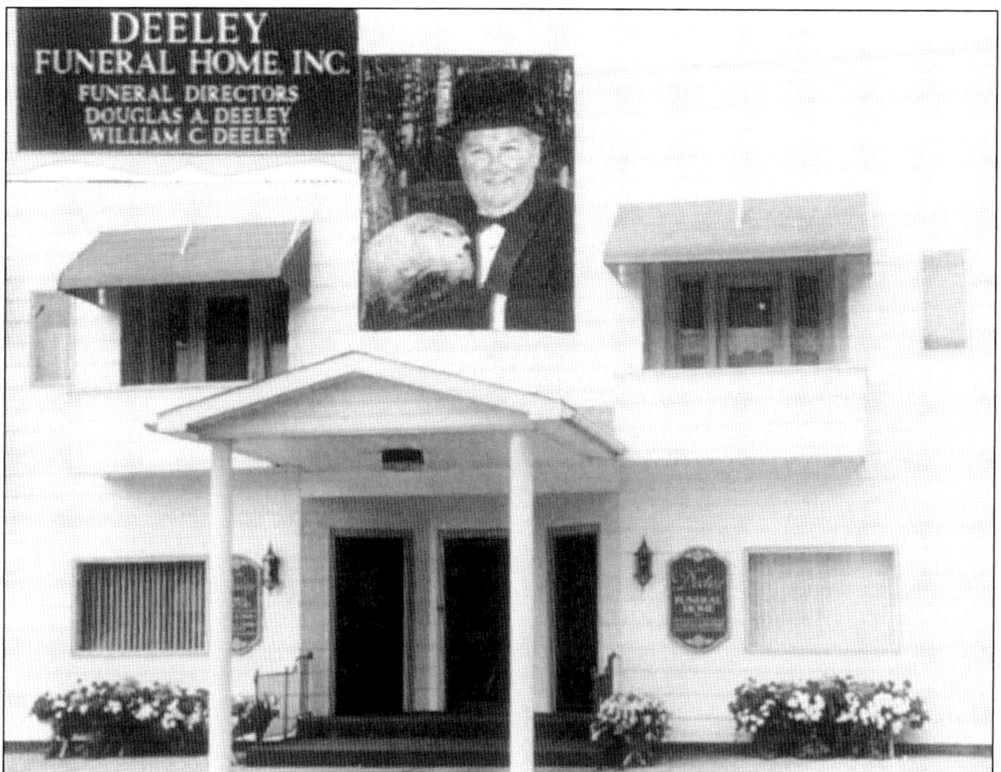

The Deeley Funeral Home was established by William (Bill) Deeley on Gilpin Street in 1976. He is a native of Anita and a graduate of the Pittsburgh Institute of Mortuary Science. His brother, Douglas, joined him in the funeral profession. They worked together, making it a family business. Bill married Jean Bish of Frostburg; the couple have two daughters, Beth and Michele. They lived at the Gilpin Street site. Bill is also well known as the handler for Punxsutawney Phil, the famous groundhog.

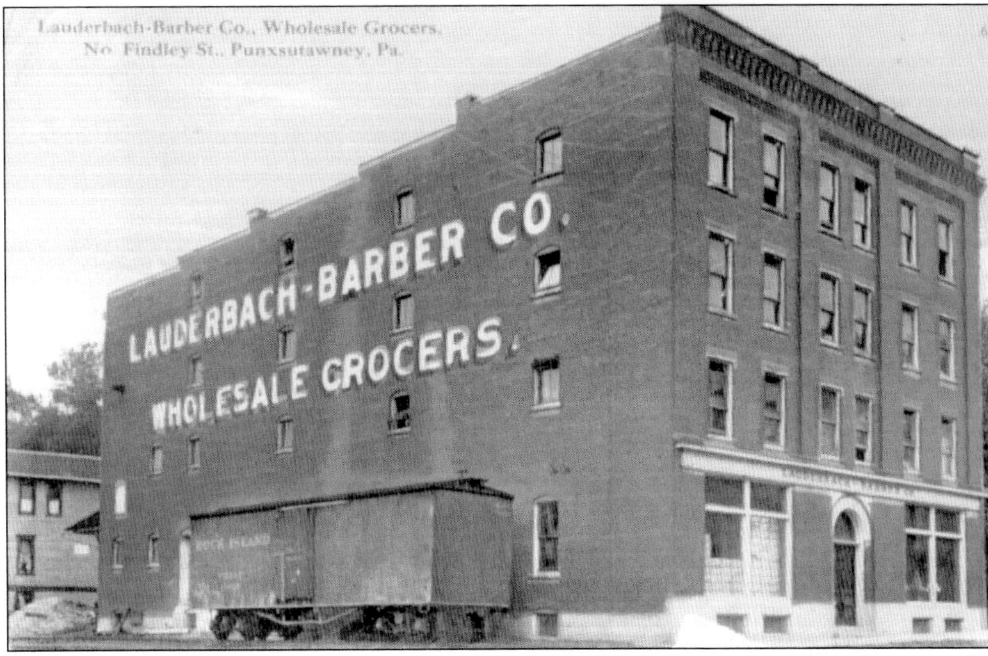

The Lauderbach-Barber Company was established in 1902. Sites that have been home to this firm include the Old Brewery, the Ford Building, and the North Hotel. In 1910, a four-story building was constructed on North Findley Street to house the business. Lauderbach-Barber was the only wholesale grocer in town and served Punxsutawney as well as many surrounding coal towns. Salesmen traveled by train and horse-and-buggy to make deliveries. The company was always limited to wholesale distribution.

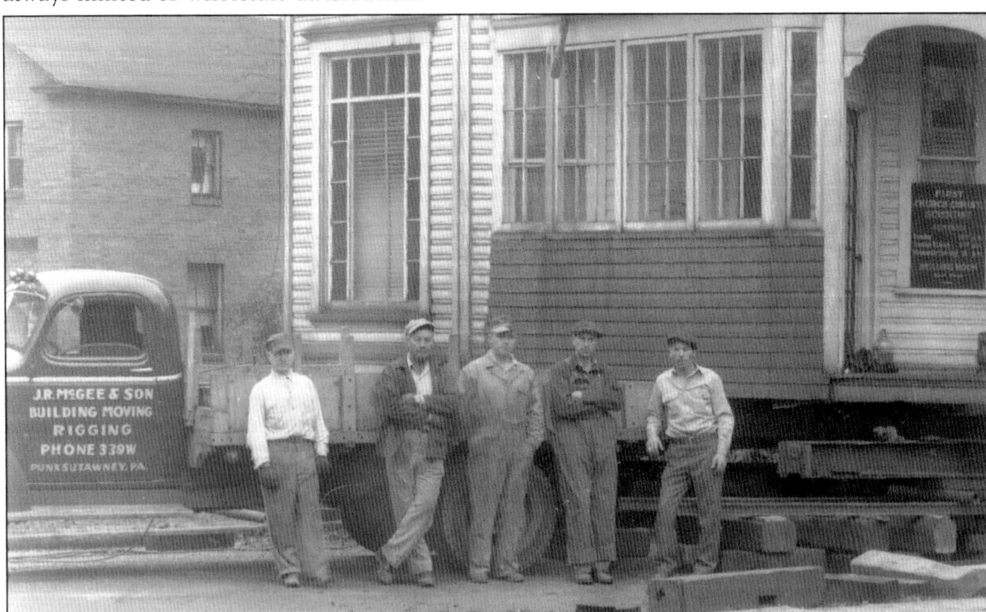

The McGee & Son Moving and Razing Company was founded by J.R. McGee in 1900. The company specialized in building and house moving. It was located on Virginia Avenue and was taken over by Willis McGee, the founder's son. He appears fourth from the left.

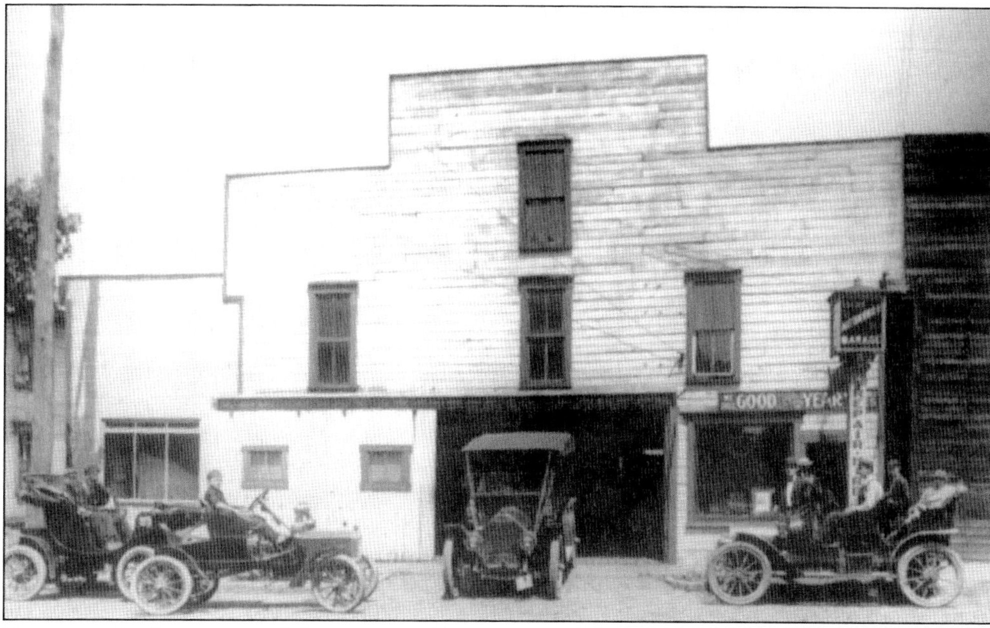

Freas was the first automobile garage in Punxsutawney. It was established on North Jefferson Street in 1909 by P.O. Freas. He was a bicycle, electrical, and auto merchant. Initially located in the Carl North building, the business relocated in 1926 to a newly constructed site. Freas brothers Jay, William, and Philip initially sold Templar, Graham Paige, Hupmobile, and Marmon automobiles along with Bessmer trucks. In 1922, the Dodge franchise was granted to the firm.

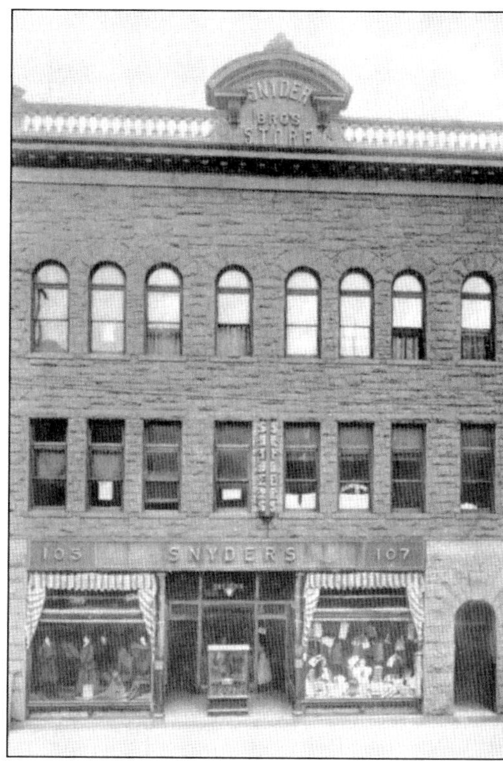

Snyder established a large dry goods store on Mahoning Street. He offered the best products from cloth mills around the world. He employed expert tailors who worked with only the most serviceable, fashionable fabrics in imported and domestic goods. Snyder kept endless displays of cloth for the entire family. Business was so good that his staff of six was increased to ten on weekends. His motto was, "Quick sales, small profit, only cash trade."

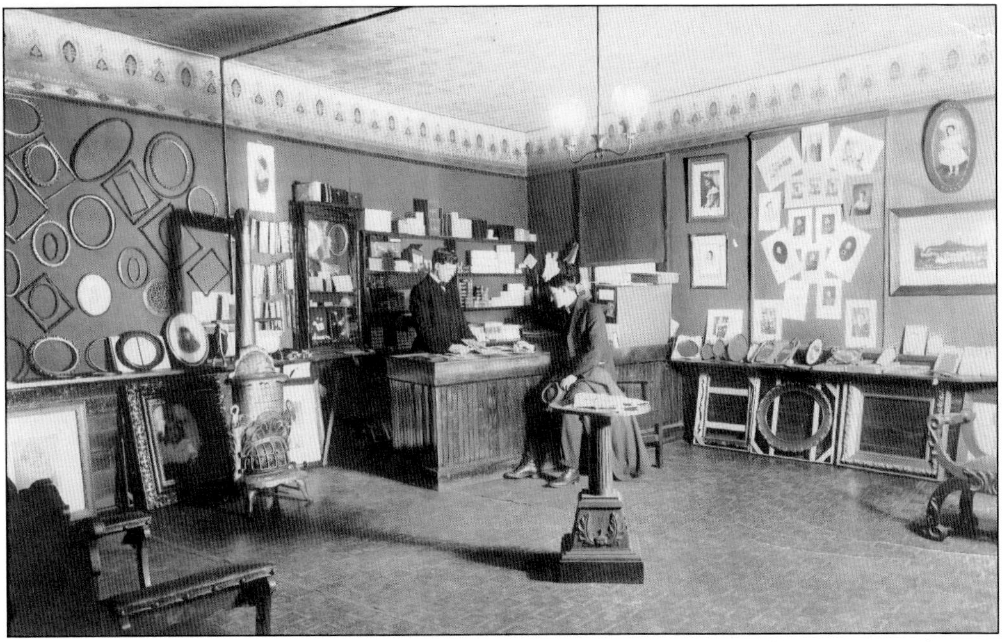

Jean H. White founded the White Photograph Studio in 1897. Located on West Mahoning Street, the studio had a northern exposure skylight, which was necessary for taking pictures at that time. White initiated the idea of candid shots at weddings and school activities. Negatives date back to 1897 and were produced on glass. They yielded sparkling new photographs. In 1920, he inaugurated the use of newly developed portrait film. Many of the images in this book were taken by the White Photograph Studio.

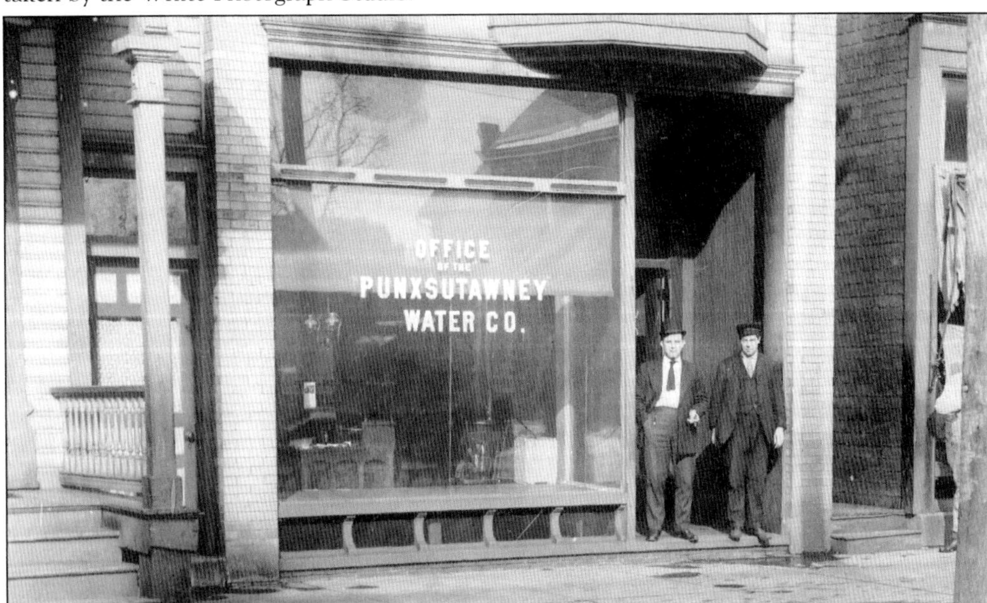

The water company was formed in 1886. Six wells were drilled 1,000 feet from Front Street, and huge tanks were sunk at the north end of town. Fire hydrants were installed. The water works was complete in 1887, and with its completion came the rates. These monthly rates cost hotels \$6, livery stables 25¢, saloons \$2, barbershops \$1, and dwellings 75¢, with baths being 50¢ extra.

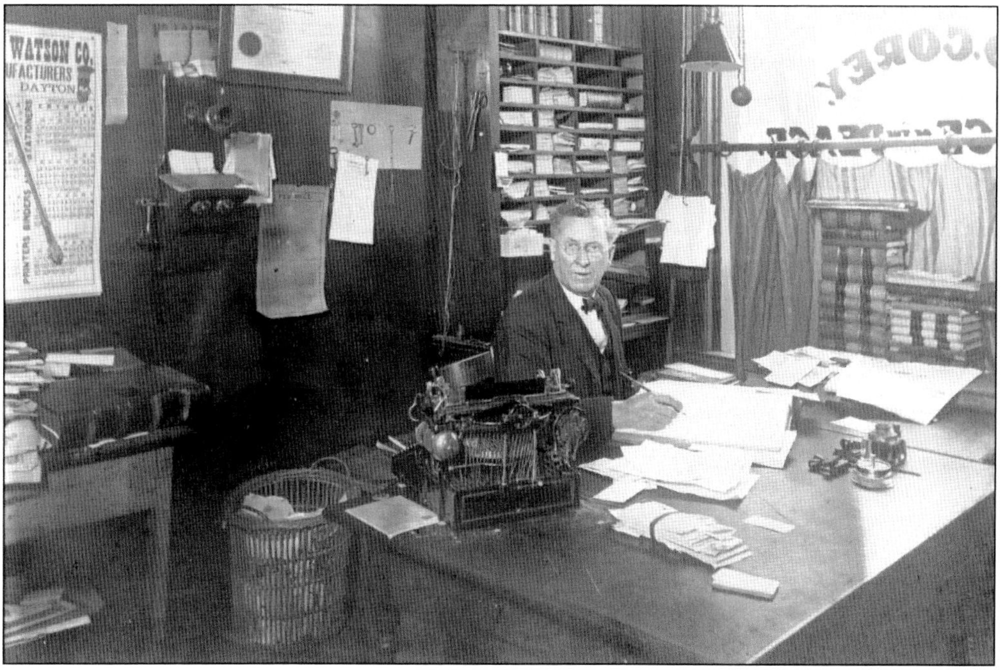

N.D. Corey was the justice of the peace in 1909. Note the vintage Oliver typewriter and the classic telephone. His position as local magistrate included maintaining justice, administering oaths, performing marriages, and enforcing the law. Ordinances of the era regulated local government, physical expansion, and public industries. Fines were given for placing obstructions in the Public Square or for permitting livestock on the public thoroughfare.

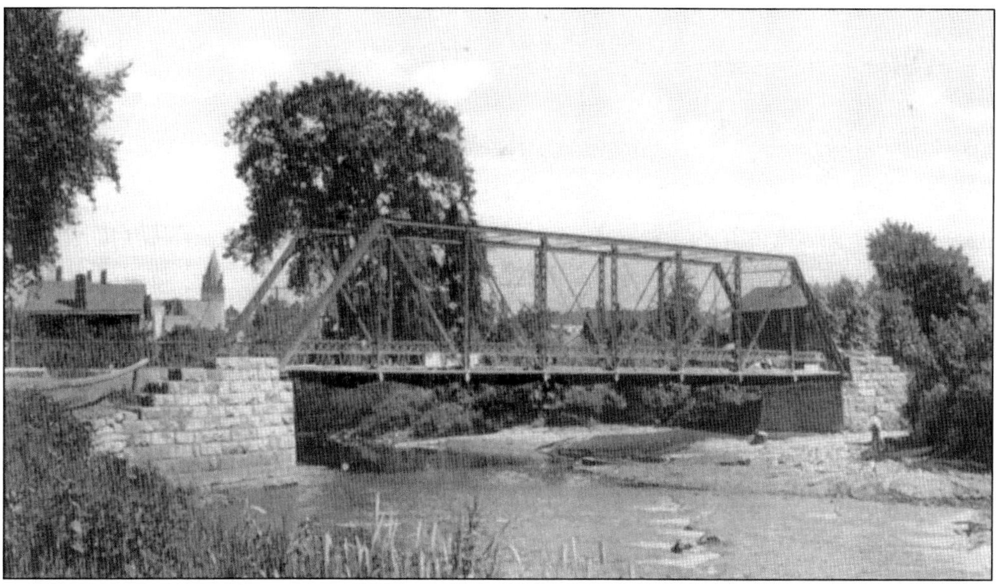

The Old Indiana Bridge spans the creek in Punxsutawney. The creek is shallow, but this serviceable stream of water provided a backdrop for fishermen, hikers, and youngsters. It proved most beneficial in the days of rafting and logging. It has its source in several streams above Big Run. These form the 30-mile Mahoning Waterway that eventually flows into the Allegheny River near Kittaning, Pennsylvania.

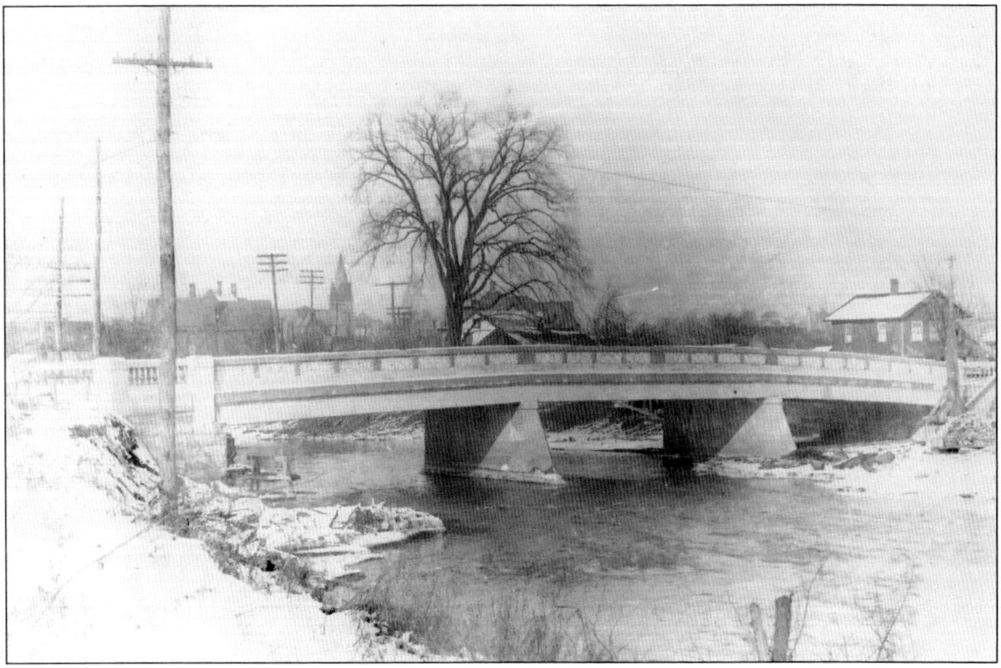

A new bridge was constructed over Mahoning Creek. Punxsutawney is a land of bridges. The creek usually remains calm and has always been an aid to the many industries in the area. The town is forever intertwined with the stream that flows through it. The spacing of the many bridges creates a scenic view as one looks down the creek.

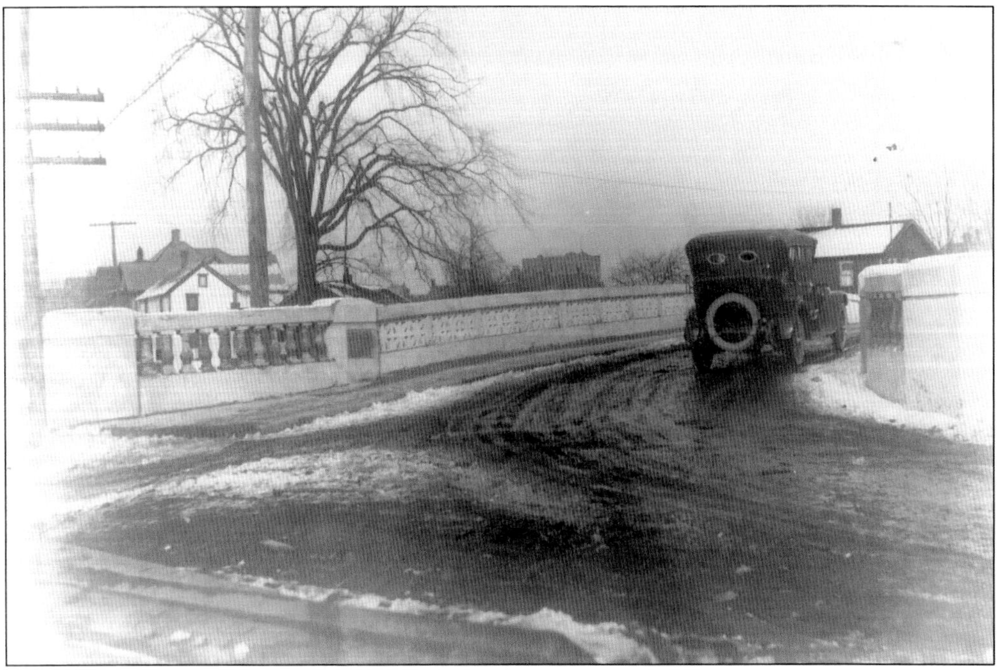

A car crosses the new bridge in the mid-1930s. Bridges were always a necessity in a settlement where a picturesque creek winds its way through the town. Industries continued to locate on the creek after the logging industry had run its course.

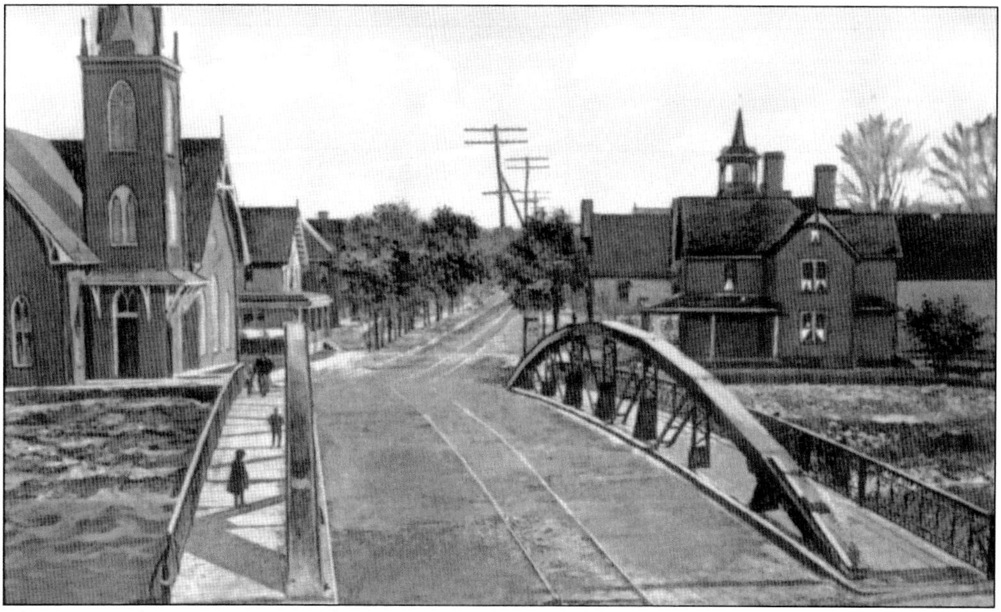

The East Mahoning Street Bridge spans the creek at the hub of activity near Barclay Square. Beneath the bridge, high school students have designed artwork along with the word "Punxsutawney" inscribed in big, bold letters on the wall of the dike.

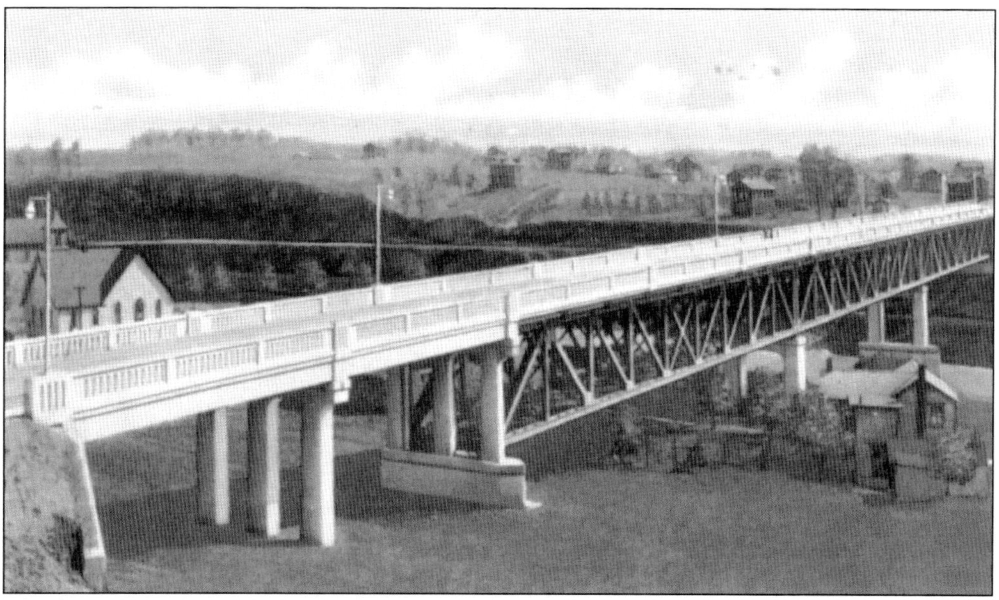

Charles Margiotti was a native of Punxsutawney. He became the Pennsylvania state attorney and earned the title "Tiger at the Bar," which became the title of his biography. He was responsible for the construction of this bridge at the west end of town. Margoitti was influential in aiding his hometown. He arranged for the state police troop and for the Pennsylvania State Highway Department to be headquartered at Punxsutawney. He also maintained close ties with the Groundhog Club. He brought many dignitaries to town for Groundhog Day.

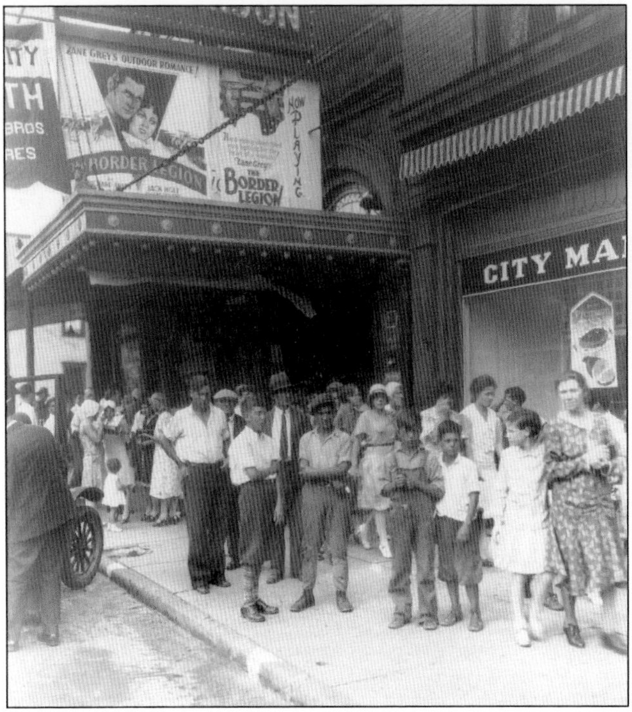

People gather around the Jefferson Theater on North Findley Street before a performance. The theater was opened in 1906 by a stock company and succeeded the old opera house. The new theater was an elegant, modern playhouse with a seating capacity of 1,280 people. Before the advent of silent movies, it catered to live plays produced by the locals. It was named for Joseph Jefferson, whose son was an actor. The first play staged at the Jefferson was *The Princess Chick* in the fall of 1906.

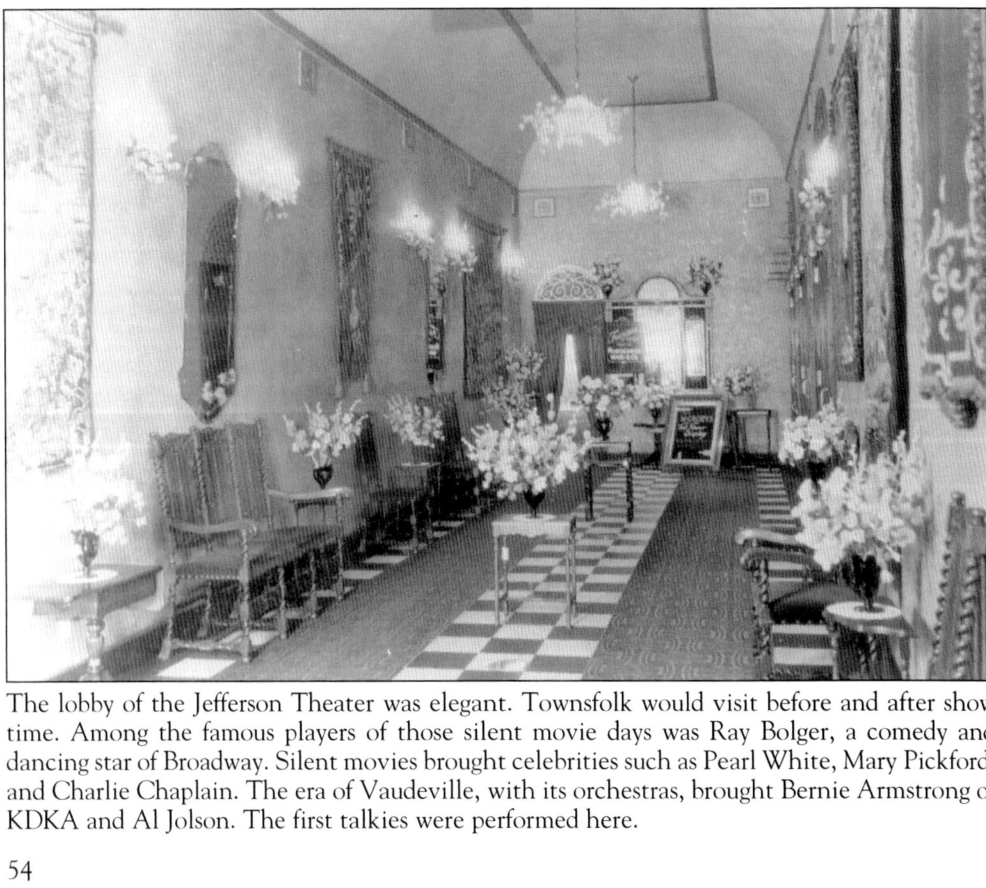

The lobby of the Jefferson Theater was elegant. Townsfolk would visit before and after show time. Among the famous players of those silent movie days was Ray Bolger, a comedy and dancing star of Broadway. Silent movies brought celebrities such as Pearl White, Mary Pickford, and Charlie Chaplain. The era of Vaudeville, with its orchestras, brought Bernie Armstrong of KDKA and Al Jolson. The first talkies were performed here.

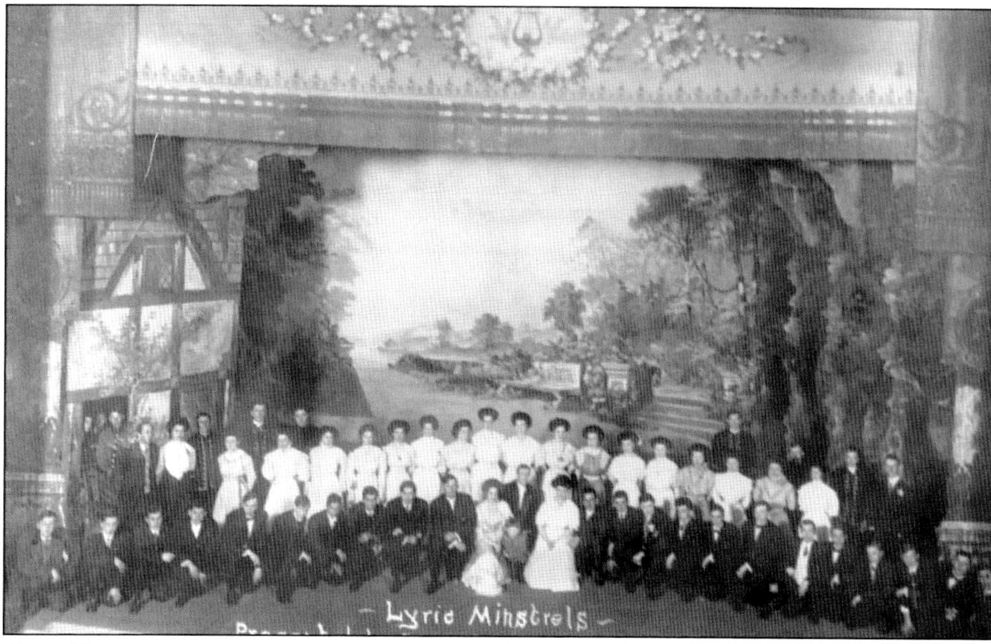

The Jefferson Theater was host to many minstrels through the early years. These minstrels were often medieval musical entertainers. Programs of music, melody, and impersonations proceeded the era of the silent moving picture. They performed throughout town as well as on stage. Minstrels phased out with the coming of talkie motion pictures. The Mask Wig Club presented this lyric minstrel on March 17, 1909.

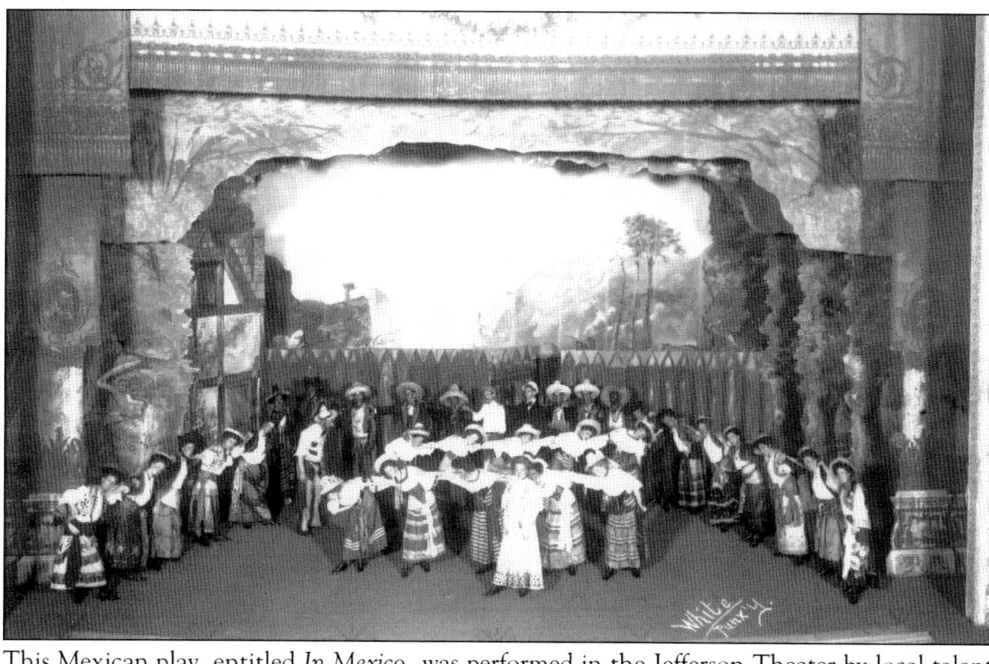

This Mexican play, entitled *In Mexico*, was performed in the Jefferson Theater by local talent on May 25 and 26, 1908. Plays by locals were a highly prized form of entertainment. The Jefferson Theater was built solely for entertainment. It was heated by steam and lighted by electricity. Zana Grey's outdoor romance *The Border Legion* played at the Jefferson in 1929.

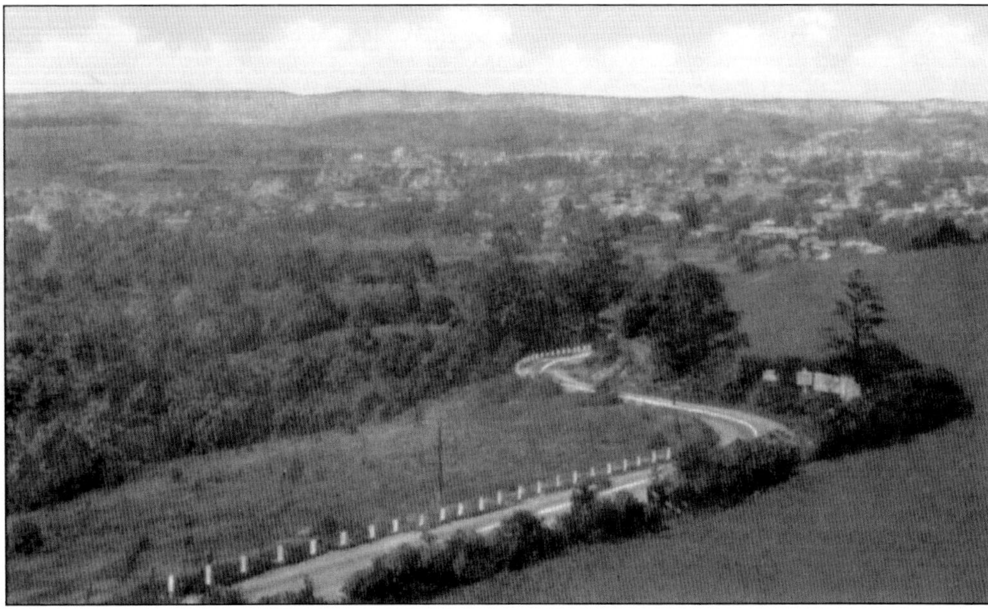

The Buffalo-Pittsburgh Highway was paved early in the era of automobile travel. It connected the two major cities on a picturesque drive through the country. A segment of the 350-mile stretch wound its way through Punxsutawney. Many local roads were constructed to branch out from this major highway.

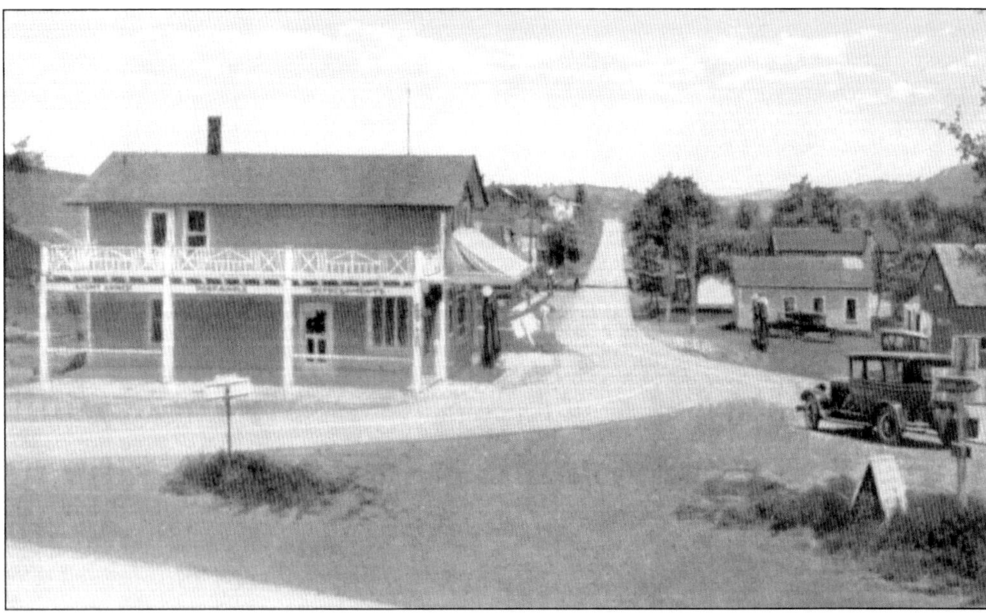

The triangle on the Buffalo-Pittsburgh Highway was a landmark. It was a rest stop for travelers along the 27-mile span connecting Punxsutawney and Indiana. The road evolved into what we now know as Route 119. The Rose Angle Restaurant catered refreshments and lunches; it was a favorite stopping place for the Model T citizens of the Roaring Twenties.

Four

Yesteryear around Town

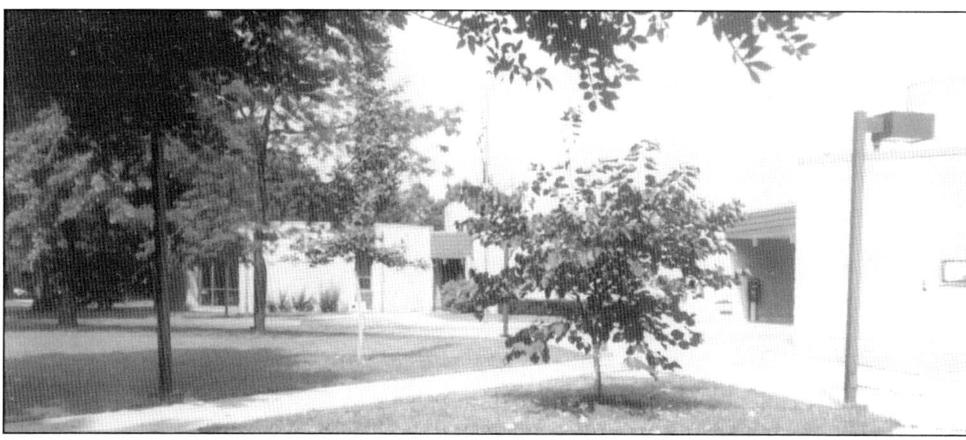

Groundbreaking for the East Mahoning Civic Center Complex took place in August 1973. The edifice contains 23,000 square feet of fluted concrete blocks. The buildings display unity in diversity with geometric shapes and abstract sculpture. It is a multipurpose facility that combines all civic functions. The buff-colored complex contains administrative offices, a court chamber, a police department, a jail, the central fire house, a library, and the Groundhog Zoo with Punxsutawney Phil, the world-famous groundhog.

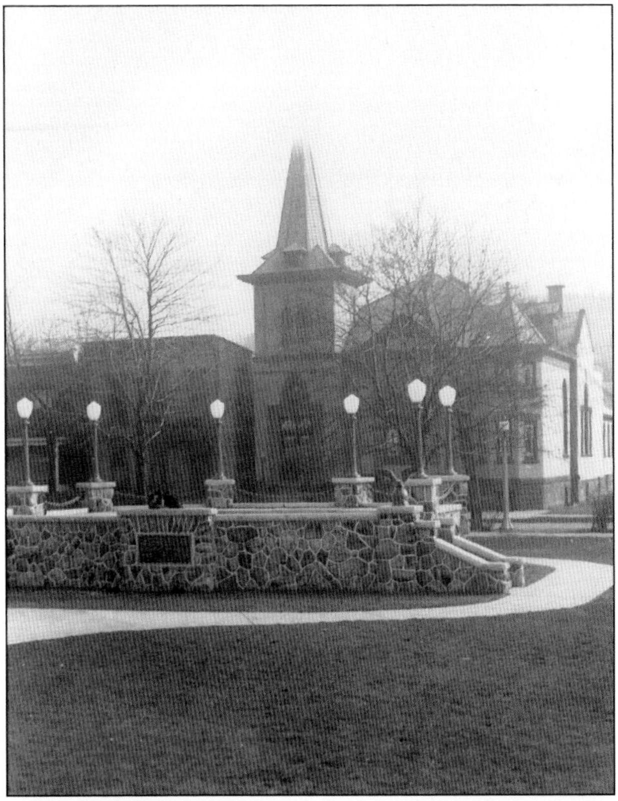

The First Baptist congregation was formed in 1840. The congregation met in a school building on the Public Square and later on the northwest corner of Farmer's Alley and Jefferson Street. In 1904, a permanent site was purchased on East Union Avenue, between Jefferson and Penn Streets facing Barclay Square. The church was constructed of yellow brick and featured stained-glass windows. Pastor Henry Madtes brought in high-grade entertainment to defray the expenses of completing the church.

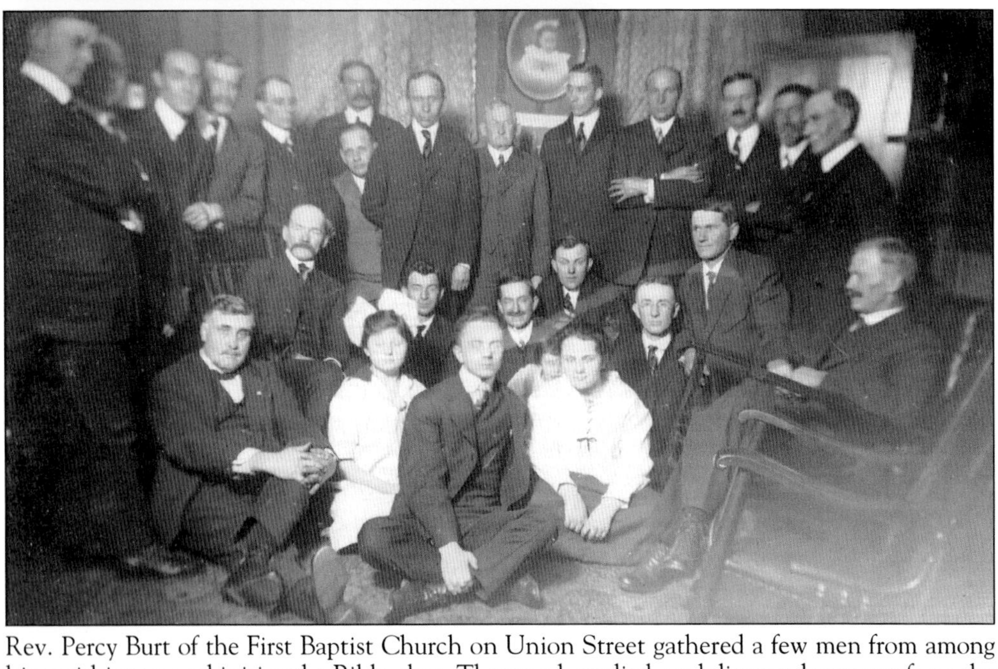

Rev. Percy Burt of the First Baptist Church on Union Street gathered a few men from among his parishioners and initiated a Bible class. They read, studied, and discussed passages from the Bible. It gave them a greater knowledge of the Bible and an opportunity to talk about the text with others of the same religious persuasion.

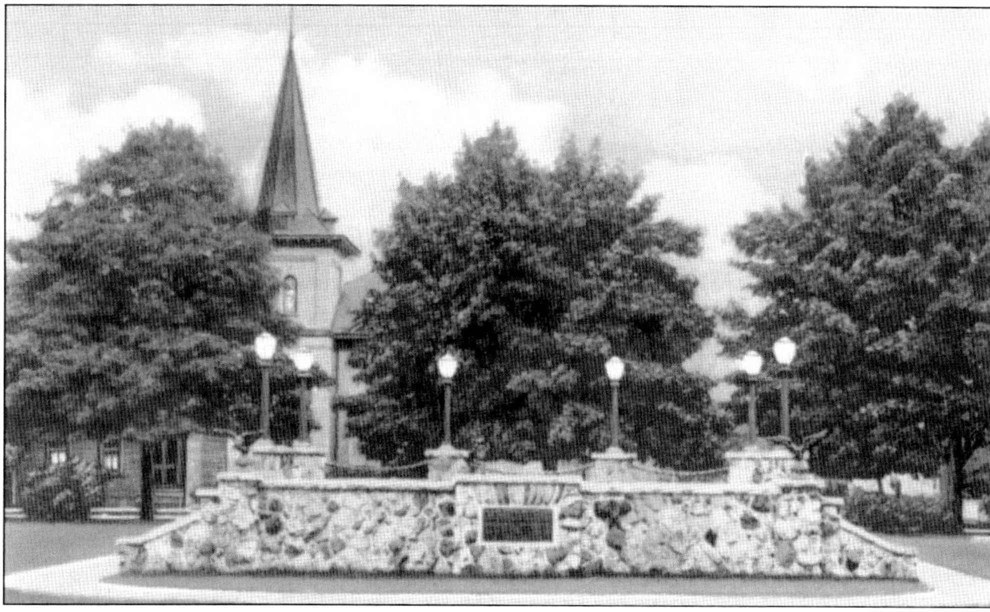

The Soldiers Memorial Bandstand was built on Barclay Square in 1911 at the request of the Citizen's Band. Constructed of wood in an octagonal shape, it stood on 16 feet of cement at the northwest corner of the park. In 1932, the old wooden bandstand was removed, and one made of native stone was constructed 100 feet from Mahoning Street. It was dedicated to the veterans of all wars in recognition of their valiant service. The ceremony took place on Armistice Day, November 11, 1932.

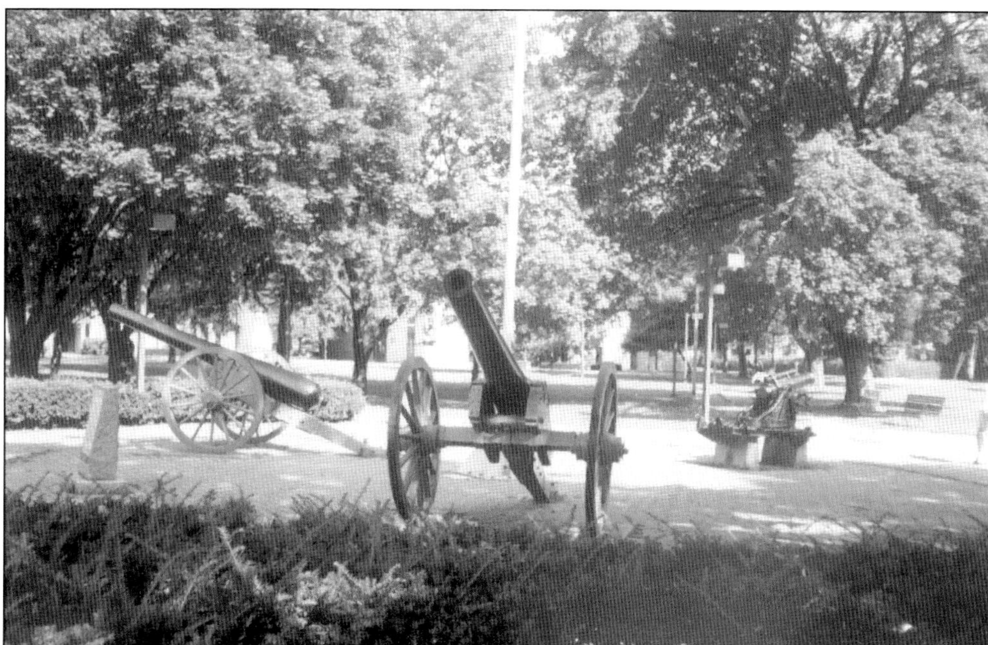

In 1897, the U.S. War Department presented two large Civil War cannons to E.H. Little of Punxsutawney as a gift. They were conferred in a formal ceremony dedicated to peace. The cannons were officially placed in Barclay Square after it was refurbished in 1910.

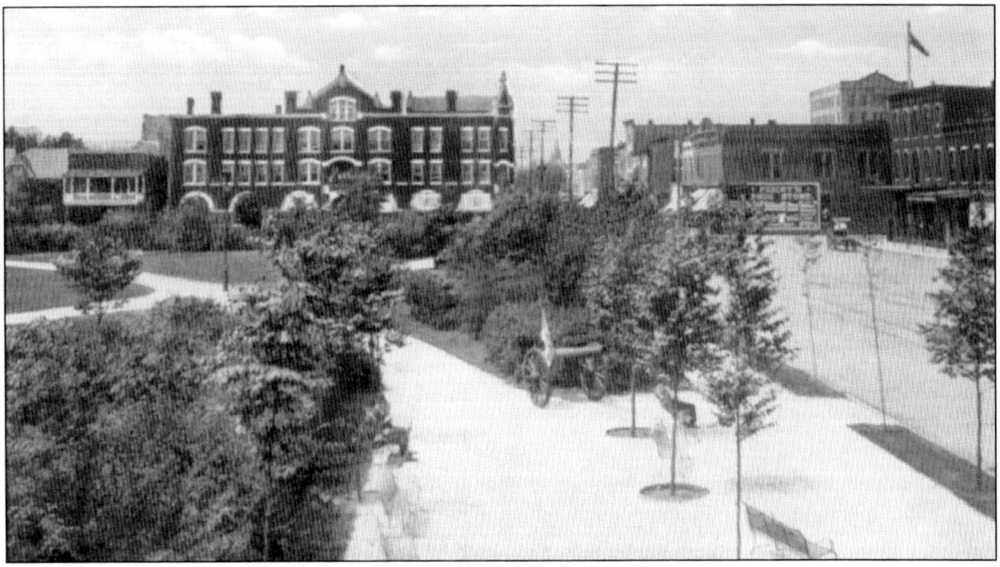

This image looks west in downtown Punxsutawney toward the Public Square in 1915. The Pantall Hotel is on the left, and Feicht's Drug Store is along Mahoning Street. The Punxsutawney Spirit building rises in the background.

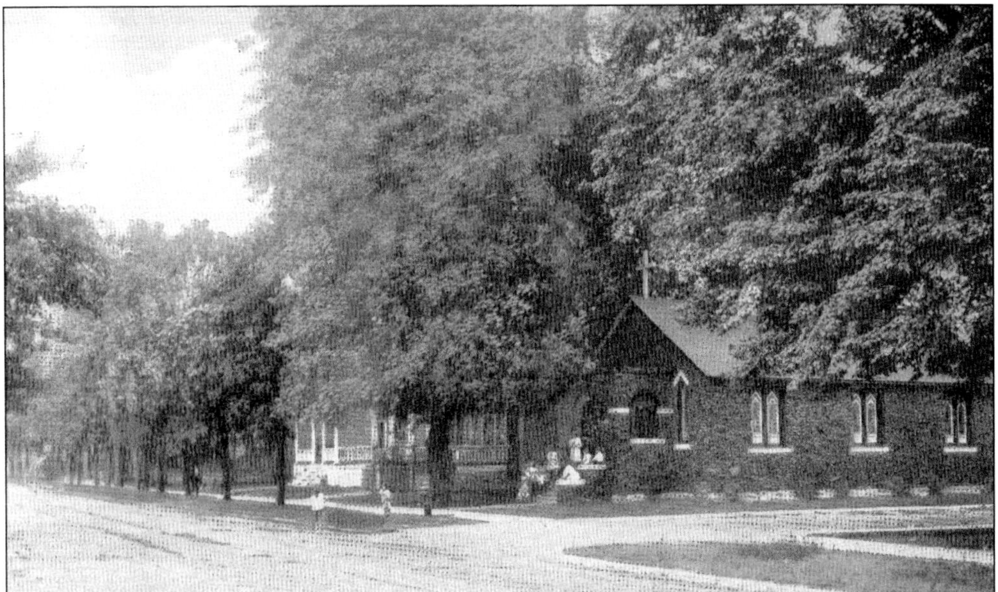

The Christ Episcopal Church was founded in 1889. Many immigrants were church members who worked in the Adrain Mines. In 1905, a frame building was erected on the south side of East Mahoning Street. Later, it was moved across the street, and a cobblestone exterior was placed on the building.

The Peter and Paul Byzantine Catholic Church was established in 1893 by Slavonic immigrants. Walston and Adrian, nearby thriving towns, were made up of Slavs and Hungarians who were all held together by a common bond, a love for their native customs and religion. Services had been held in private homes with founding pastor Father Sabo until the church was completed and blessed in 1895. On July 4, 1895, Mass was celebrated for the first time in the church.

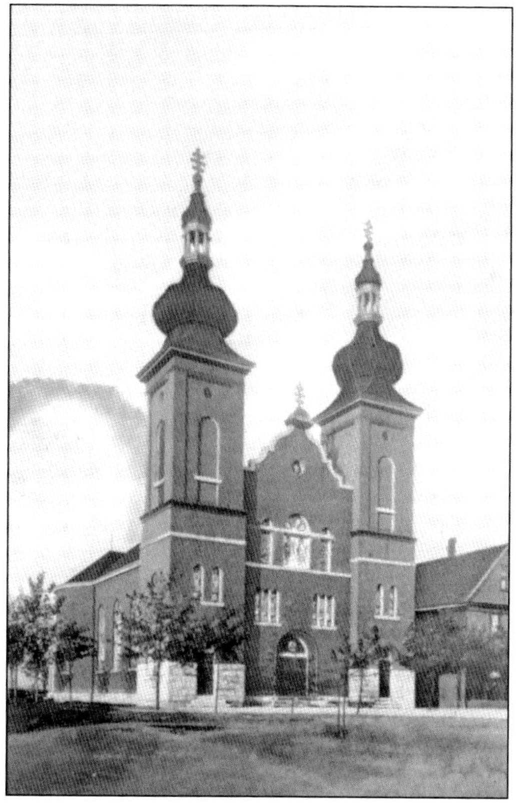

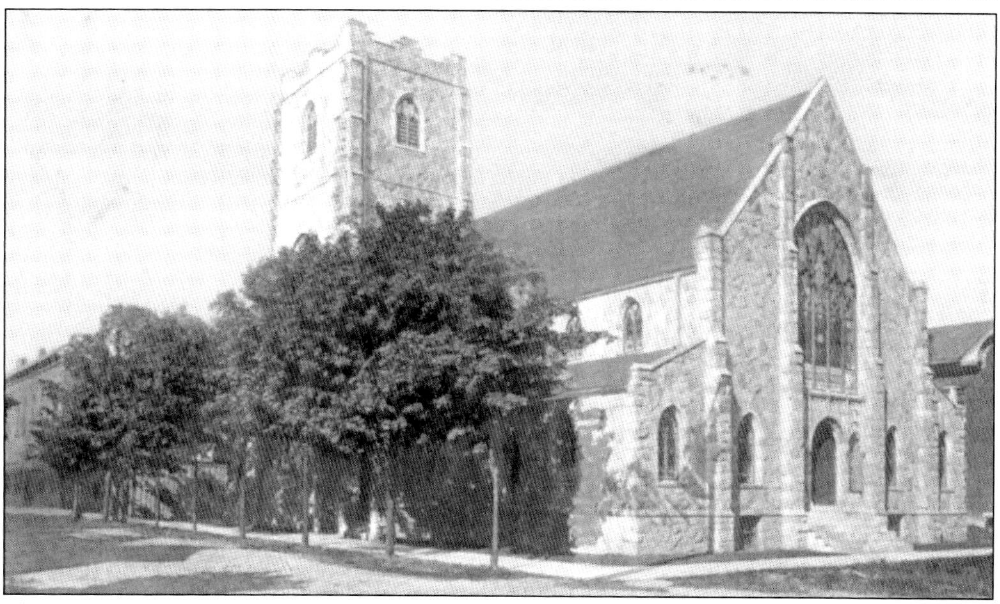

The Central Presbyterian Church dates back to 1818, when Reverend Barclay held services. A pioneer edifice of hewn logs was constructed in 1826 on the northwest corner of the Public Square. In 1860, a brick church building was dedicated on the southwest corner of Mahoning Street and Findley Street. In 1902, this building was sold to J.B. Eberhart for a department store. A new brick church was erected.

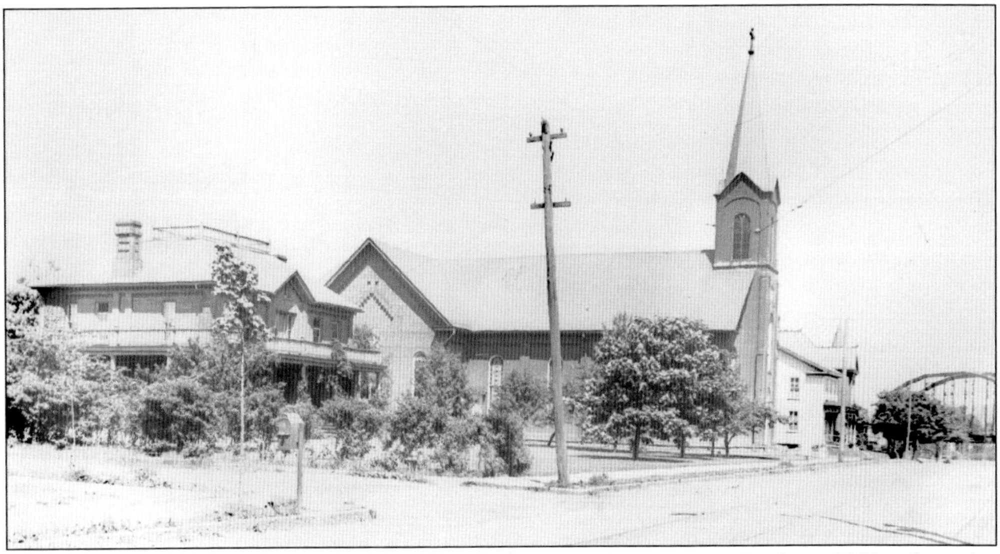

The Saints Cosmas and Damian Roman Catholic congregation goes back to 1870, when the first Mass was offered in Punxsutawney. Rev. Herman Clement Wienker ministered to many congregations in the area. In 1885, he chose a site in Punxsutawney based on the proximity of the population to the adjoining town of Walston. The church of Roman architecture was complete in 1887, and the first Mass was celebrated on July 4 of that year. The spire towered 90 feet into the heavens. The rectory is in the foreground.

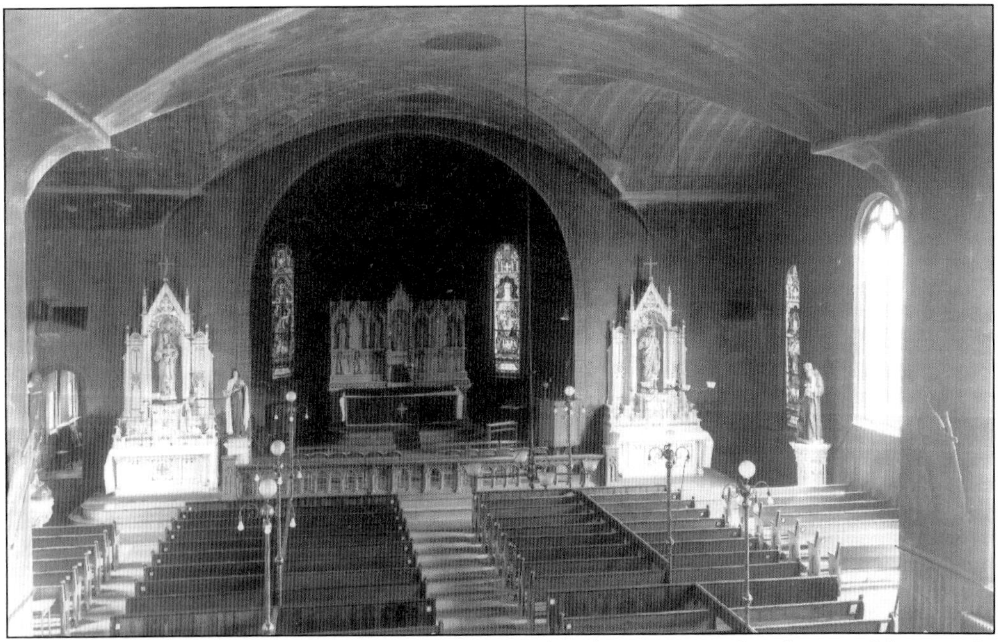

The interior of the Saints Cosmas and Damian Church was steeped in liturgical beauty. In 1892, a parish school was added and staffed by the Sisters of Mercy. The name "Saints Cosmas and Damian" was chosen by the founding pastor, Fr. H. Wienew. His brother had joined a monastery in England and was known as Brother Cosmas. The population continued to expand, and additions were added to the church. In 1939, the church building was razed to make way for a larger edifice.

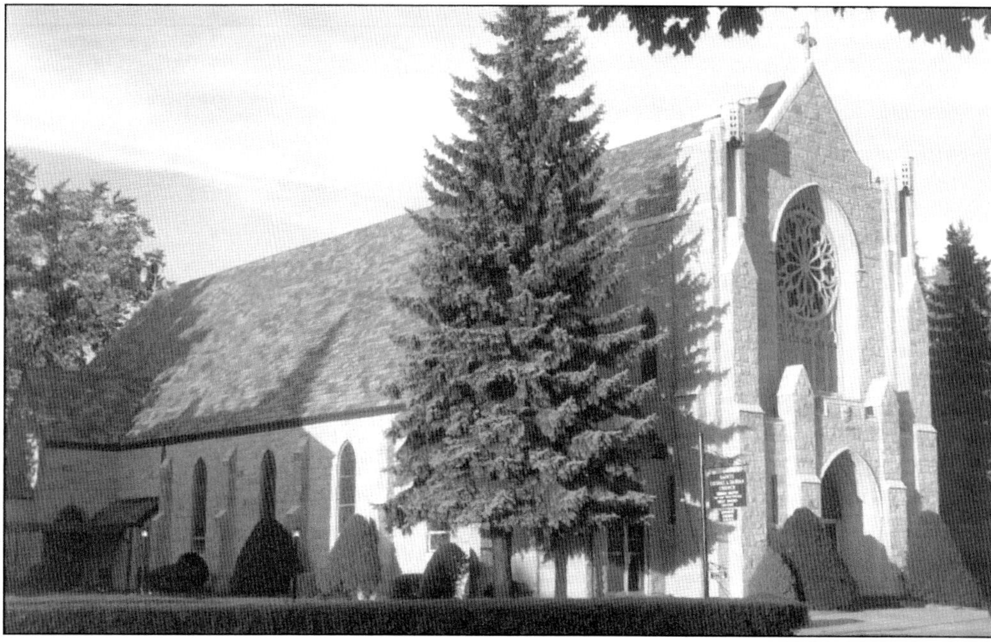

The new Saints Cosmas and Damian Roman Catholic Church was located on the same site as its predecessor. Construction was in progress when World War II was declared. Fortunately, the basic materials had arrived before the outbreak of the war. Marble came from Italy and Germany; glass came from Venice. The Gothic design exterior was constructed of Brier Hill Ohio sandstone. The windows follow the mysteries of the Rosary. Bishop Gannon blessed the cornerstone of the new edifice on August 31, 1941.

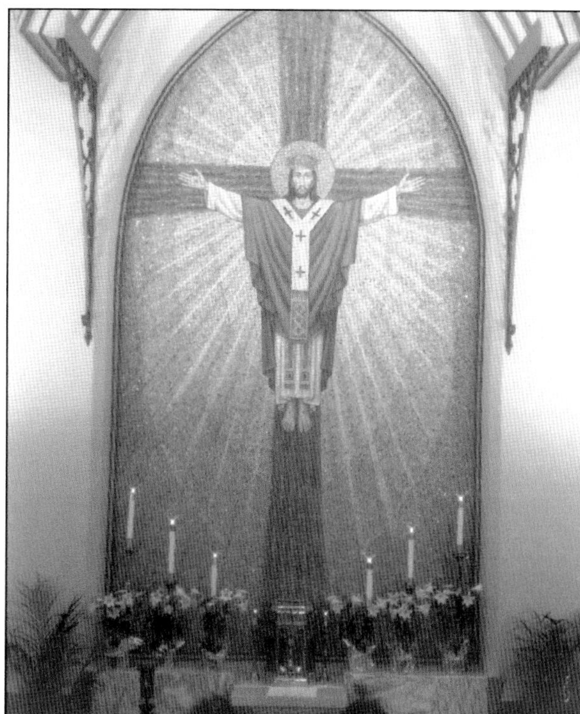

A magnificent mosaic frames the main altar at Saints Cosmas and Damian Roman Catholic Church. It depicts Christ the King as a high priest and king. Designed from miniature squares of Venetian glass, the intricate design was placed in harmony. The main altar is German marble. The 12 pillars in the church represent the 12 apostles, whose names appear between the pillars.

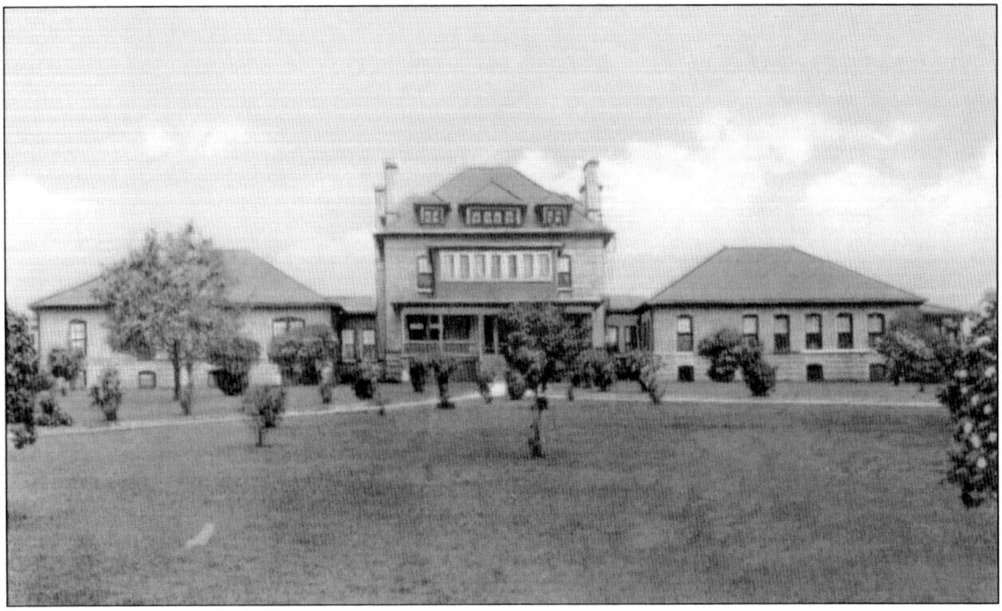

Adrian Hospital was founded in 1889; Adrian Iselin of New York donated $5,000 toward its establishment. The facility was intended to serve injured miners; however, it rapidly became a general hospital. Services expanded and a new site was purchased in 1898 with state aid; hence, it is sometimes referred to as a state hospital. Adrain Hospital merged with Punxsutawney Hospital in April 1932. The fee per week was $5 in the wards or $15 for a private room.

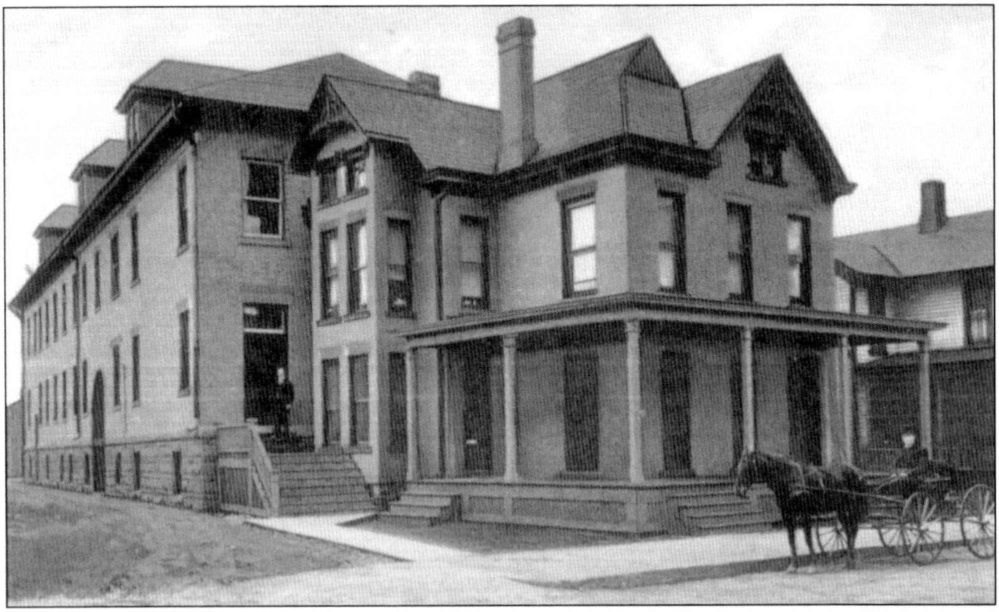

Punxsutawney Hospital was founded in 1900 by Dr. John E. Grube. Located first in the Dinsmore building on West Mahoning Street, it operated until 1908, when necessity deemed it move to larger quarters. The J.B. Eberhart home on Gilpin Street was purchased, and operations continued. The hospital was chartered in October 1908. A new wing was added when the need for more space became paramount. The first instructor in the nurses' training school was Susan Heitzenrater. The hospital merged with Adrian Hospital in April 1932.

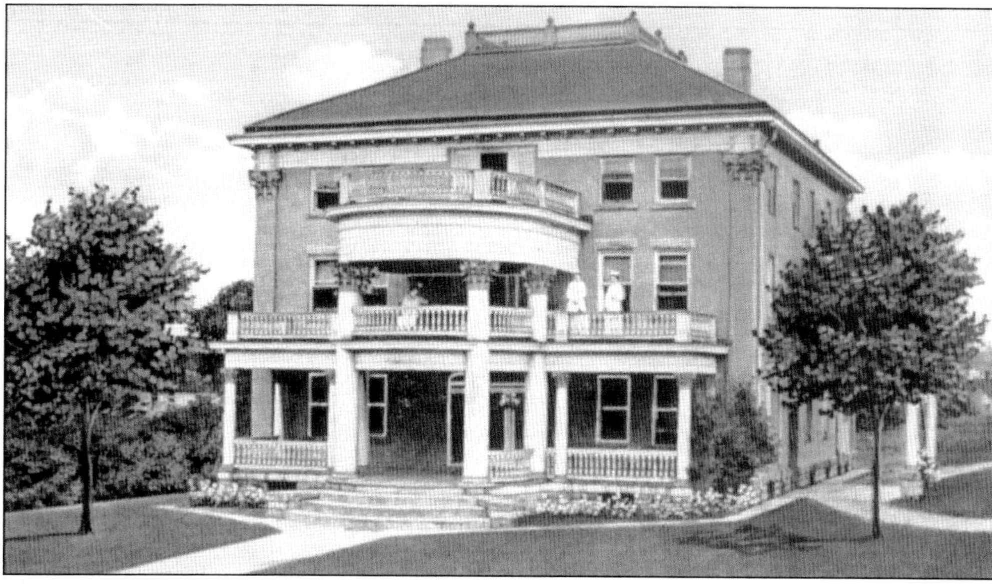

The Murray Sanitarium was established by Dr. J.H. Murray on October 25, 1911. He bought the W.A. Bowers residence on the corner of Dinsmore Street and East Mahoning Street; it accommodated 20 patients. The institute became well known for the treatment of stomach diseases. Patients came from across the United States to seek help at the sanitarium. Drs. Smathers, Black, and Dove were also on the staff, along with a team of nurses.

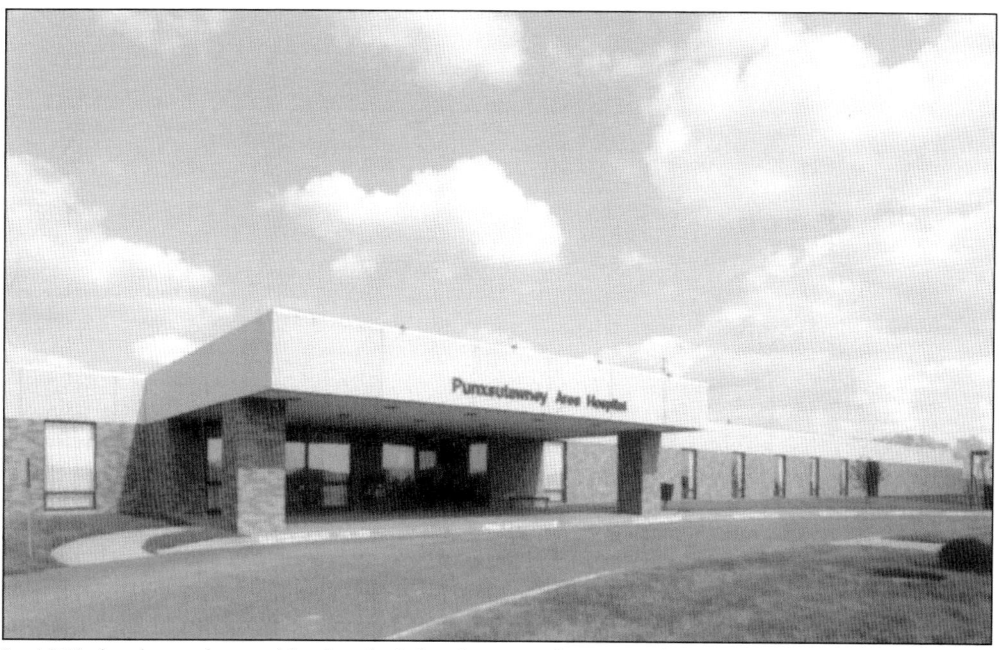

In 1975, land was donated by local philanthropists for a new hospital. The one-story, 50-bed hospital was constructed on Hilltop Drive, west of town. Originally considered a primary care facility, it has adjusted its services to meet the needs of the area. The new hospital holds the distinction of being in the top 100 hospitals in the United States and has the highest rating in Pennsylvania for patient satisfaction.

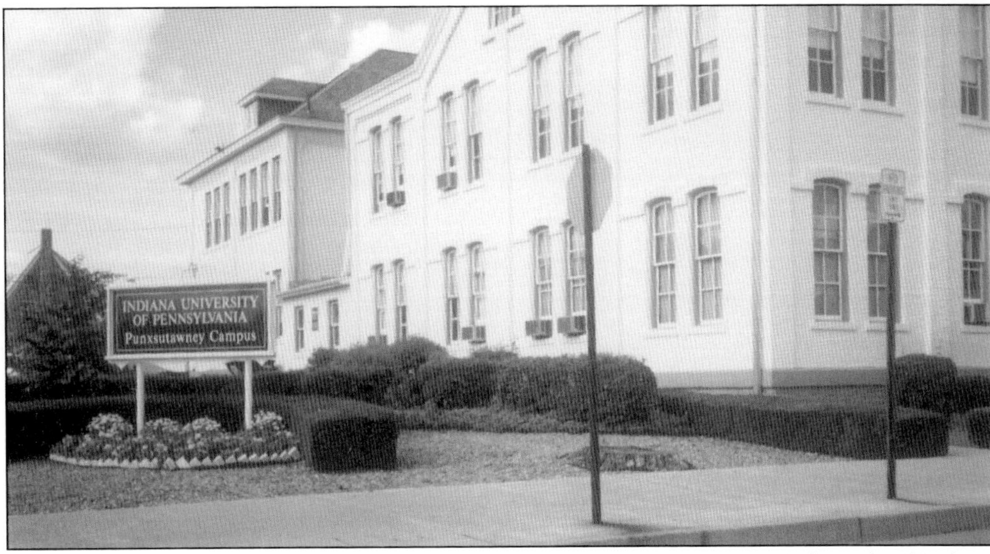

The University of Indiana maintains a branch campus in Punxsutawney. A branch of Indiana State College, the Indiana University of Pennsylvania (IUP) was opened in 1962 in a former elementary school. The initial enrollment included 51 students. In 1965, the college became a university. The branch currently accepts only freshmen. Seventy-three percent go on to the main campus in Indiana. The enrollment hovers around 175.

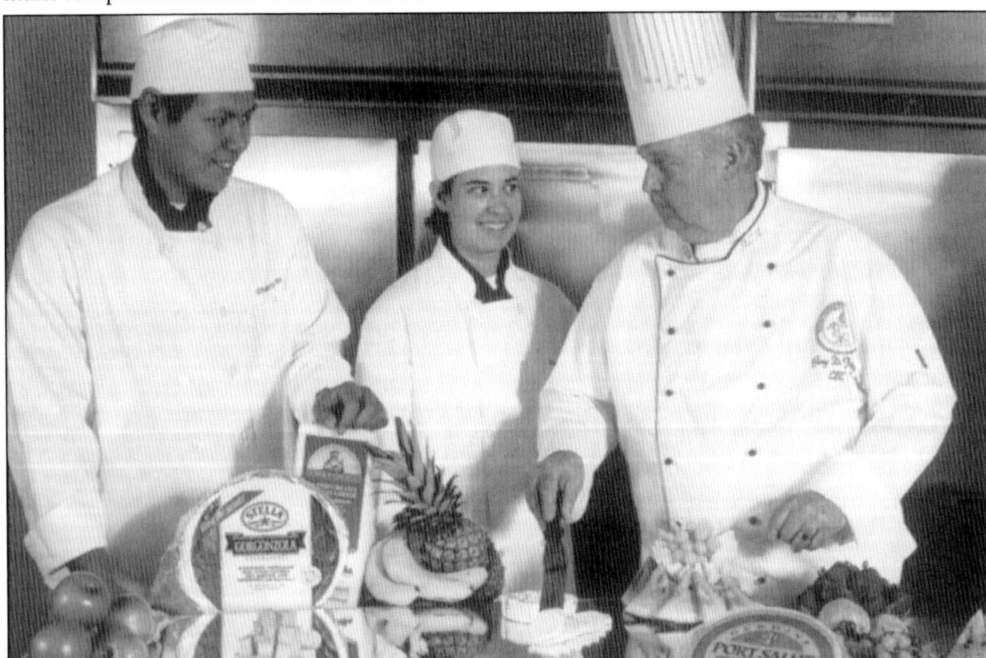

The IUP Academy of Culinary Arts is housed in a 13,000-square-foot facility on Gilpin Street, one mile from the Punxsutawney campus. It is dedicated to the training of future cooks and is equipped with five kitchens and adequate classroom space. The rigorous, intensive, and thorough yearlong program balances creativity and business. The school combines quality education with artistry. Classical and international cookery are learned in a small setting. Students realize that a chef is an artist who can apply skills both creatively and profitably.

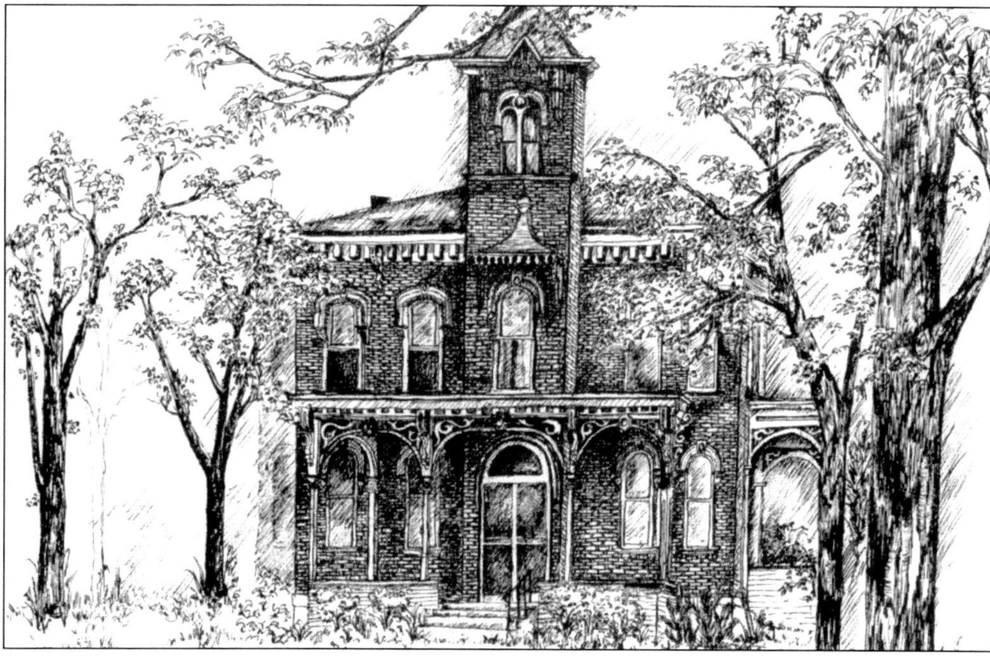

The Winslow House was built after the Civil War. Rueben C. Winslow began construction on the Victorian-style house that he wanted to tower over Punxsutawney. He purchased 12 acres along Torrence Street in 1864. His large, imposing residence was similar to suburban Italian villas with towers and overhanging eaves. The house remained in the family until 1994. Winslow was a prominent lawyer who joined in a law firm with P.W. Jenks.

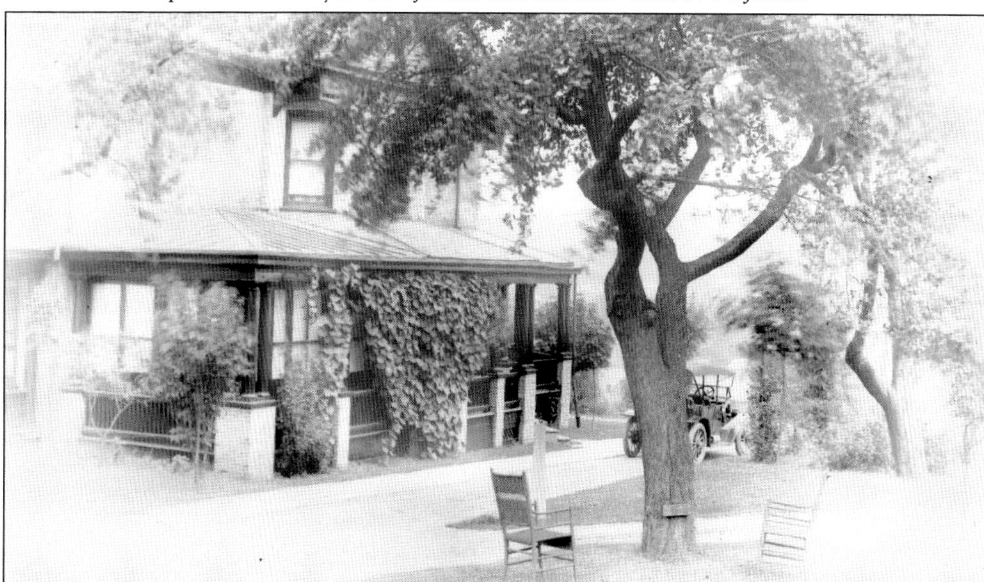

D.H. Clark came to Jefferson County in 1893. He was a lumber merchant who built his home on Record Avenue. He became involved with the railway business and was active in the construction of the Jefferson Theater. Note the chairs that have been moved outside for the day. Outdoor furniture had not yet became popular. Note also the vintage car. In inclement weather, isinglass windows were snapped over the windows.

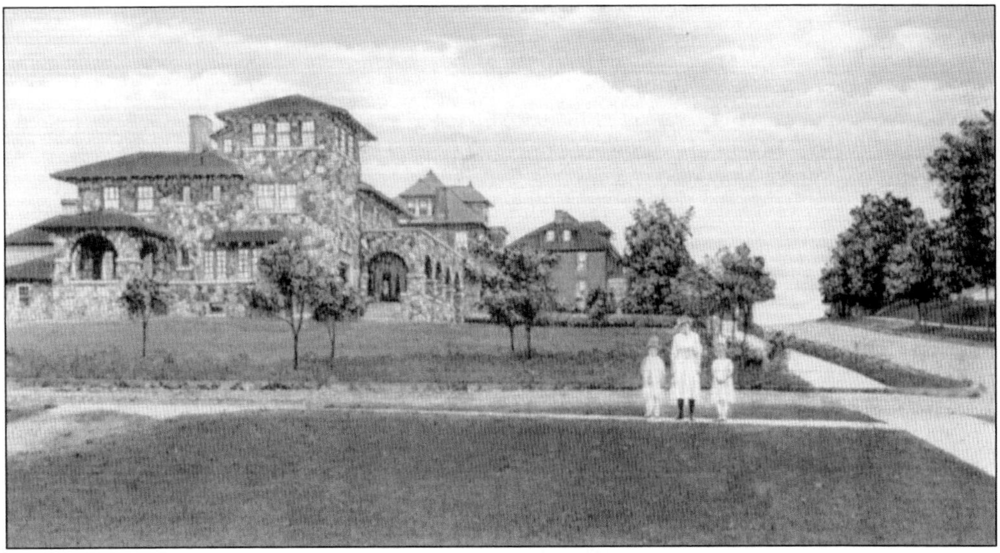

A stately stone house stands on the north side of East Mahoning Street. David Brown, an oil and lumber tycoon, traveled across the United States and twice around the world collecting stones to build this unique house. Its low style with tower and patio creates a Spanish-like architecture. It was constructed by J. Grier Sparkle in 1915–1916. The house represents part of nearly every state in the union, every historic shrine in the country, and many places around the globe.

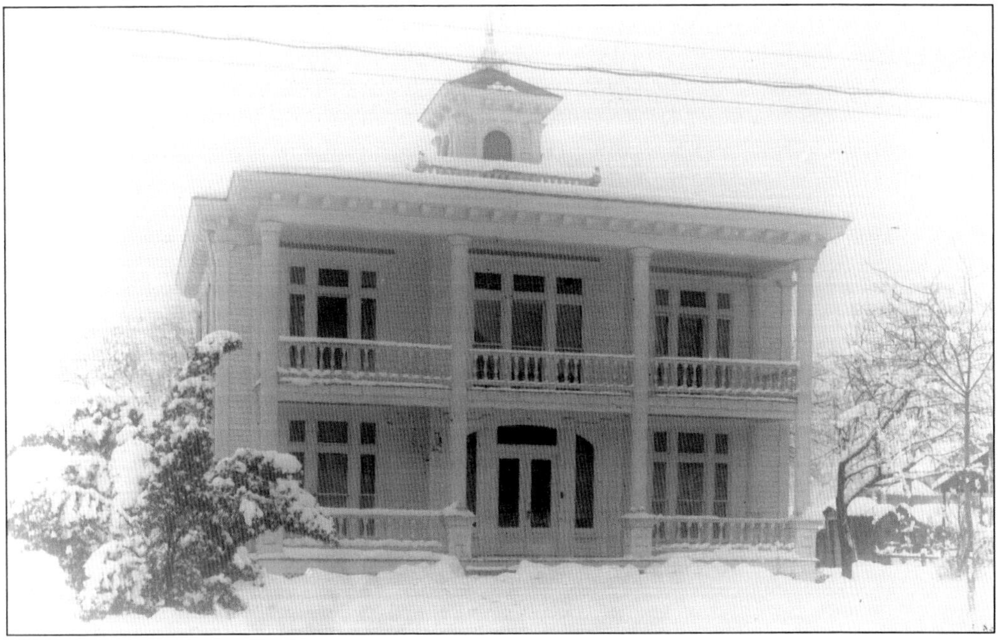

The Gillespie House at 809 West Mahoning was built in 1859 by W.E. Gillespie. This edifice was the site of the first Roman Catholic Mass offered in Punxsutawney. It was celebrated by Rev. H. Clement Weinker, who walked from Brookville. The Gillespie brothers, John Berger, and a few Catholics who would form the nucleus of the new Saints Cosmas and Damien parish attended the ceremony. Father Weinker chose a site for the new parish that was accessible to the neighboring hamlets as well as Punxsutawney.

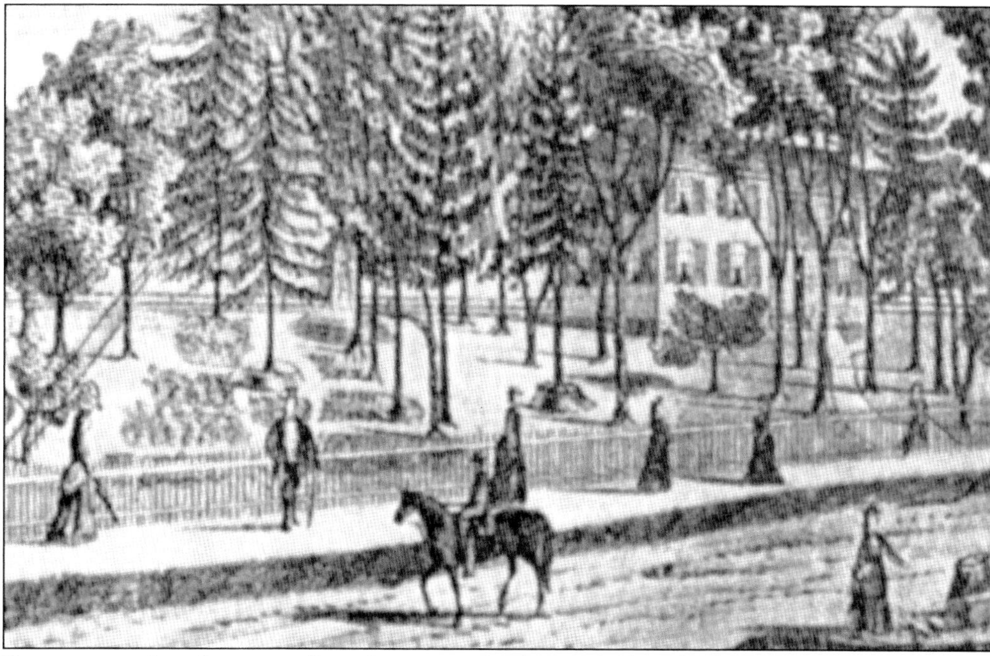

Rose cottage, later known as Betts home, was built in 1835 by Charles C. Gaskill. Roses, many other flowers, and a white picket fence surrounded the house. In 1868, it was sold to William Davis and later to Theodore Pantall. Due to construction of the flood control project, the house was moved to Maple Avenue.

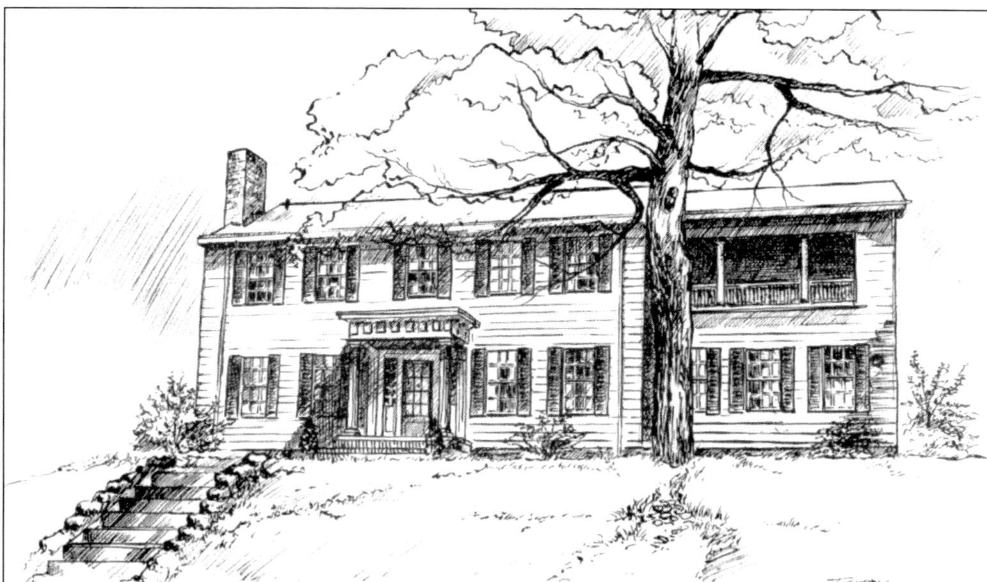

The Jenks House is among the oldest residences in Punxsutawney. John W. Jenks built it as a farmhouse in 1819; it was renovated in 1920. Jenks graduated from the University of Pennsylvania Medical School and was the town's first physician. He was elected to the first Punxsutawney Board of Commissioners. He opened the first tannery in town and became an associate judge. He did not depend on the medical practice for livelihood. He was instrumental in major contributions toward the Findley Street cemetery and the land for Barclay Square.

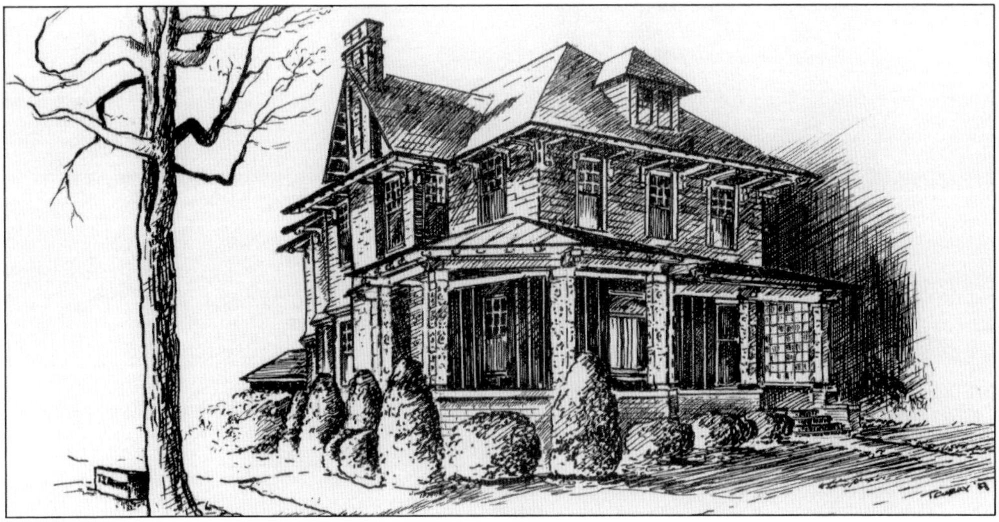

Bennis's Victorian-style house was constructed in 1903. Located on the corner of Morrison Avenue and Mahoning Street, it was designed by Stanford White, a prominent New York architect. The house was built for E.C. McKibben, secretary of the Punxsutawney Iron Works. It was purchased in 1918 by T.E. Bennis. The house stands out with its unusual porch, its detailed dormers, the low pointed roof, and the elaborately carved columns. It currently houses the Punxsutawney Historical and Genealogical Society.

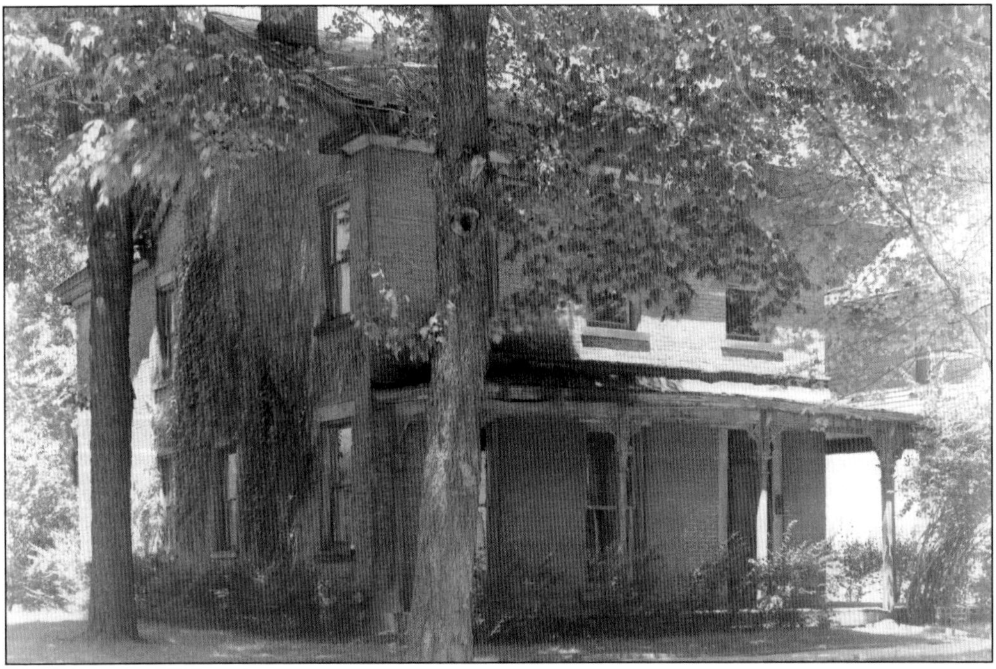

The Minish House contained a slave pit in the cellar. It was a two-story, red-brick home at 504 West Mahoning Street. A trapdoor was inserted in the flooring beside a big fireplace in the dining room of the house. Slaves, fleeing from their owners before the Civil War, were kept here on their way to freedom in Canada. The slaves remained until they could be safely transported during the night to the next station. The pit was reached by steps beneath the trap door. The house has since been demolished.

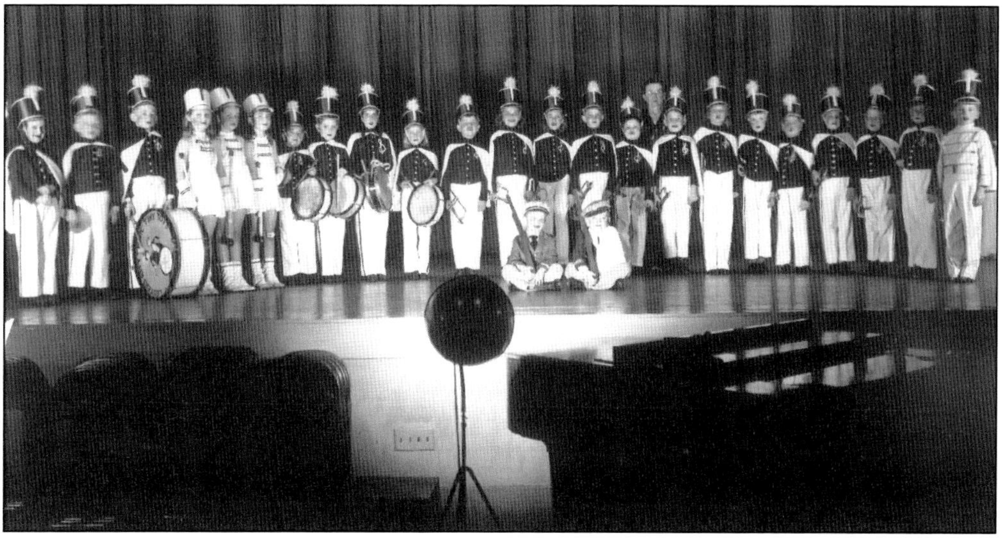

The Tiny Tots Orchestra was directed by a Mrs. Lester and was known as Lester's Rhythm Orchestra. This performance took place on November 20, 1942, to an audience of more than 1,000 people. During the World War II era, the show was arranged by the Civil Defense Council. Attired in colorful uniforms, the tots enjoyed their time on the stage. Other attractions included a magician and a ventriloquist.

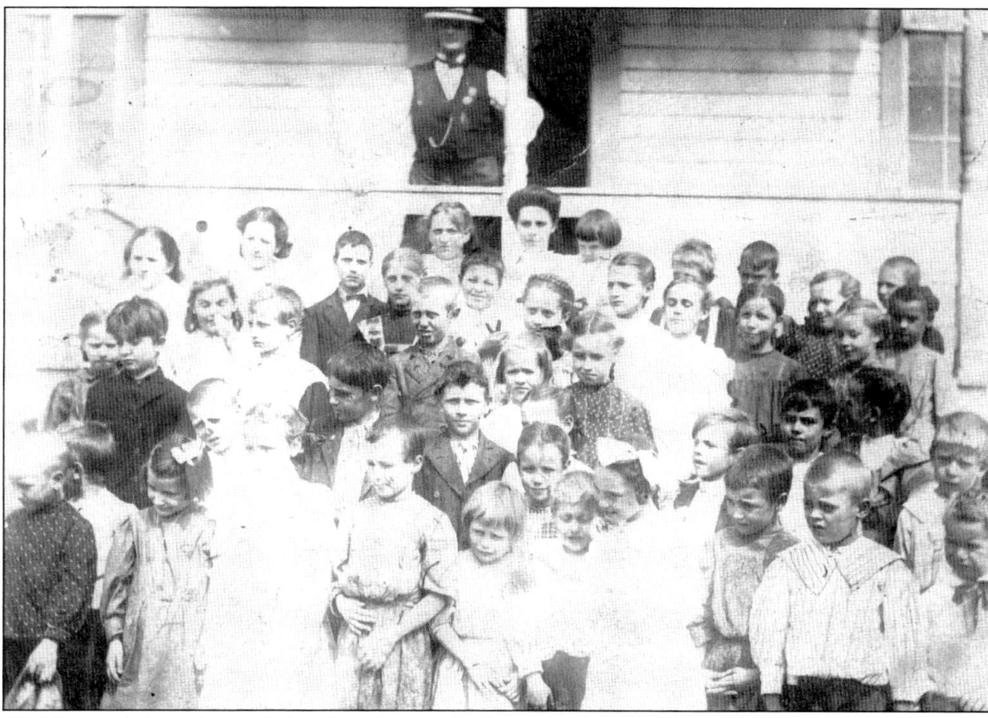

Children of the Morris School gather with their teacher, Miss Carr, during the 1907–1908 school year. The earliest school in Punxsutawney was a round building made of logs. By 1836, a schoolhouse had been built on the north central part of the square. The population increased rapidly, and a second school, this one with two stories, was built on the southern part of the park. By 1856, the school was moved to Jefferson Street.

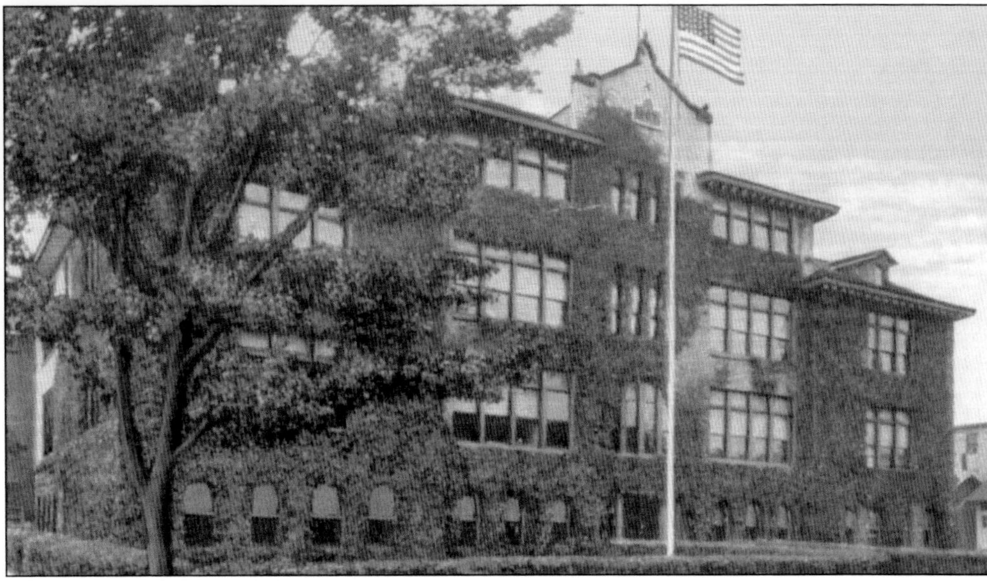

The Jefferson School, constructed in 1908, replaced a four-room brick building that had stood for four decades. The first schoolhouse of 1822 was constructed of round logs. The seats were made of broad pieces of split logs; desks were boards nailed to the wall. The second schoolhouse was located on the southwest corner of the Public Square. The third was an 1867 brick structure, which was replaced by the Jefferson School.

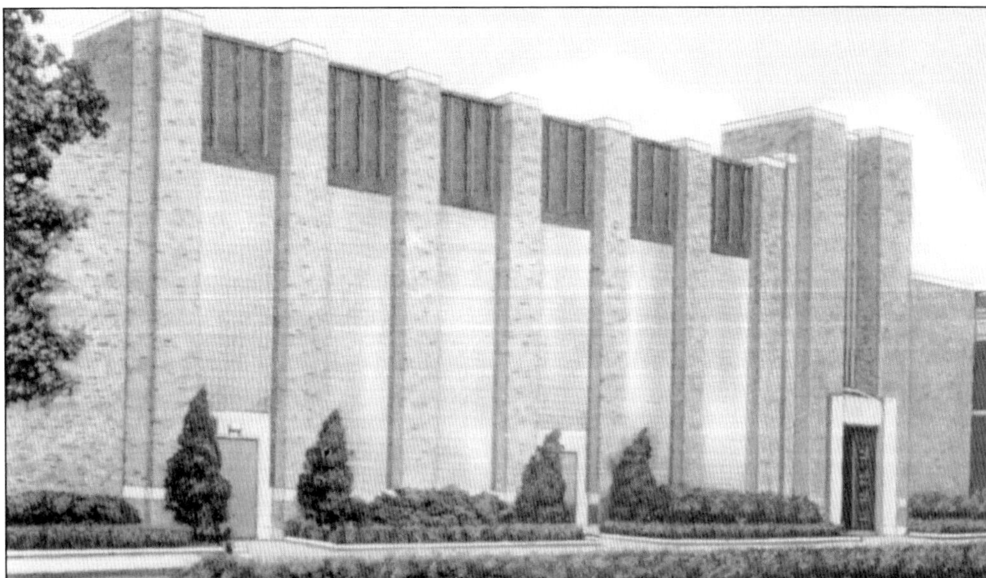

A crowd of 12,000 attended the dedication of the Punxsutawney area joint school. It was a multimillion-dollar senior high school dedicated in November 1959. The ceremony was followed by tours of the massive building.

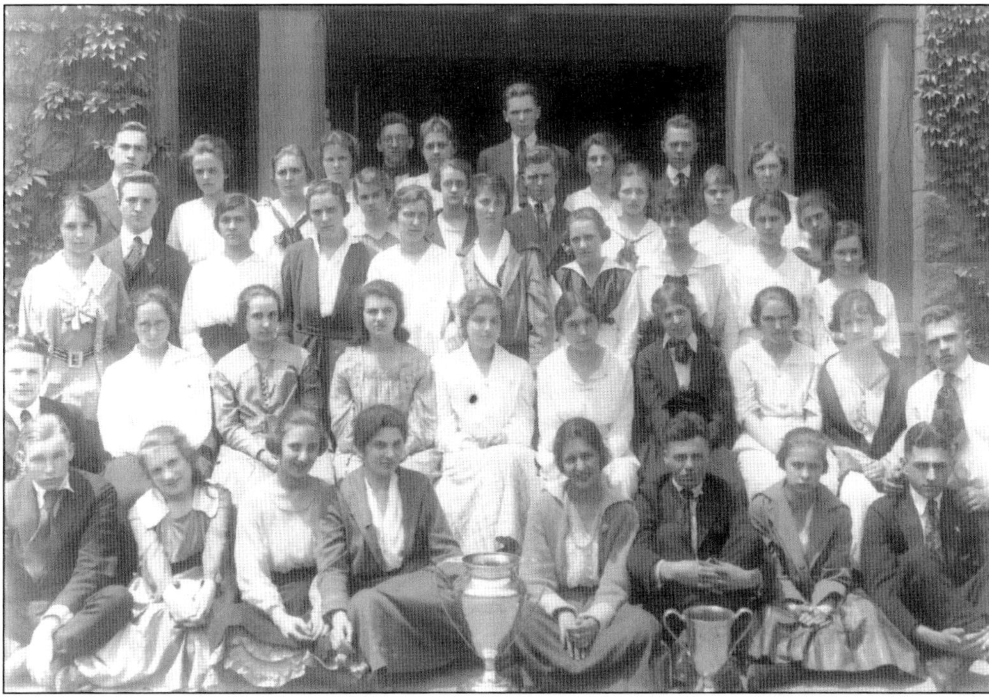

The Punxsutawney High School (PHS) Class of 1918 is about to graduate. In those days, commencement exercises were held in the Jefferson Theater. Students from outlying districts rode the train to school, and hiking through snowdrifts was common. The girls had a basketball team. The boys had a basketball team as well as a football team, known as the Chucks.

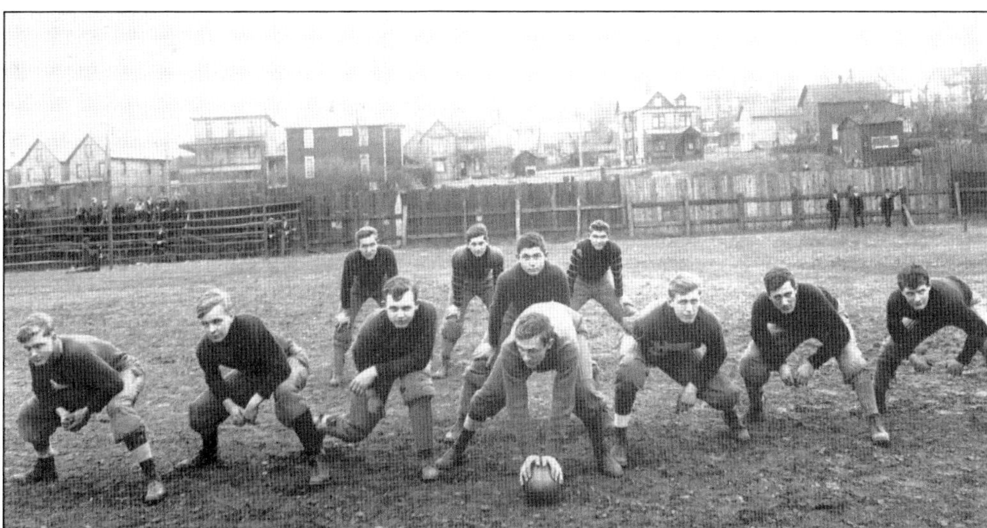

PHS always had a rich tradition of athletic excellence. The many sports included boys' and girls' basketball, track, cross-country, wrestling, and baseball. There was always stiff competition between local teams, as well as those from other high schools around the state.

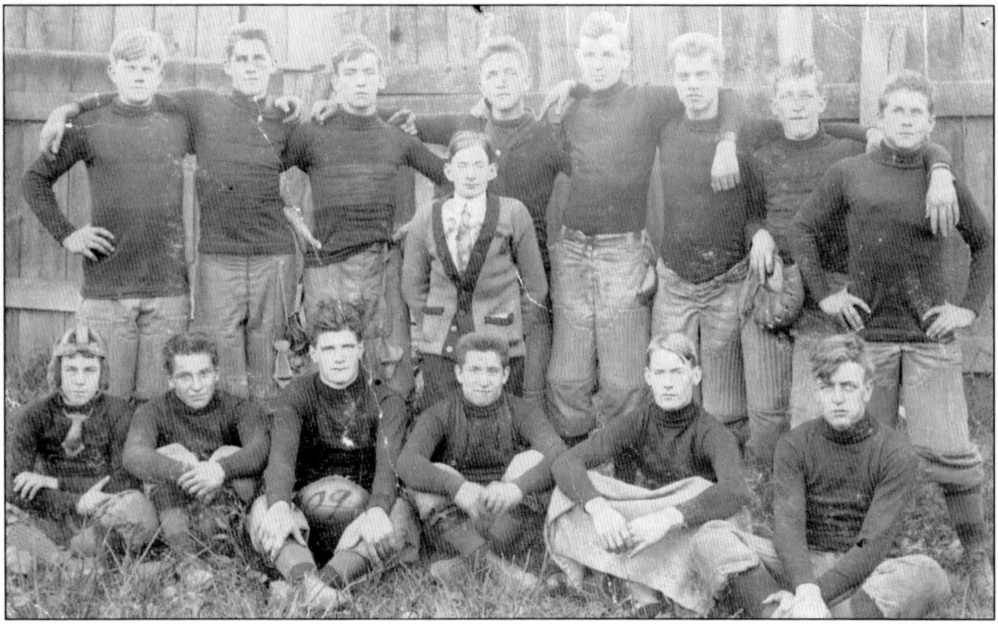

The 1909 PHS football team includes, from left to right, the following: (front row) Corsey Williams, John Maivbuco, Ralph Conway, Tony Manbuca, Lynn McGinnis, and Paul Weherle; (middle row) Charles Eberhart; (back row) Dick Alberts, J. Crissman, Clyde Fetterian, P. Dock, Hubert Wilson, George Brady, Red Shirk, and Fred "Skeets" Gordon. Many of these teams were founded by Troop D of the Pennsylvania State Constabulary.

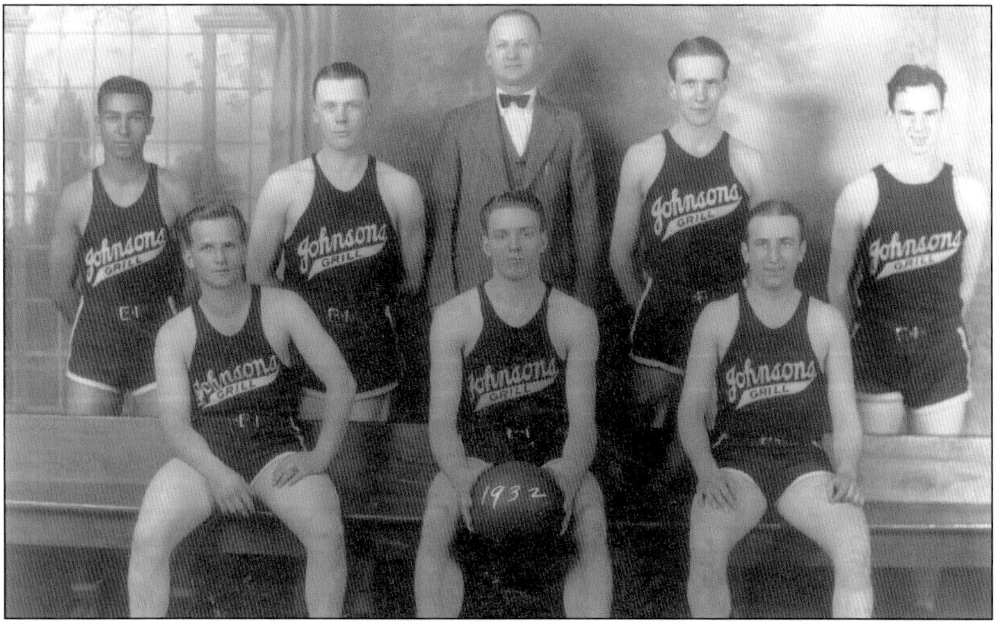

The members of the Johnson's Grill basketball team are, from left to right, as follows: (front row) Ben Jones, Jay Simon, and Fred Levy; (back row) Joe Catanzarits, Joe Kohler, coach Gordon Bloom, Sid Parsons, and Pete Johnson. The grill was established in 1932 by Peter Johnson on East Mahoning Street. It opened in the Zeitler building, also known as the Feicht building. Johnson came from Constantinople in 1907 and originally operated a candy store in Punxsutawney.

Five

Coal, Coke, and Our Neighbors

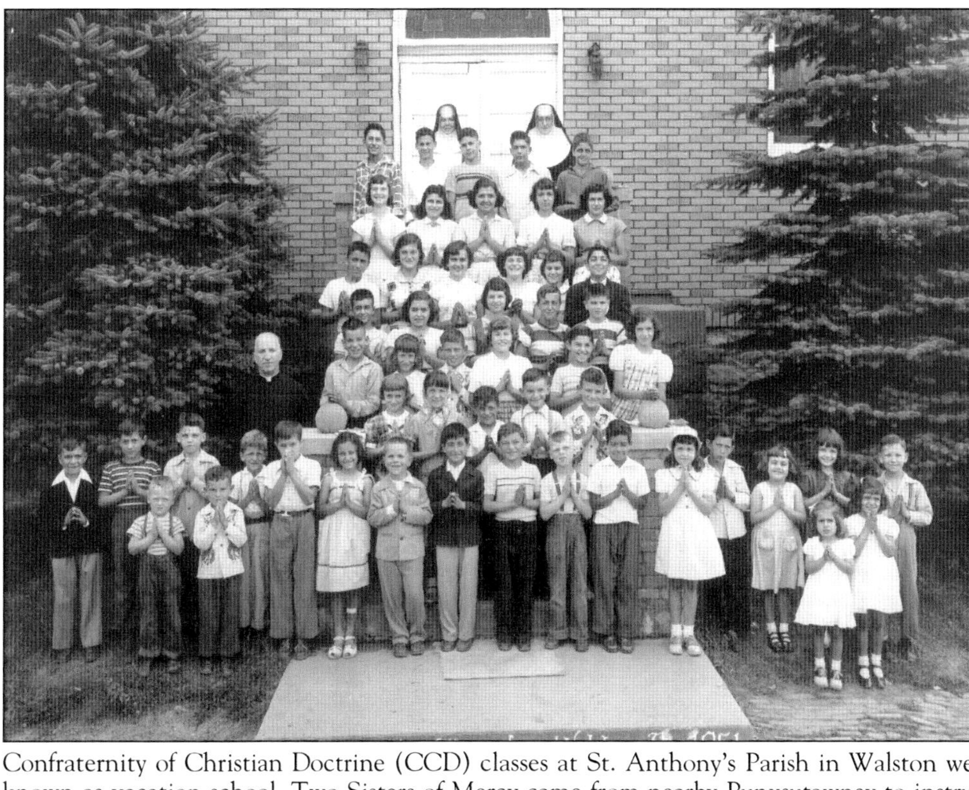

Confraternity of Christian Doctrine (CCD) classes at St. Anthony's Parish in Walston were known as vacation school. Two Sisters of Mercy came from nearby Punxsutawney to instruct the children, usually for two weeks, shortly after school was finished for the year. The children were prepared for the sacraments at that time.

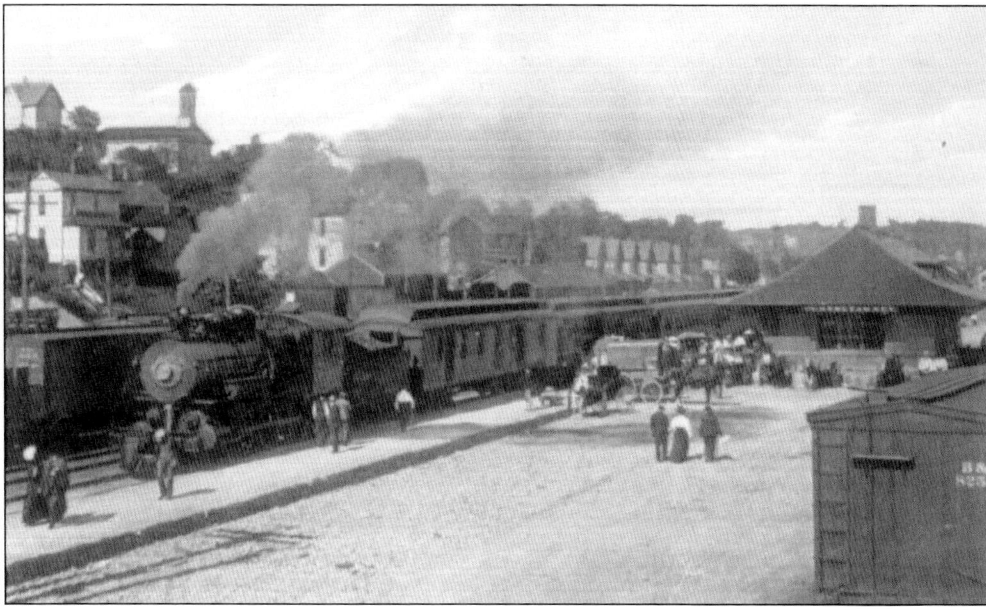

The first train of the Buffalo, Rochester, and Pittsburgh Railroad arrived in Punxsutawney in September 1883. This arrival resulted in access to vast coal fields. In 1898, the road was double tracked and provided passenger travel between Ground Hog Town and the Smoky City, Pittsburgh. In 1932, the railroad was bought out by the Baltimore and Ohio Railroad. Note the row of company houses in the background. The engine is followed by the mail freight car and then by the passenger cars.

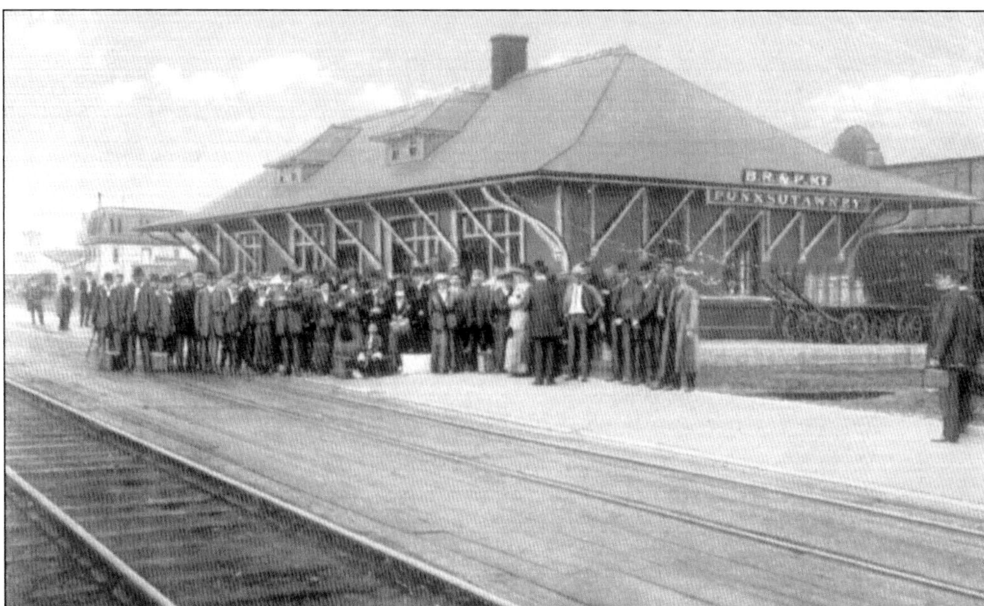

The railroad was the fastest and most efficient mode of travel before the automobile took its place. Men traveled to and from work on the train for many years. Public transportation had become a necessity that was part of every town and village.

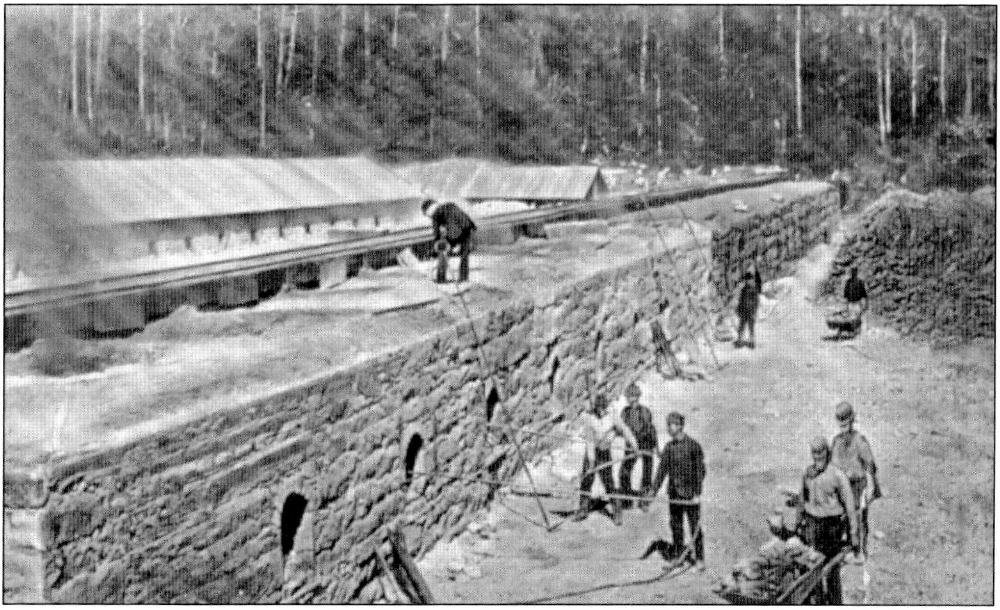

Walston gained prominence in 1882 when the Rochester and Pittsburgh Coal and Iron Company purchased land and laid the slender steel rails that would give this community a renowned place in history. Named for Walston H. Brown, an executive of the railroad, the little hamlet housed the largest unbroken string of coke ovens in the world. Coke was a necessary commodity in making steel. Seven hundred ovens produced 3,000 tons, or 100 railroad cars of coke per day.

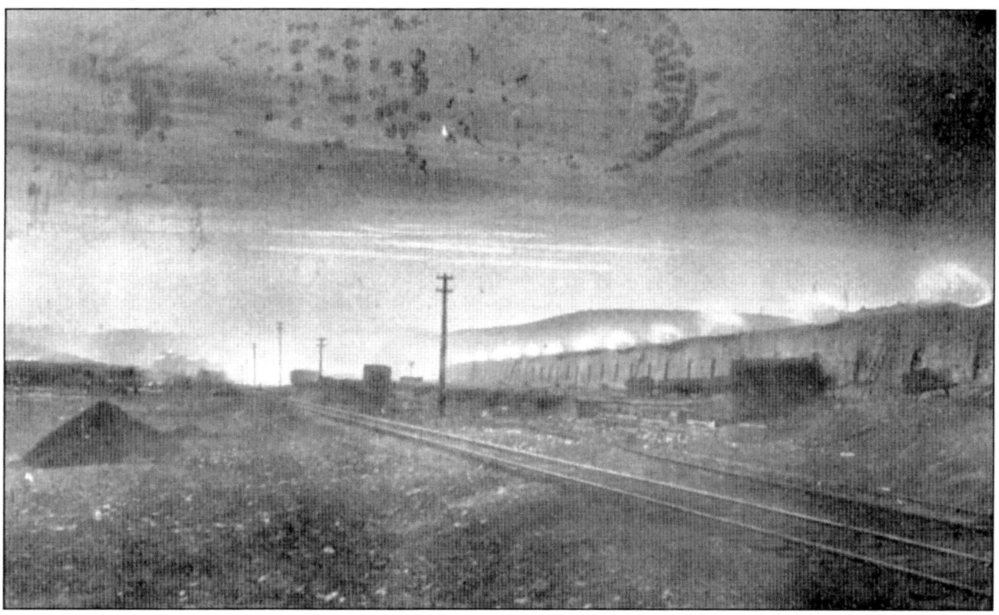

Coke is produced from coal. Ovens constructed for this purpose were filled with crushed coal. A dinky (coal car) dropped the coal into the oven, which was then leveled by reaching through the door at the front. The oven was sealed with bricks and mud. The coal was exposed to extremely high temperatures for three days. It was then drenched with water and the gases thrown off. The result was the coke that was shipped to Punxsutawney and Pittsburgh.

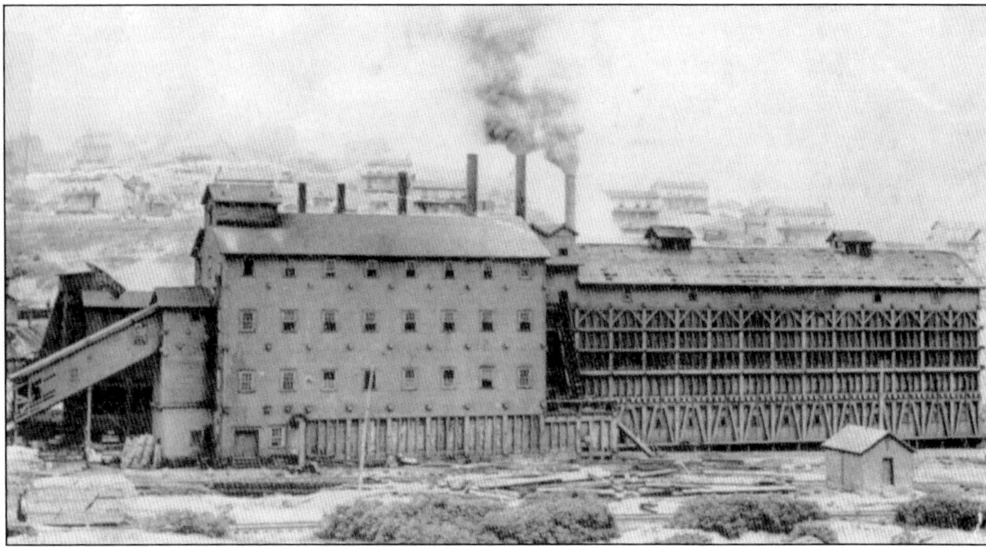

The washery and company houses dot the hillside. The coke ovens created a glow in the sky that became a trademark of Walston. Italian and Slavish immigrants made up its nearly 2,000 inhabitants in 1888. Two hundred company houses sprang up, and the ovens stretched 1.25 miles in length. However, the Walston operations eventually closed because of a declining need for coke, the depletion of coal seams, and the competition from other coke-producing areas.

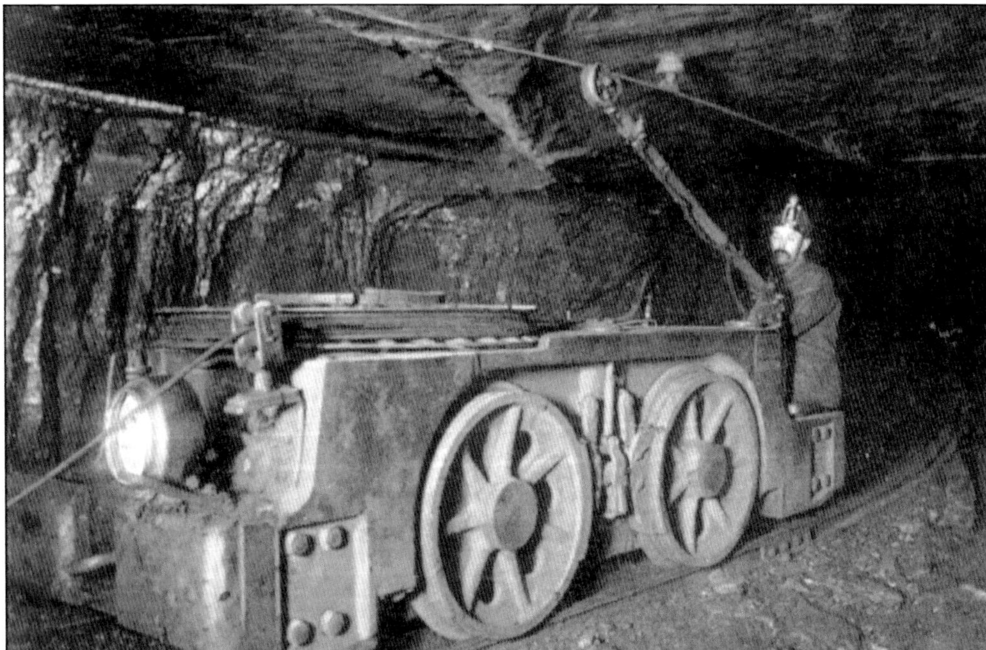

A shuttle car in the coal mines near Punxsutawney transports miners and coal to the mines. The first coal mine in the county was opened by the Diamond Gas & Coal Company at Reynoldsville in 1873. A year later, the first car of coal was shipped from Jefferson County to Buffalo by rail. Coal production in the county reached a peak of 318 million tons in 1947. This volume was produced by 2,260 employees. Coal production declined a decade later.

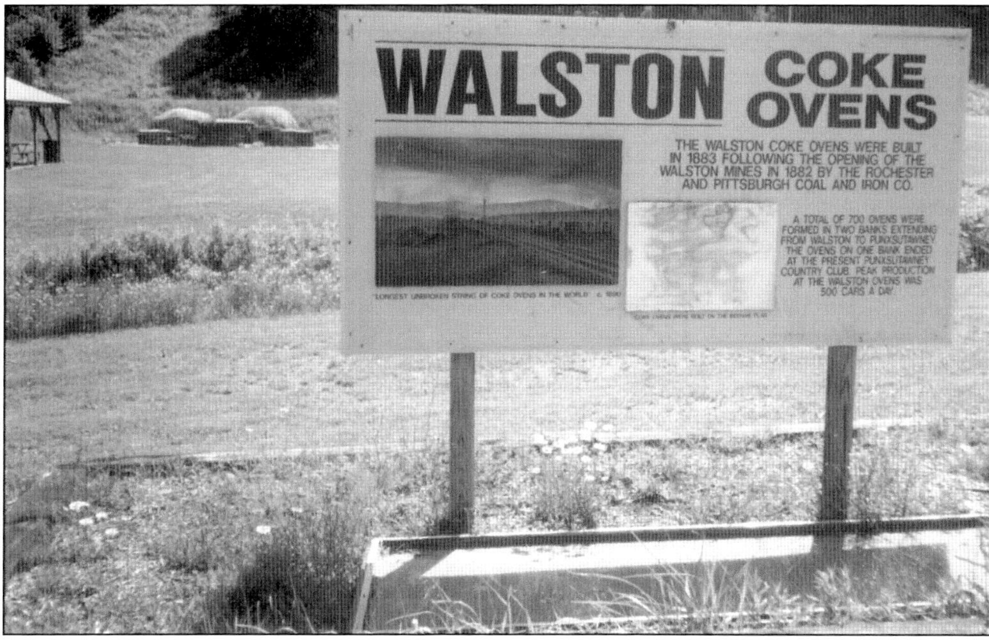

This sign describes the Walston coke ovens, which were built in 1883 by the Rochester and Pittsburgh Coal and Iron Company: "A total of 700 ovens were formed in two banks extending from Walston to Punxsutawney. The ovens on one bank ended at the present Punxsutawney Country Club. Peak production at the Walston ovens was 500 cars a day."

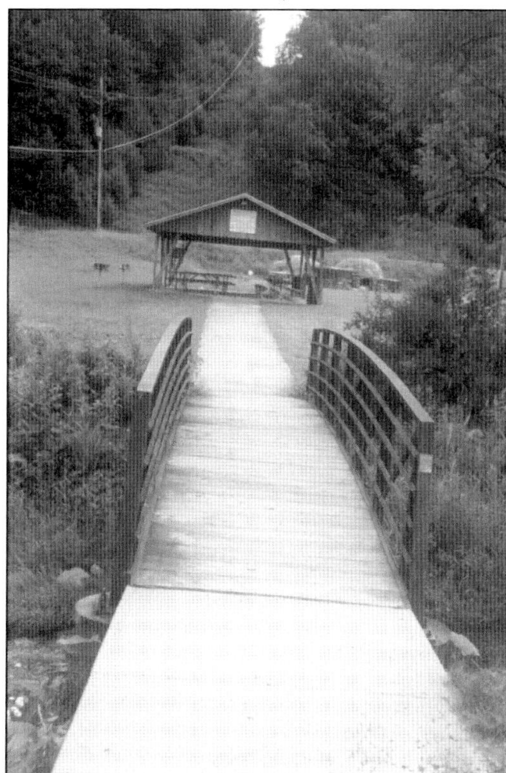

This quaint bridge spans a rippling mountain stream. It creates a practical yet charming spectacle as it affords access to the community park that borders a scenic mountainside. This picturesque setting maintains a peaceful, serene atmosphere with its singing birds and fluffy clouds. This was one of Jefferson's County's most thriving hamlets just a century ago.

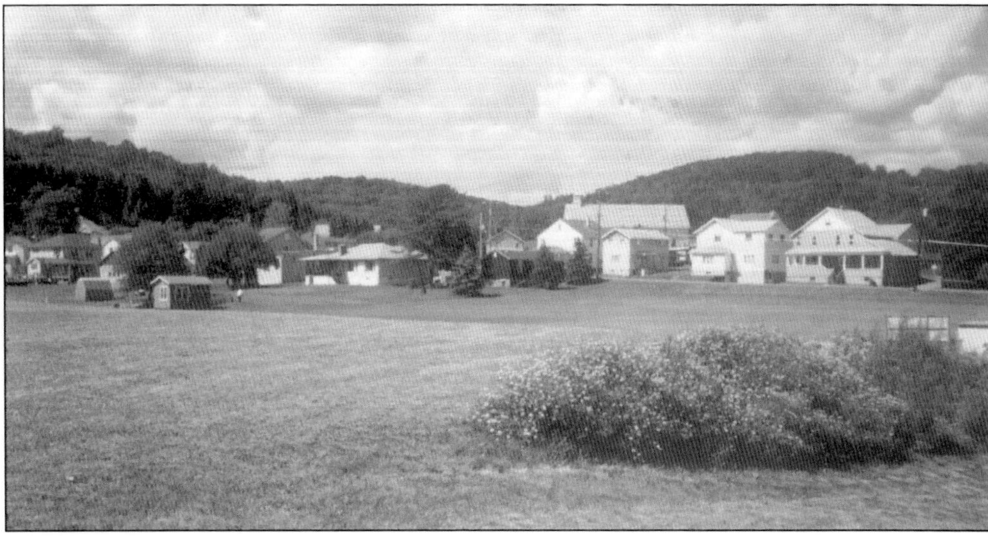

The Walston Community Park was established as a gathering place for the townsfolk. It serves as picnic grounds, a baseball field, and a meeting point. It also provides a safe place for the last two existing beehive coke ovens that were so prevalent in this locality. The park is a lasting tribute to those many immigrants who settled here.

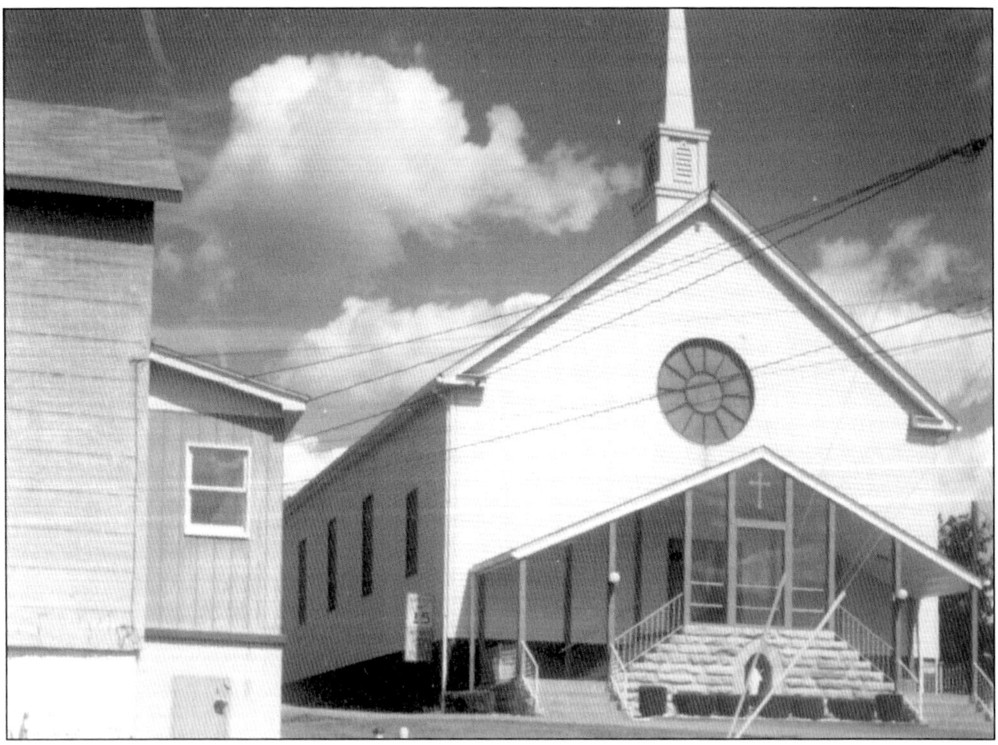

St. Anthony Church, established in the 1890s, served many immigrants from Italy and Slovakia. Immigrants arrived, seeking employment in the mines and coke ovens. The first Mass was offered in Walston on May 16, 1897, and the congregation increased rapidly. In 1900, the St. Anthony Society of Walston was formed and festivals were begun in connection with the annual St. Anthony Procession.

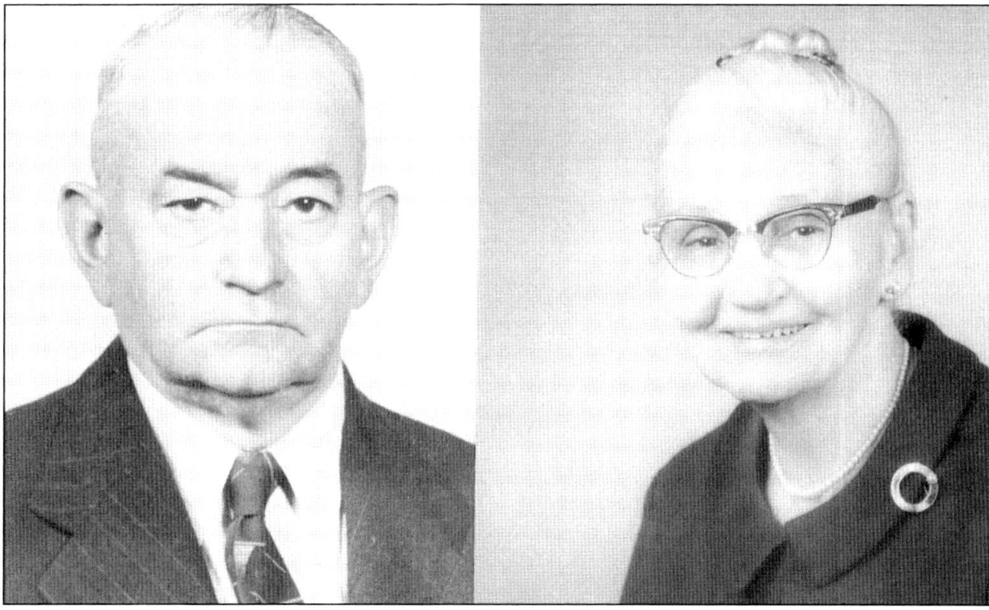

Stephen and Anna Fairman Farcus were closely associated with St. Anthony's. Steve, born of Hungarian parents, was the first child baptized in the parish. The historic ceremony took place on January 8, 1897. He spent four decades as a coal miner and, in his later years, turned to carpentry. Anna was born in 1899 of Austrian parents. She was sacristan and caretaker of the church for many years. The couple were married on January 25, 1915, in St. Anthony's and had seven children.

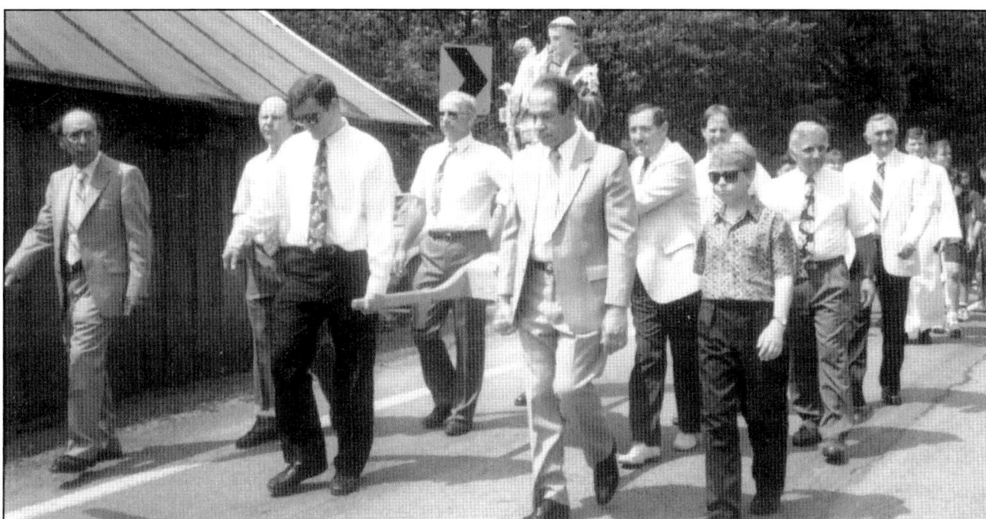

The St. Anthony Society of Walston initiated a tradition of annually sponsoring the St. Anthony Procession. These celebrations are held on his feast day, June 13. Society members carry the statue in procession through the town. Appropriate prayers are recited and hymns are sung by those in the procession. This celebration gives the parish a distinctive identity. The procession concludes with the Benediction of the Blessed Sacrament. A celebration always follows in the form of the annual festival. Entertainment, music, a concession stand, and the spirit of festivity accompany the Feast of St. Anthony.

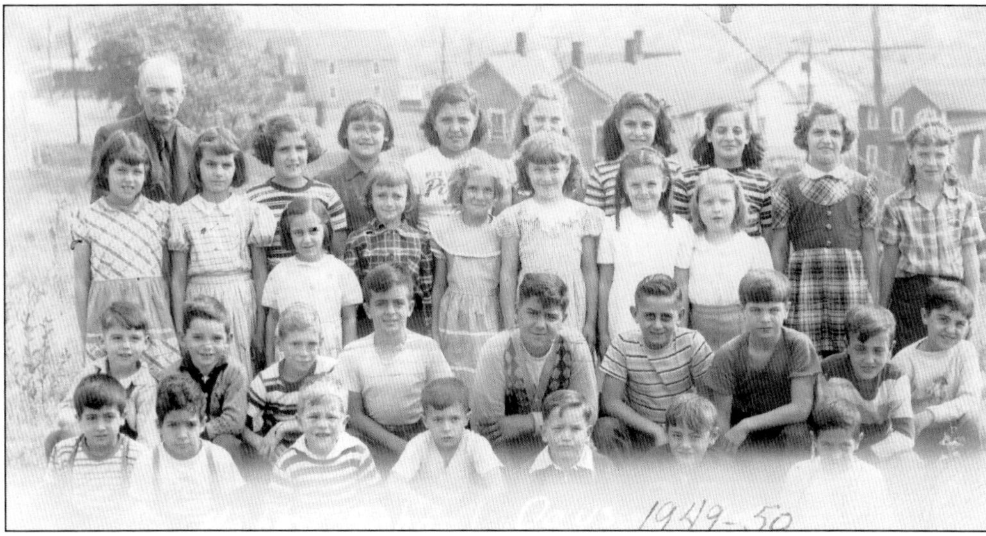

Youngsters of the Walston School pose for this photograph during the 1949–1950 school year. They are, from left to right, as follows: (first row) Tom Mondi, Hyacenth Bianco, Philip Fye, Frank Bianco, Paul Farcus, Tony Ritz, and Sam Parise; (second row) Steve Farcus, Sam Adams, Lloyd Fisher, Rich Gigliotti, Nick Ritz, Anthony Villella, Bruno Farbo, Steve Yasolsky, and John Ritz; (third row) Margie Farcus, Anna Marie Farcus, Mary Villella Molinare, Marie Elena Pascuzzo, Betty Fisher, Mary K. Gagliardi, Loretto Bianco, and Suzie States; (fourth row) teacher Lott Nolen, Shirley Astorino, Connie Monde, Rosalie Astorino, Regina Yasolsky, Eileen Faibo, Caroline Martino, Cecile Astorino, and Carolyn McQuown.

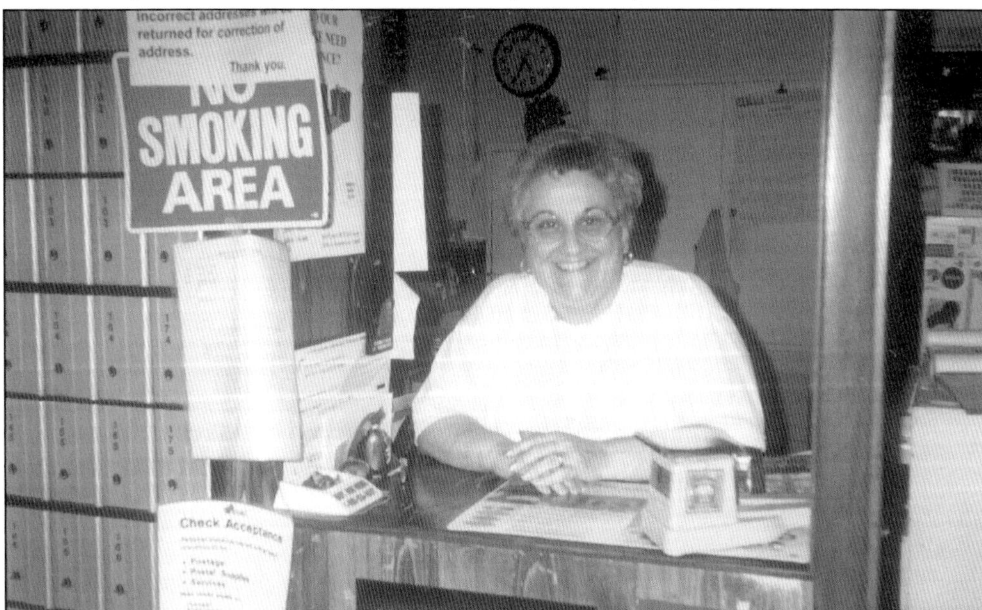

Mary C. Villella Molinare has been serving as postmaster of the Walston Post Office since 1980. She was married to Joseph Molinare, and the couple had three sons—Joseph, Jonathan, and Timothy. The post office was established in Walston on November 18, 1885, and the first postmaster was David McIntire. Postage stamps had been issued for the first time in the United States in 1845. Before that time, one paid the postmaster to send a letter.

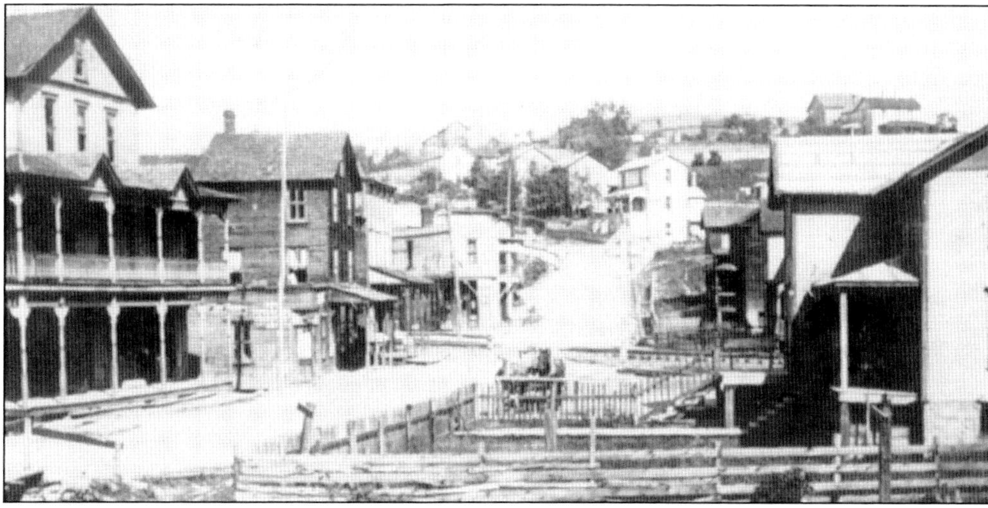

Main Street meandered through the thriving hamlet of Anita when coal was discovered beneath its hills. It had become a close-knit coal mining community, complete with shops, a church, and a community center. On July 7, 1910, Edyth Galbrath of Frostburg, Pennsylvania, received this postcard from her sister in Anita, indicating a "moonlight picnic" would be held that evening. These picnics, held during a full moon, would feature candlelit picnic tables, hors d'oeuvres, and champagne or wine.

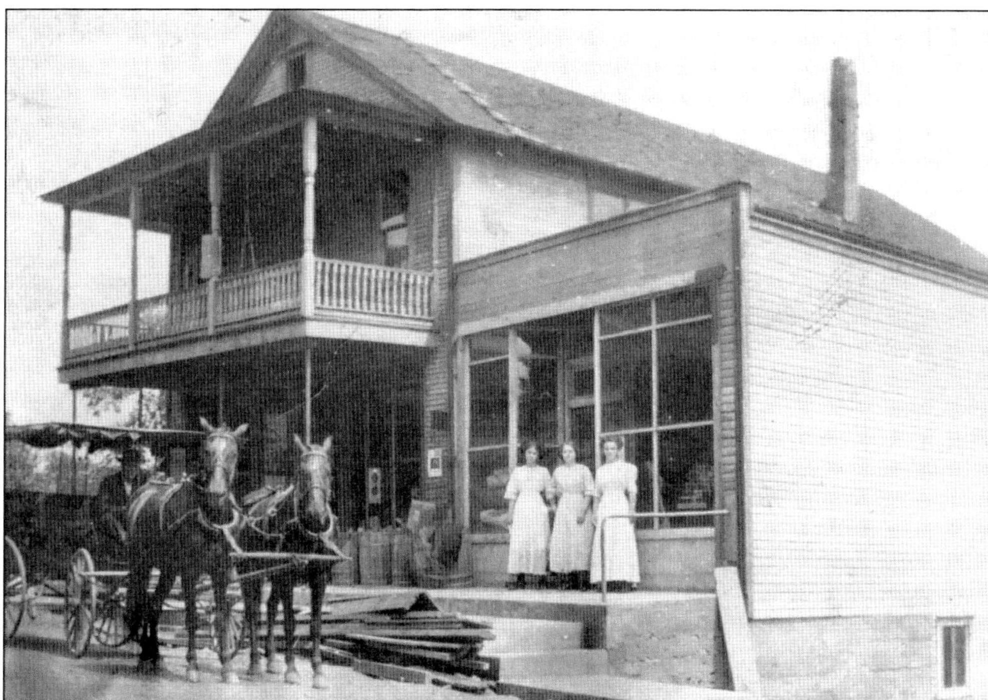

The little hamlet of Anita, named for the wife of a coal mine owner, is nestled close to Punxsutawney. In 1911, the entire area was thriving with coal mines, company houses, and immigrants who had come to seek a new life in America. This tiny settlement gave the Roman Catholic Church scores of its sons and daughters in a religious realm. Among these was Bishop Richard Thomas Guilfoyle, the third bishop of the Roman Catholic diocese of Altoona Johnstown.

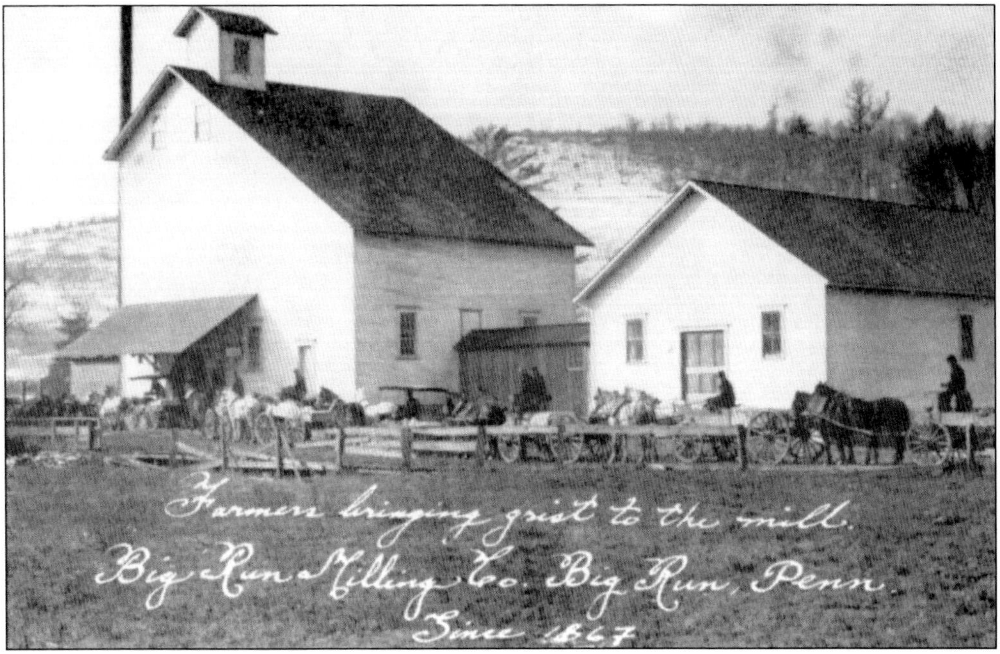

Big Run Mill stands stark and stately to greet visitors to Big Run. In 1867, Philip Erlerine gathered men and materials to begin construction on a mill. The settlement of Big Run had just been designated a borough. Its Native American name, *Gar-yar-nese*, had been retained and translated into English. Supplies for the rising mill flowed in on the Mahoning Creek. The mill became a vital part of life in Big Run. The virgin forests supplied the lumber.

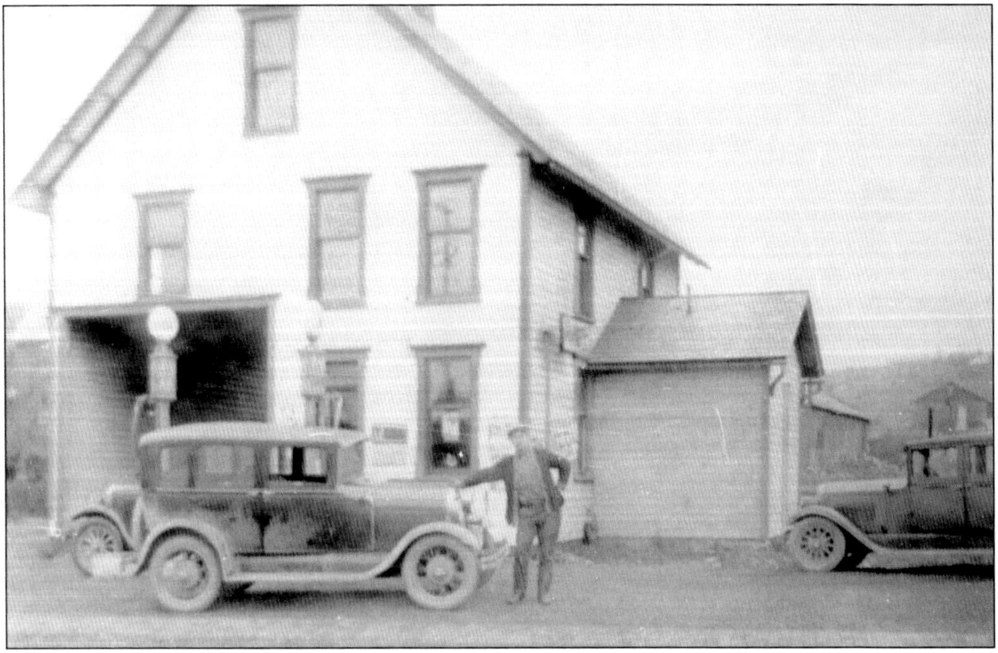

The Big Run gas station was one of the earliest in the area. The automobile era created the need for gas and service stations. The idea of sinking a huge gas well into the earth was considered dangerous by many pioneers. Many early refill stations found one pump sufficient.

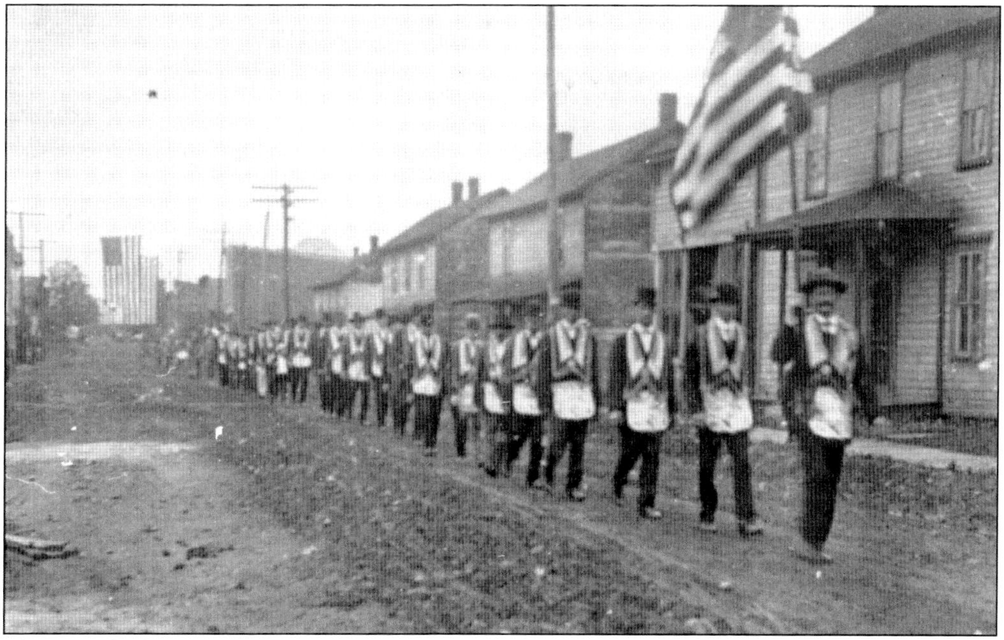

This parade down Main Street, Big Run, early in the 20th century demonstrates the patriotism and public spirit of this close-knit community. The muddy road did not deter these staunch patriots, many of them immigrants, from demonstrating their Americanism and showing gratitude for the blessings their adopted homeland afforded. They formed a band and constructed a band shell in 1903 near the old post office. Music from across the sea could often be heard floating on the evening air.

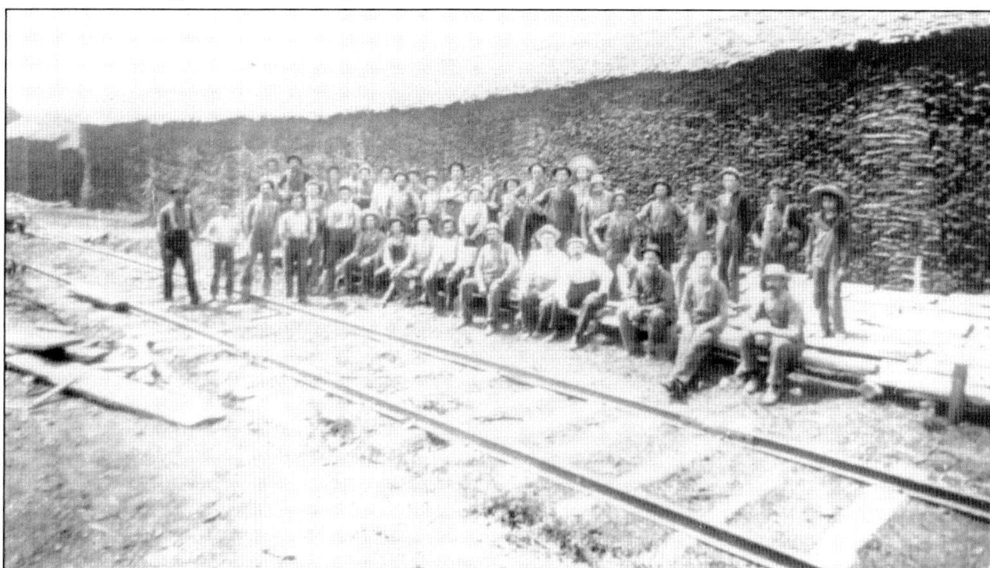

Bark stacks at the sawmill in Big Run indicate a thriving logging industry. Here, the logging crew pauses beside the railroad. Much of the bark will be shipped to Pittsburgh. The first sawmill in Big Run was built by a Mr. Farnsworth in 1840. It was located on Main and Union Streets where the medical center now stands. The dense forests of pine, hemlock, cherry, poplar, chestnut, beech, and birch trees led to the development the lumbering industry.

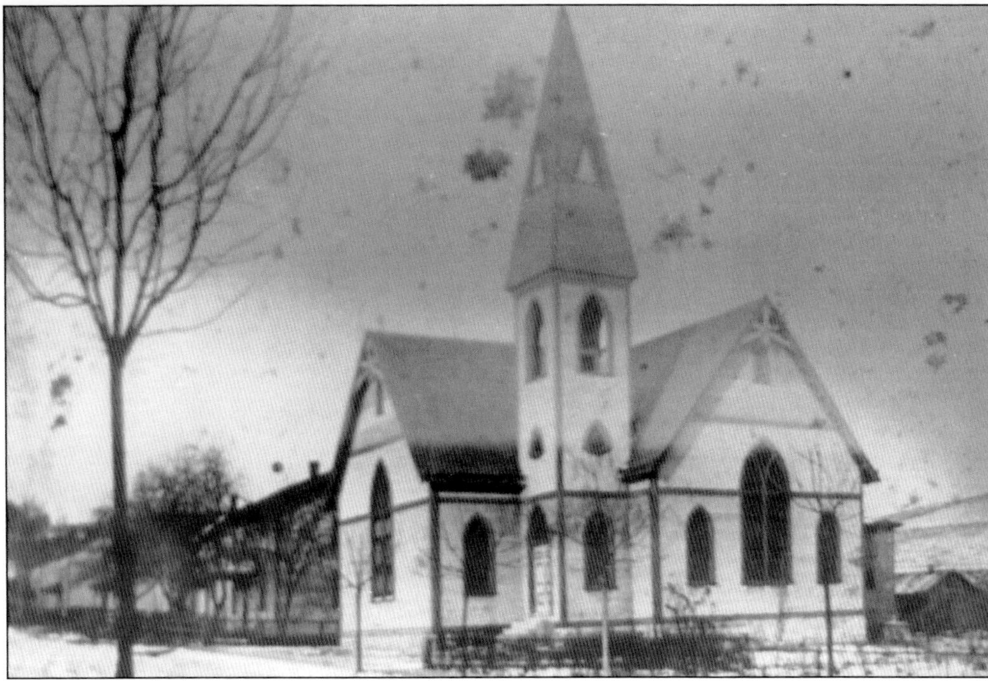

The First Christian Church was organized in Big Run in 1891. Faith in God had been nurtured through the years by early itinerant preachers who braved the perils of riding the circuit to spread the Word of God. The Methodist congregation had been formed in 1858. They and the Baptist congregation conducted services in the school building. In 1888, the Presbyterian Church was formed, and by 1893 their own church was complete.

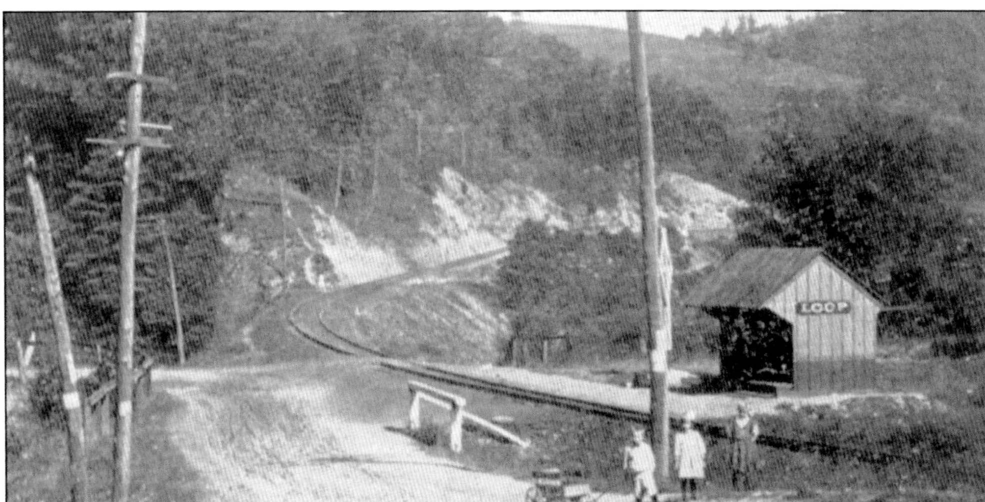

Loop was a whistle stop in 1909. Sharp curves, steep hills, deep ravines, and the rugged mountain terrain afforded a challenge to engineers and passengers alike on the Buffalo, Rochester, and Pittsburgh Railroad. Rail travel had become increasingly common, and mountaineers grew accustomed to the unusual deep ravines that swept gracefully around the mountainside. These curvatures prompted Charles Dickens to ponder the depths and later record it in his writings.

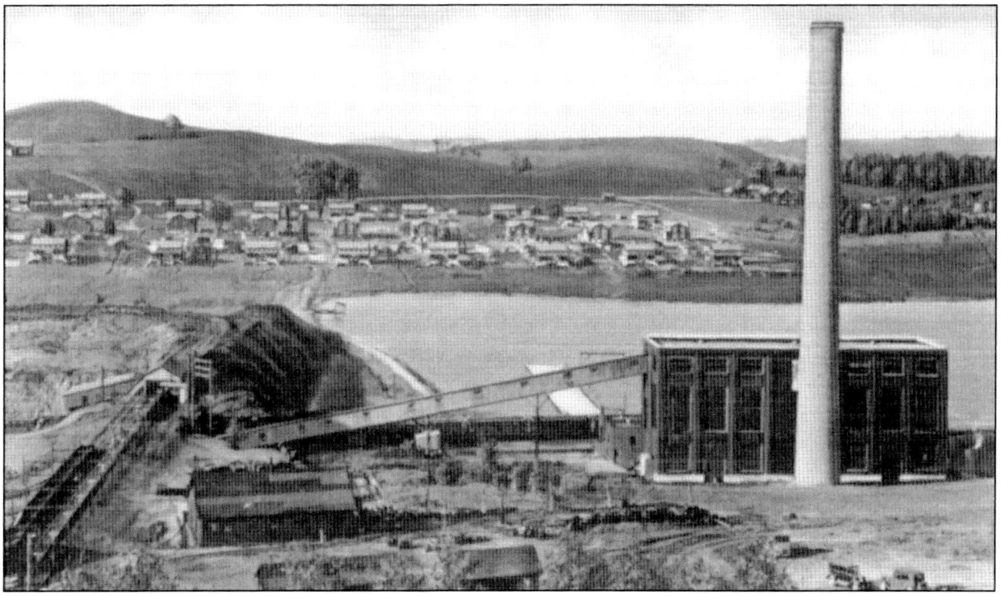

Helvetia Mine was opened in 1886 and outlasted many of the other mines. Mining has been the most lucrative and productive industry in Jefferson County, and Punxsutawney has been the center of this industry. Coal is the most valuable mineral in the county. Millions of tons of bituminous coal is still available. Much of it has been mined by the open pit method. This procedure is becoming extinct in the vicinity. Note the many company houses in the background.

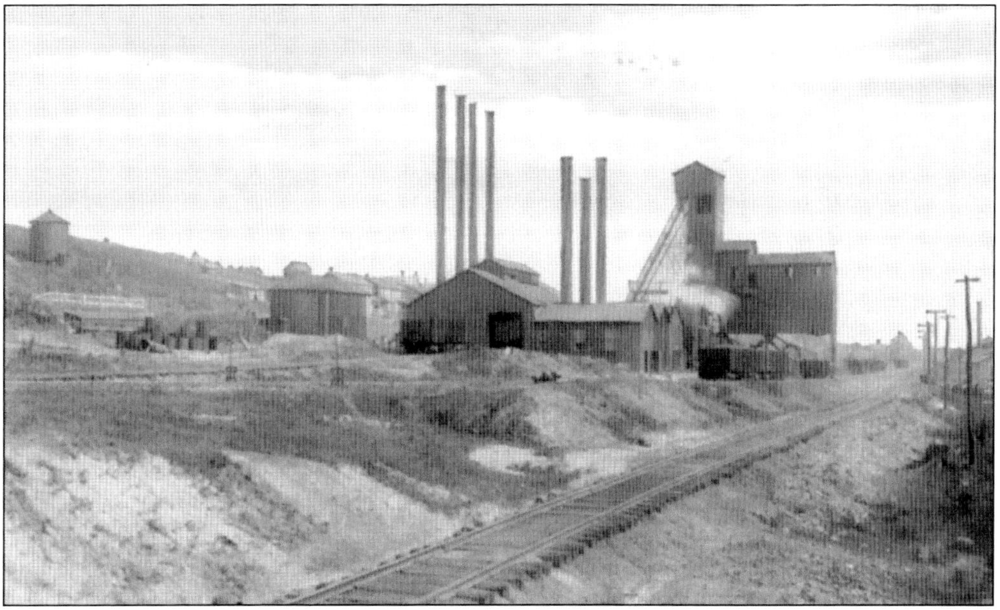

The Elk Run Mine was opened late in the 1890s. The principal producing coal company near Punxsutawney was the Rochester and Pittsburgh Coal and Iron Company. Other mines in the vicinity included the Horatio Mine, which was named after ex-congressman Horatio G. Fisher. Cloe Mine was opened in 1904 by the Buffalo and Susquehanna Company. Called the Onondaga Shaft, it operated for 30 years and employed 400 men.

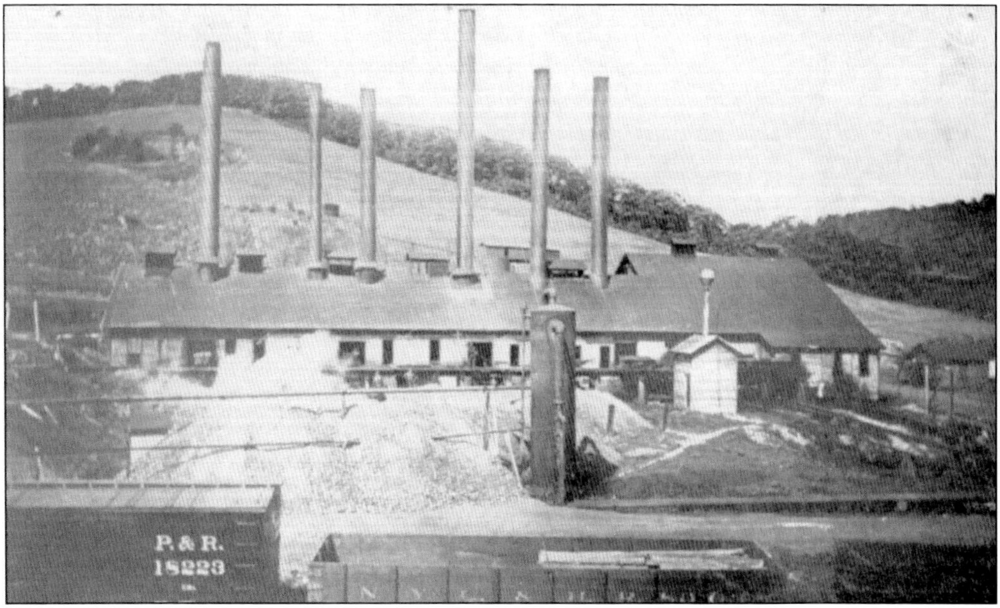

The Rossiter Coal Mine was opened in 1902 by the New York Central Railroad. When it reached peak production, the mine employed more than 700 men. Rossiter was among the small mining towns that looked to Punxsutawney as the industrial hub of activity and greatly contributed to its prosperity.

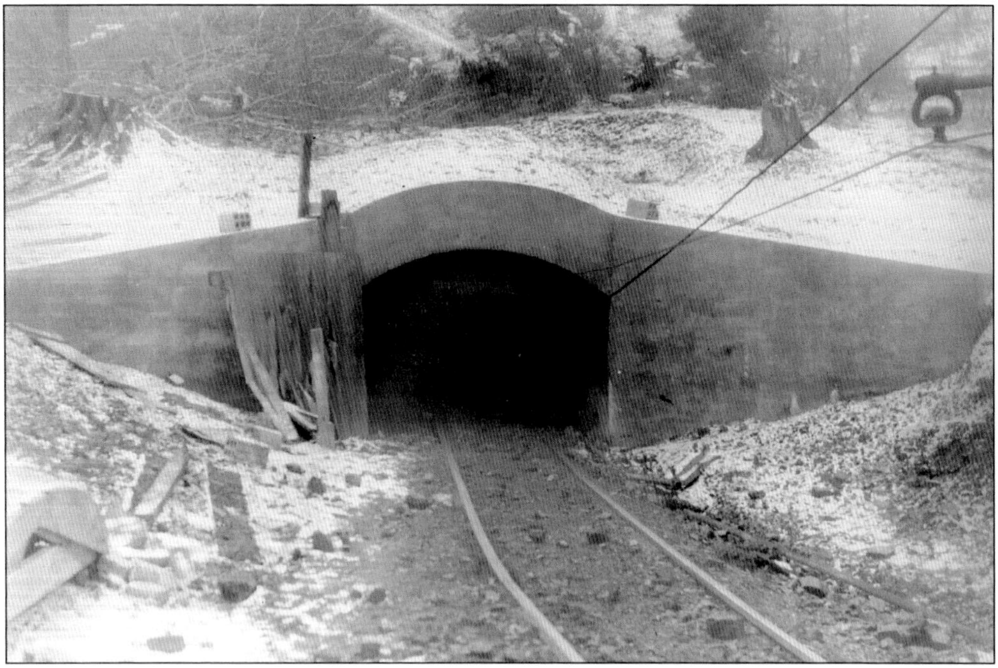
The draft, or entrance, to the mine takes the miner on a stark, prehistoric journey. He leaves daylight, fresh air, weather changes, and natural beauty as he boards the shuttle that will transport him to his austere workplace. This journey could be many miles into the mine, where primeval vegetation has been transformed into coal. The extraction of coal from deep within the earth became the life of Punxsutawney and its surrounding hamlets.

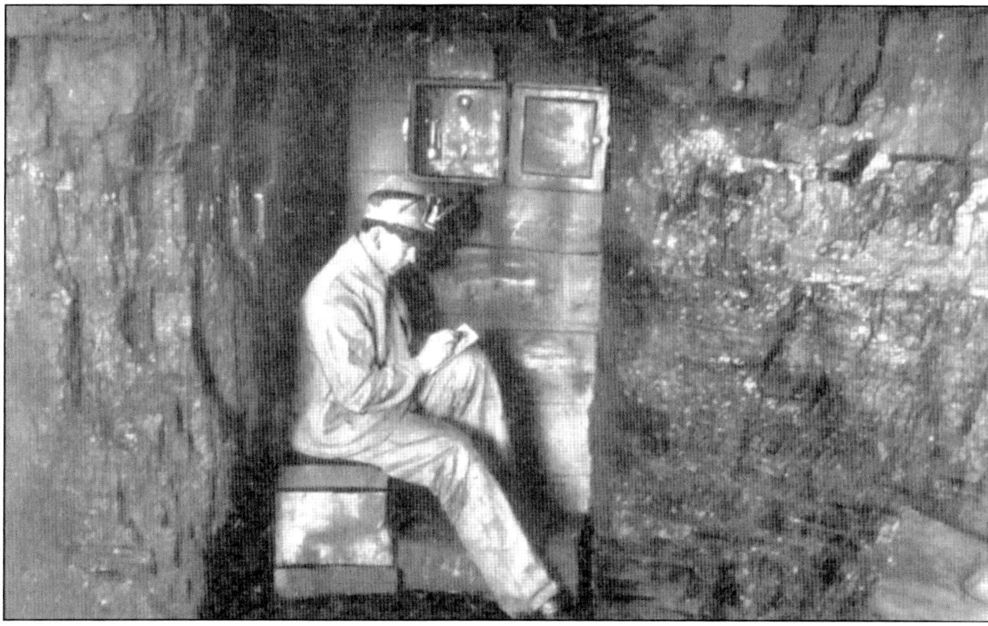

A miner surrounded by coal uses the telephone. Punxsutawney is situated in Jefferson County. The peak production of coal in the county was 318 million tons of coal produced by 2,260 employees in 1947. The first mining in the county was done in Reynoldsville by the Diamond Gas & Coal Company in 1873. The first coal was shipped by rail from this mine in 1874. It was transported by wagon to the railroads and then shipped to Buffalo, Pittsburgh, and other markets.

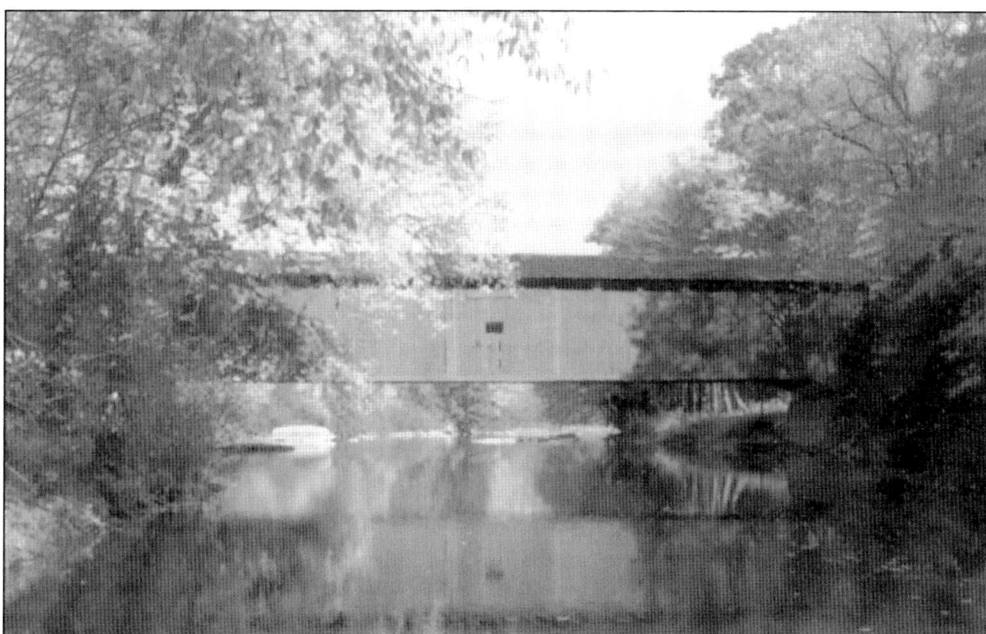

Thomas A. McGee built McGees Mill's covered bridge in 1873. It is the only covered bridge in Clearfield County and the only one that crosses the west bank of the Susquehanna River in Pennsylvania. This Burr arch truss bridge covers a 100-foot span. It was renovated in 1978.

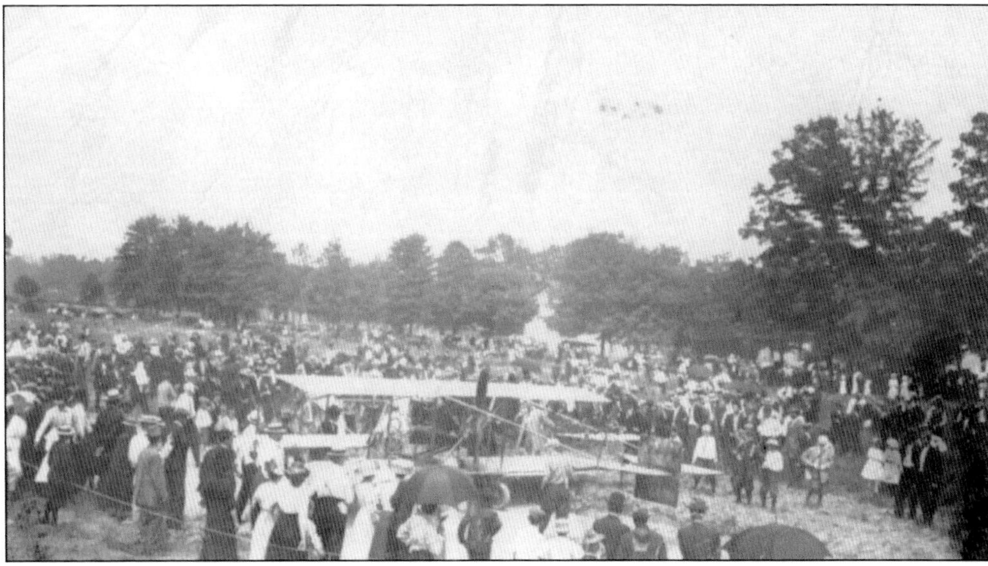

Earl Sandt was one of Punxy's first pilots. In an exhibition flight, he flew from Brookville to Punxsutawney on June 29, 1912. When he left Brookville, all the ironworks whistles blew and everyone rushed out to witness his arrival. Nineteen minutes later, he touched down on a designated site at the Punxsutawney Fairgrounds. This wondrous flying machine was a novelty that most Punxsutawneyites had never seen.

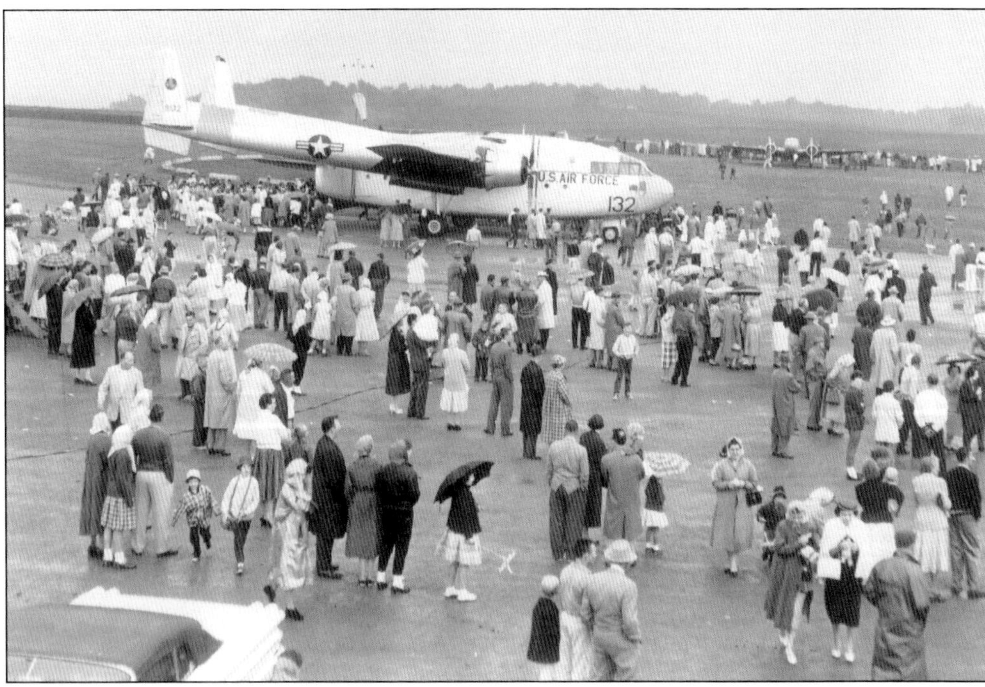

The airport is located in Bell Township and covers an area of 120 acres. It was purchased from O.P. Grube on February 20, 1945. Initially, the airport served private planes. Many successful and intriguing air shows have been staged at the airfield. Airmail pickup began on January 1, 1946, at Grube Field. Thirty spectators watched as 3,500 pieces of mail were sent out the first day.

Six

Festival Time in Punxsutawney

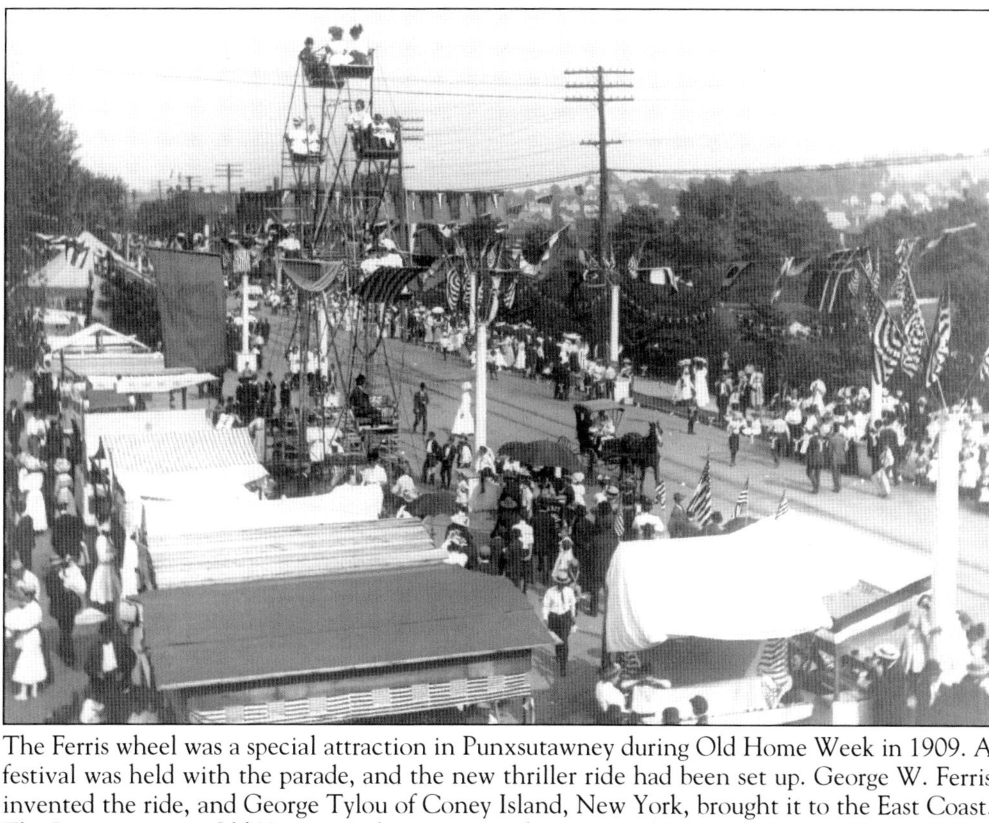

The Ferris wheel was a special attraction in Punxsutawney during Old Home Week in 1909. A festival was held with the parade, and the new thriller ride had been set up. George W. Ferris invented the ride, and George Tylou of Coney Island, New York, brought it to the East Coast. The Punxsutawney Old Home Week was initiated in 1909. The festival was among the first to acquire a Ferris wheel.

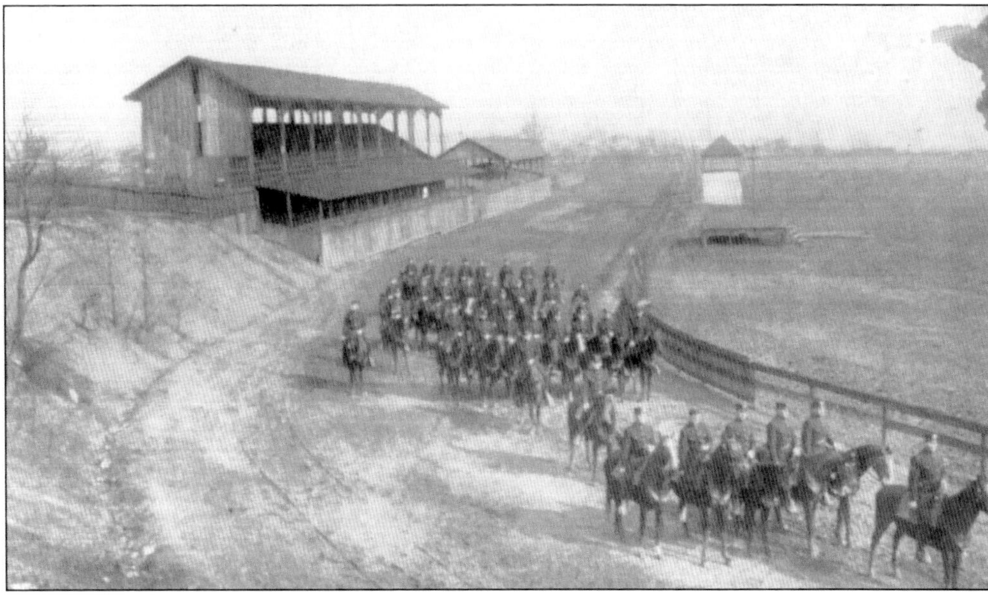

Troop D of the Pennsylvania State Constabulary is mounted at the fairgrounds. Created in 1905 for community protection and law enforcement, it was the first uniformed state police. Punxsutawney was one of four sites chosen in Pennsylvania to have such a force. Initially, 47 troopers were housed at the National Hotel. They met with some opposition and hostility until miners realized their protective purpose. They formed baseball and football teams, established a spirit of competition, founded a drama club, and established friendly relations.

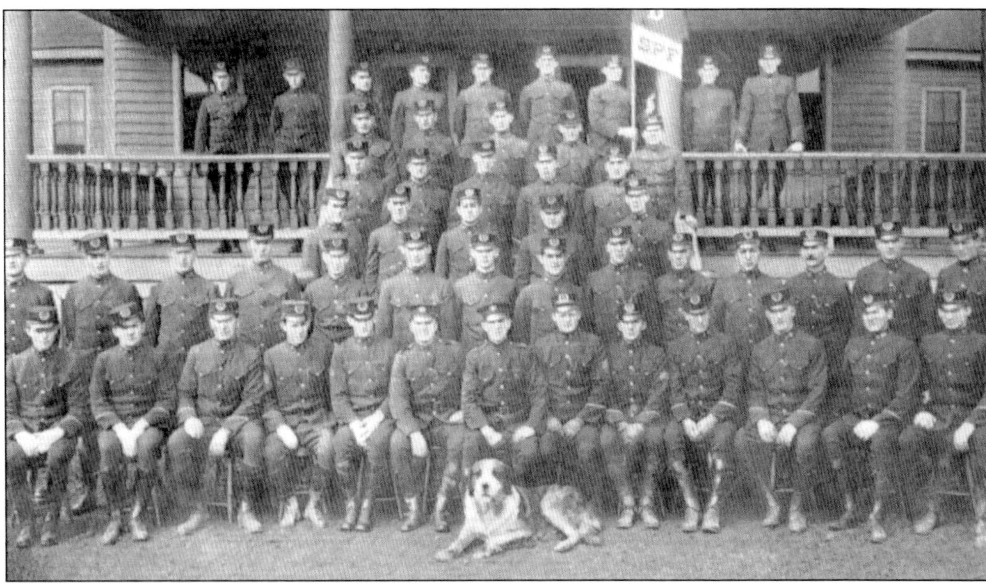

The Punxsutawney State Police had its beginnings in 1905. Gov. Samuel W. Pennypacker appointed Col. John C. Groome as the first superintendent of the first statewide police force in America. Groome studied the Royal Irish Constabulary and the Canadian Northwest Mounted Police and incorporated the best of both into his troops. Four sites were selected to pioneer the new constabulary force, including Greensburg, Reading, Wyoming, and Punxsutawney. Each was assigned a letter.

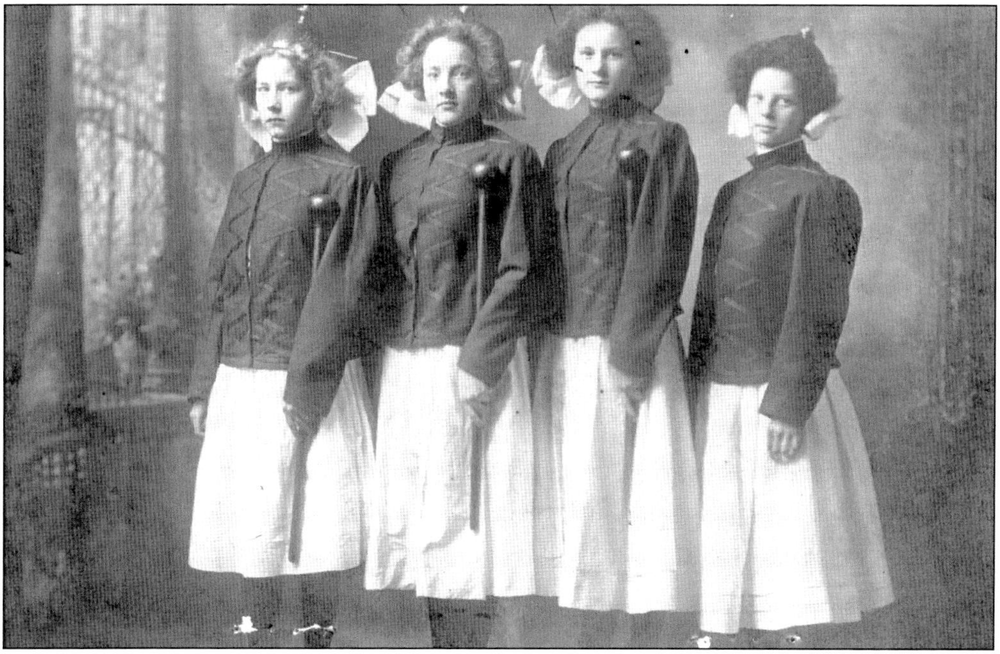

The majorettes are ready to begin their twirling act. They include, from left to right, Marge Cromley, Nelly Myers, Mary Zeitler, and Vera Harl. Their turn-of-the-century uniforms were topped off with huge white bows and black stockings. Note the wooden batons that are the forerunners of our sophisticated, gaily produced batons today. The majorettes appeared at parades and sports. They cheered the Punxsutawney team on through intense competition.

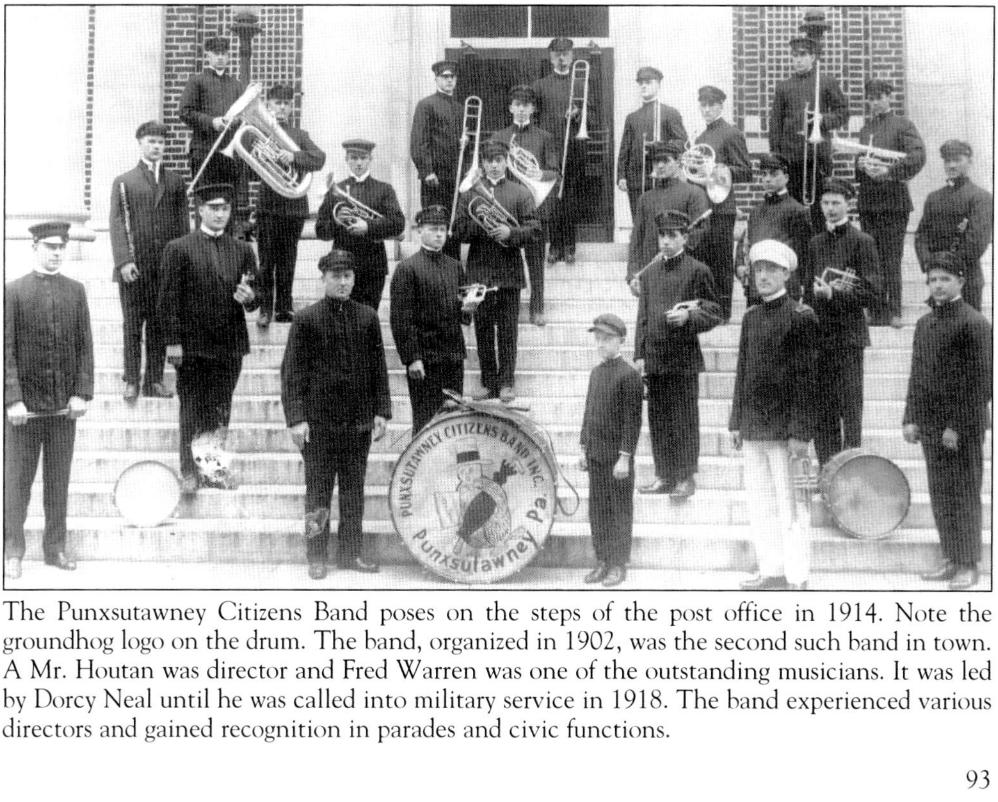

The Punxsutawney Citizens Band poses on the steps of the post office in 1914. Note the groundhog logo on the drum. The band, organized in 1902, was the second such band in town. A Mr. Houtan was director and Fred Warren was one of the outstanding musicians. It was led by Dorcy Neal until he was called into military service in 1918. The band experienced various directors and gained recognition in parades and civic functions.

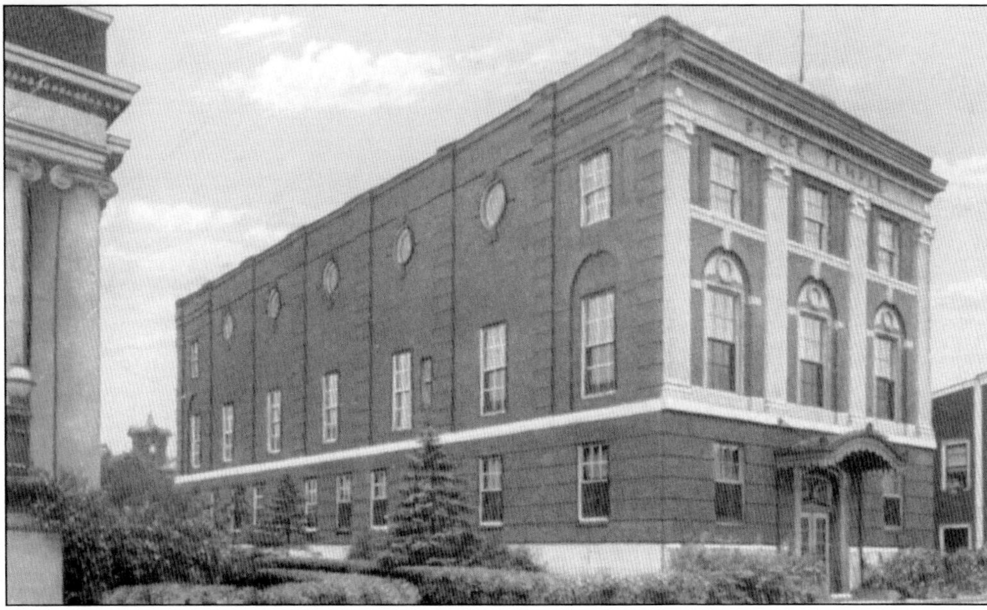

The Elks are an American fraternal organization chartered in Punxsutawney in 1895. The lodge is founded on the principles of charity, justice, brotherly love, and fidelity. In 1924, the Joseph Schooner property on Findley Street was chosen for a lodge. Rough brick with Indiana limestone make up the exterior. The first floor houses a ballroom. The second floor has a community center, and the third is for lodge use. The building has undergone extensive renovation in recent years.

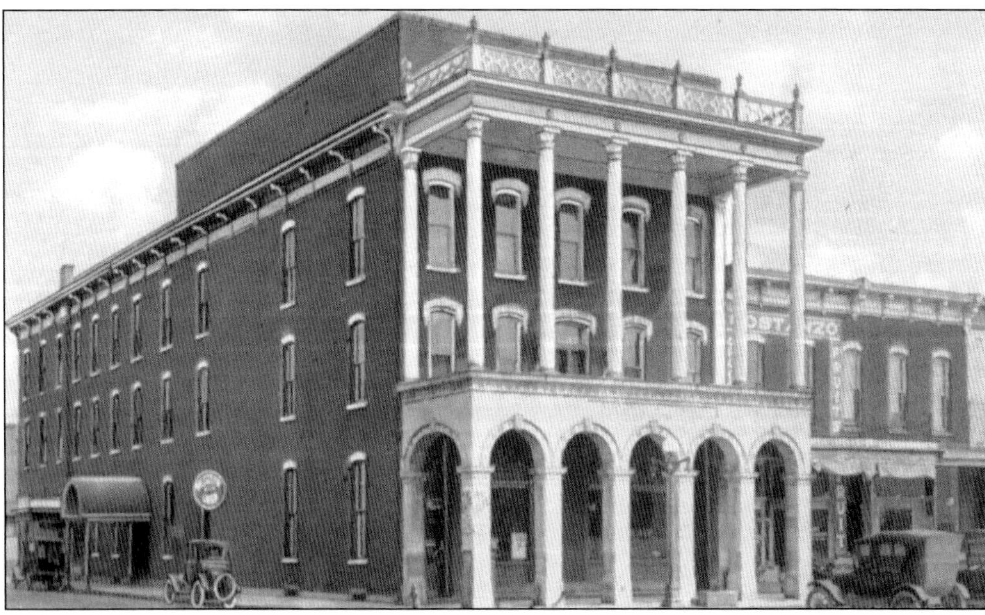

The Masonic Temple of Punxsutawney is located on West Mahoning Street. Established as the J.W. Jenks Lodge in March 1875, it consisted of 26 charter members. They met initially in the Old Shields Building. This purely fraternal organization aims to better the world and improve relations between peoples of various nations.

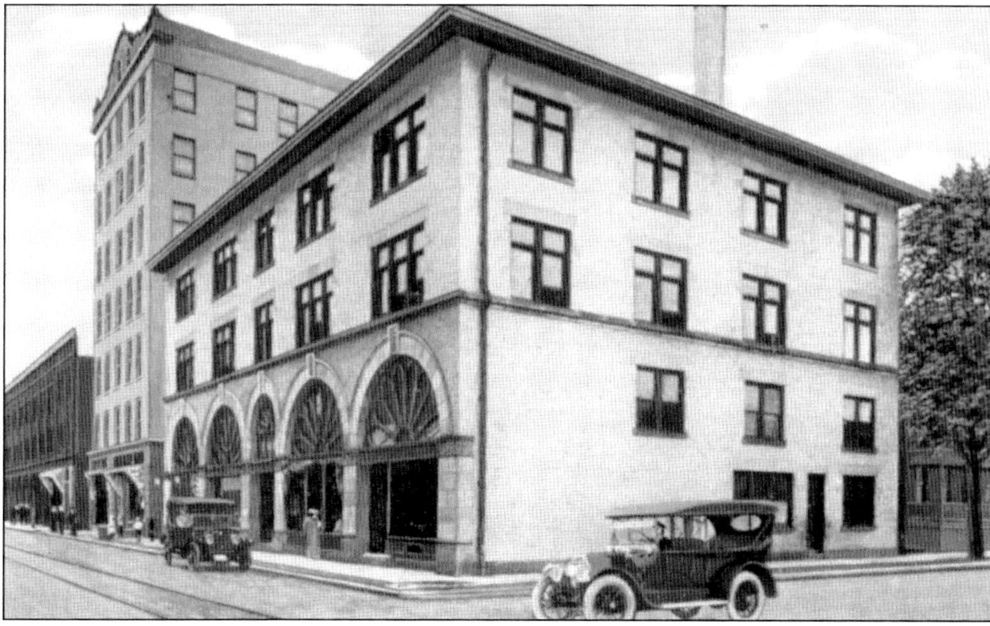

The Young Men's Christian Association (YMCA) aims to stimulate the mental, physical, and social growth of young people. The organization helps build character and proper attitudes while fostering a spirit of cooperation. Activities encourage brotherhood and Christian living ideals. Founded in 1891, the organization met initially in the Snyder Building. In 1907, the board of directors purchased a site on Findley Street and constructed the YMCA building.

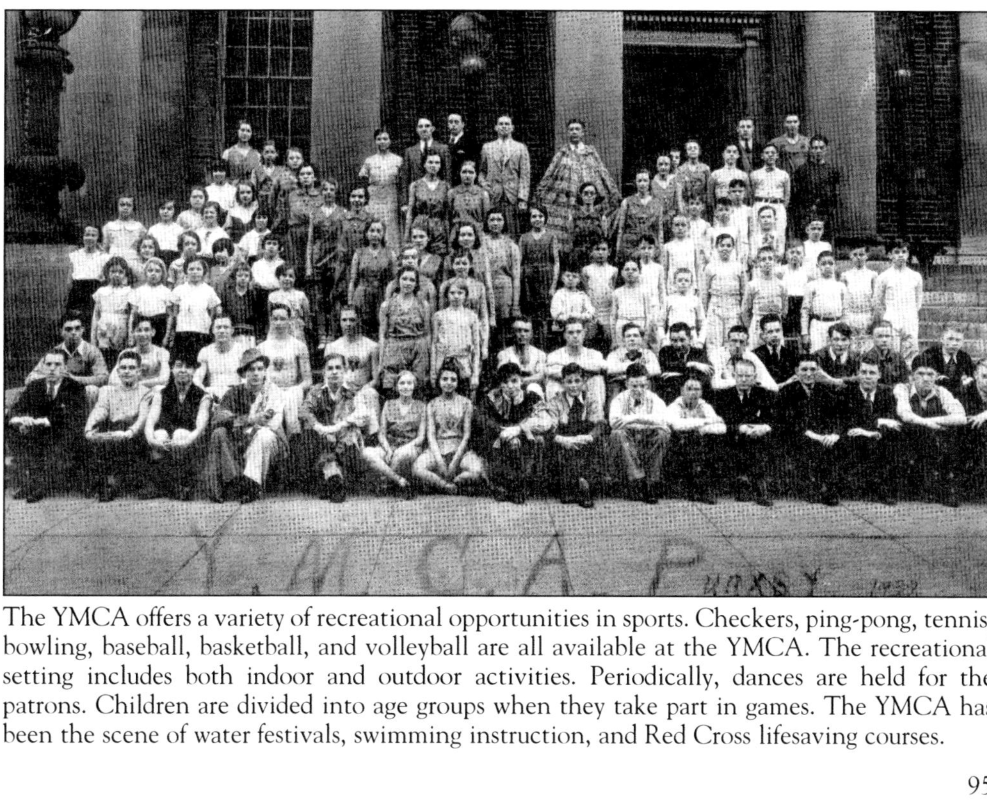

The YMCA offers a variety of recreational opportunities in sports. Checkers, ping-pong, tennis, bowling, baseball, basketball, and volleyball are all available at the YMCA. The recreational setting includes both indoor and outdoor activities. Periodically, dances are held for the patrons. Children are divided into age groups when they take part in games. The YMCA has been the scene of water festivals, swimming instruction, and Red Cross lifesaving courses.

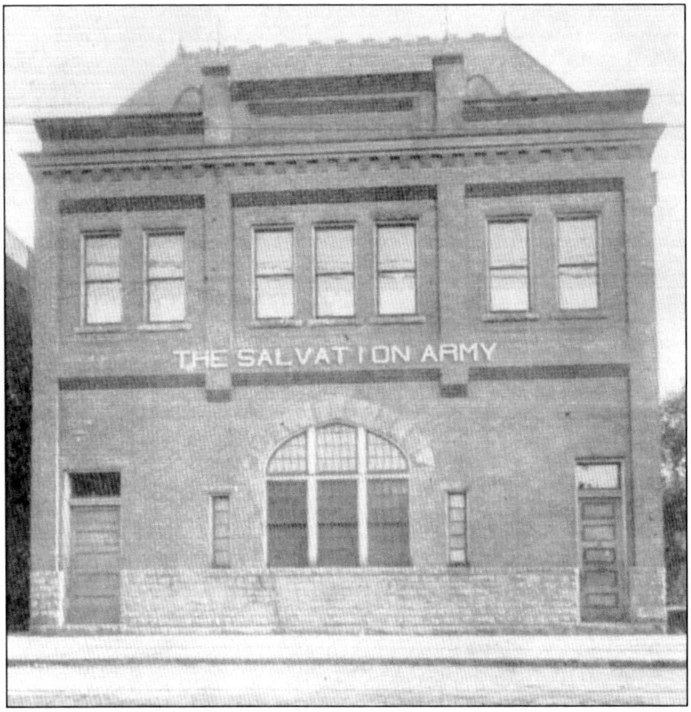

The Salvation Army has been established on Mahoning Street since 1917. It aims to build religious character and offer social welfare service to the poor and unfortunate. It is a spiritual organization with a social service purpose. The Salvation Army ministry includes open-air evangelism. It purports to embrace the principles of Jesus Christ in a practical, daily fashion. The Salvation Army is very active during the Christmas season.

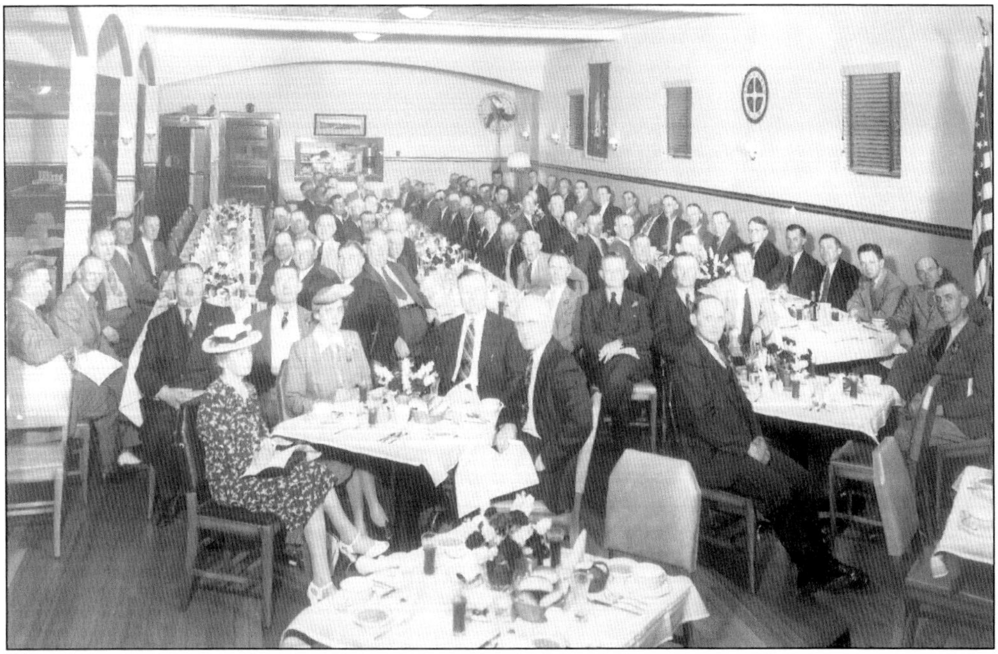

The Army-Navy Club features social gatherings for the benefit of its veterans. It was founded in 1934. Its purpose was to perpetuate the Memorial Plot of the John Jacob Fisher Post of the American Legion, Post 62, and was designed for the enjoyment of its membership. A veteran must belong to the Veterans of Foreign Wars, Disabled American Veterans, or be a veteran of the Spanish-American War to qualify. All others are considered "Class B." The club provided entertainment and sponsored bowling teams, annual picnics, and dances.

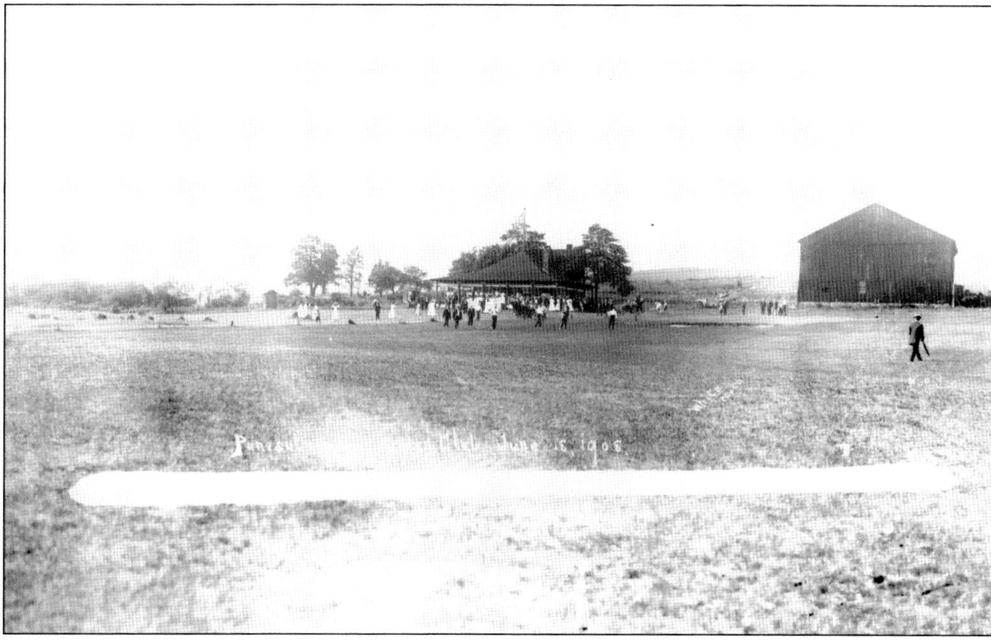

The Punxsutawney Country Club was organized in 1900 by Dr. Frank Lorenzo for the benefit of golfers. J.H. Kennedy was the first member to join Lorenzo. The others were former Rep. Jesse Whiteman, "Brick" Preston, Earl Snyder, and William Bartholomew. They bought a 110-acre farm from L. Robinson, manager of the Rochester and Pittsburgh Coal and Iron Company, to set up the club.

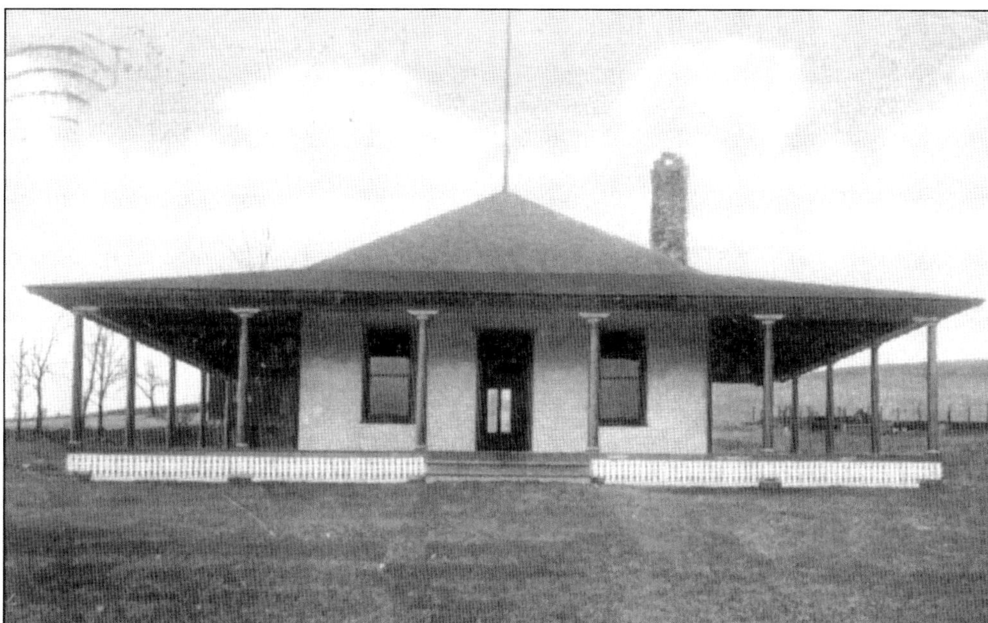

The original clubhouse at the country club was built by subscription. On August 22, 1904, the clubhouse was complete and opened to the public. Golf links were laid out on the surrounding acreage. It was the only club at the time that had been laid out beside a main street. Half of the golf course is in the borough and the other half is outside city limits.

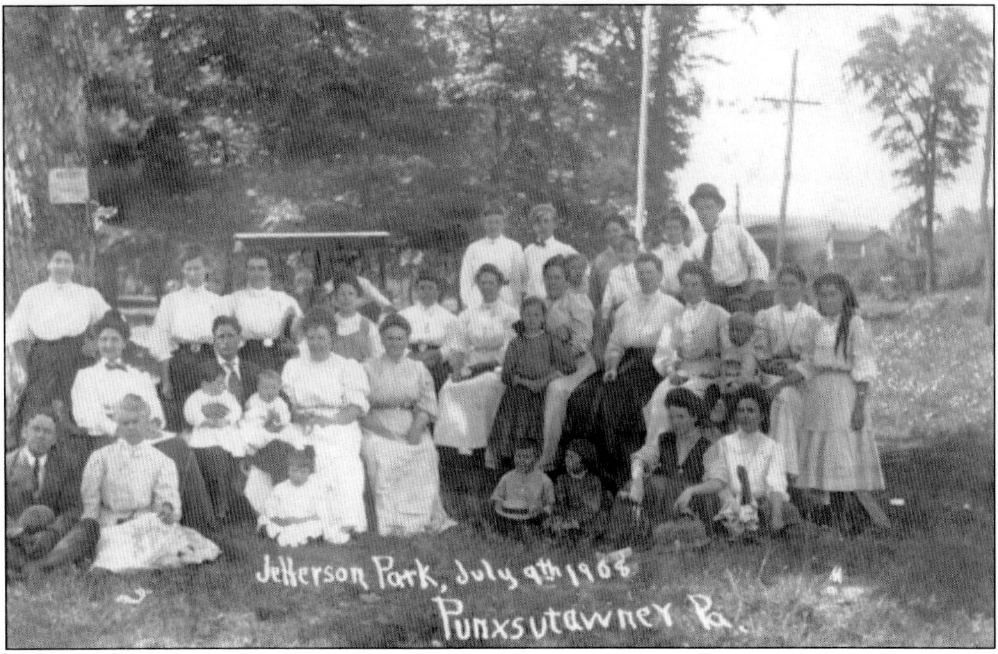

A picnic was always a welcome source of interaction for the early settlers. Here, on July 4, 1908, a group of ladies gathers in Jefferson Park for a picnic and socialization. Radio, television, and telephones were still in the future. These pioneer women were always happy when an opportunity presented itself to mingle with their peers.

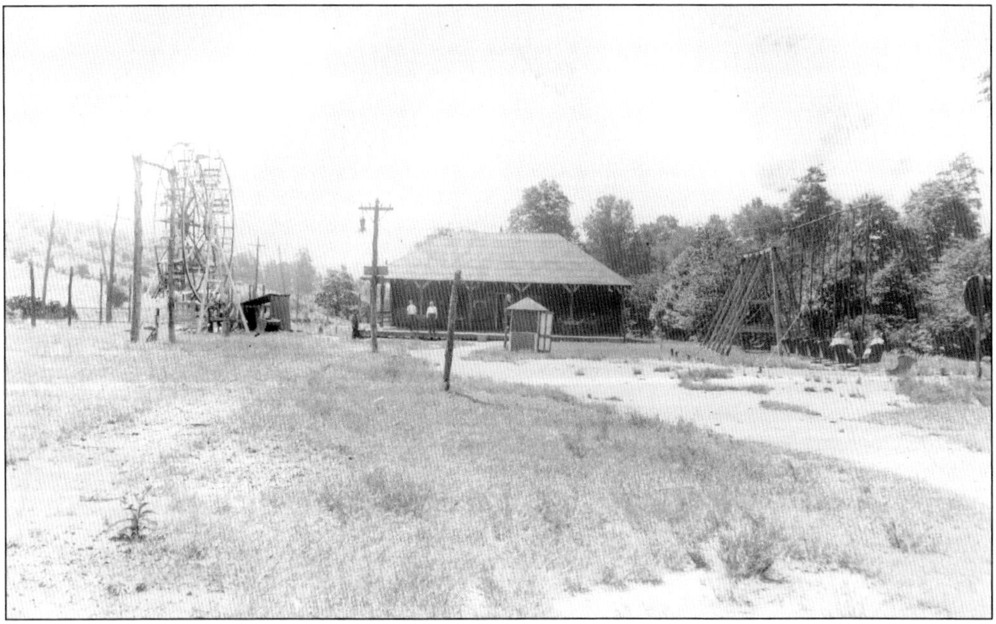

Jefferson Park was a playground for the youngsters. It contained many amusements, but the most popular was the new Ferris wheel, invented by George W. Ferris in 1893. It was first used at Chicago's World Columbia Exposition. In an era of shifting emphasis from production to consumption, from work to amusement, it was not surprising when the idea took root and was duplicated many times.

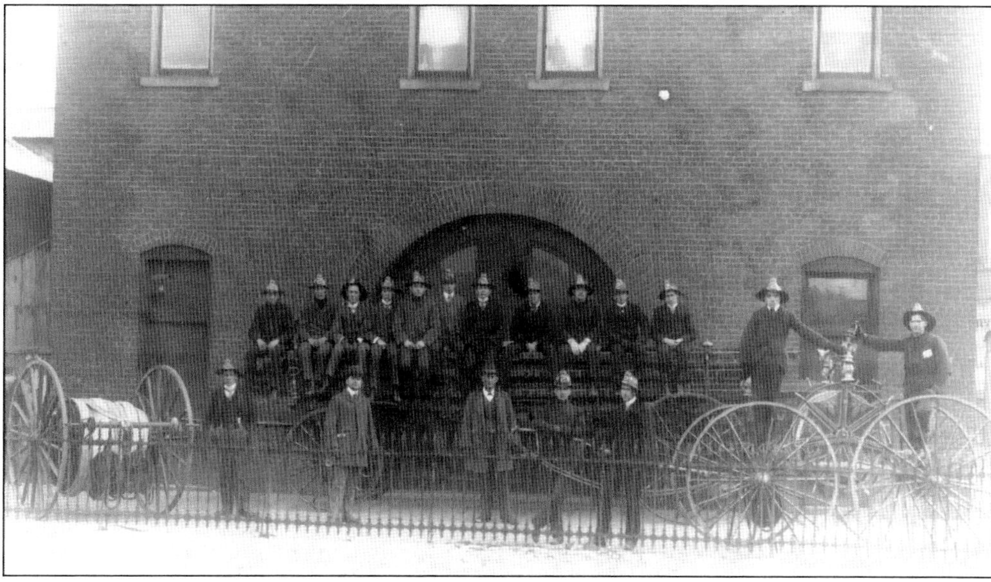

The Punxsutawney Fire Department was founded in 1900. This 1909 scene was photographed in front of the municipal building on Torrence Alley. Horse-drawn fire trucks were often pulled by the men. Frequently, the ringing of church bells sounded the alarm. Note the kerosene lanterns on the rig at the right. This was the only source of light on the dark roadways at night. There were three fire departments in Punxsutawney at one time, located in Central, Lindsey, and Elk Run.

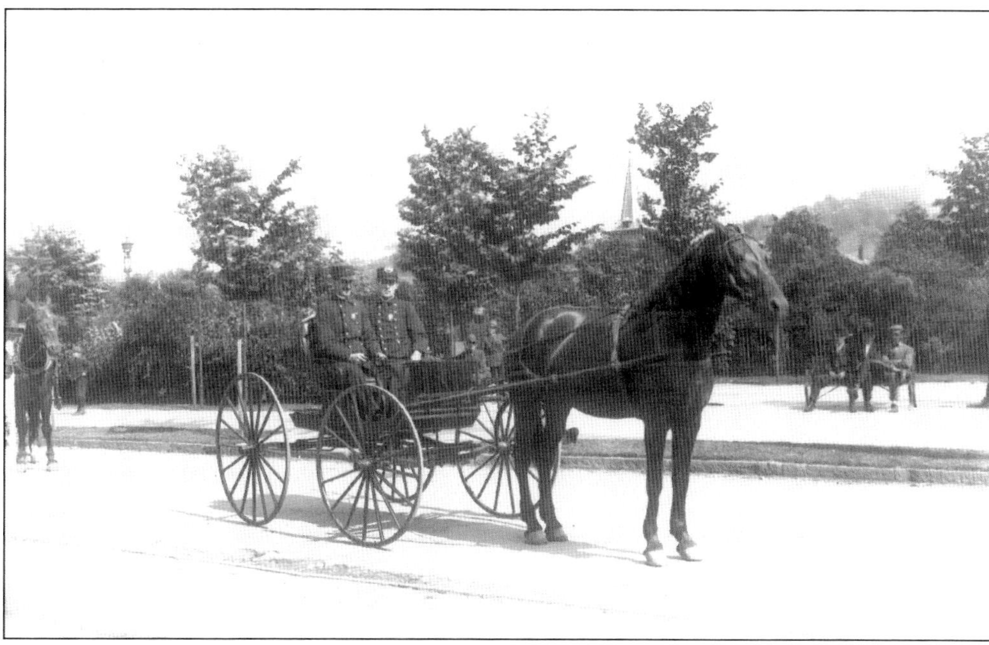

Firemen of the Central Fire Department pose in the rig usually used in parades. Their friends observe from the park bench. Their earliest equipment included buckets, grapple hooks, and ladders. They served the borough until the big fire of 1879, which clearly indicated the necessity for better equipment. The new company was organized in 1907 with Harry Euann as the first fire chief.

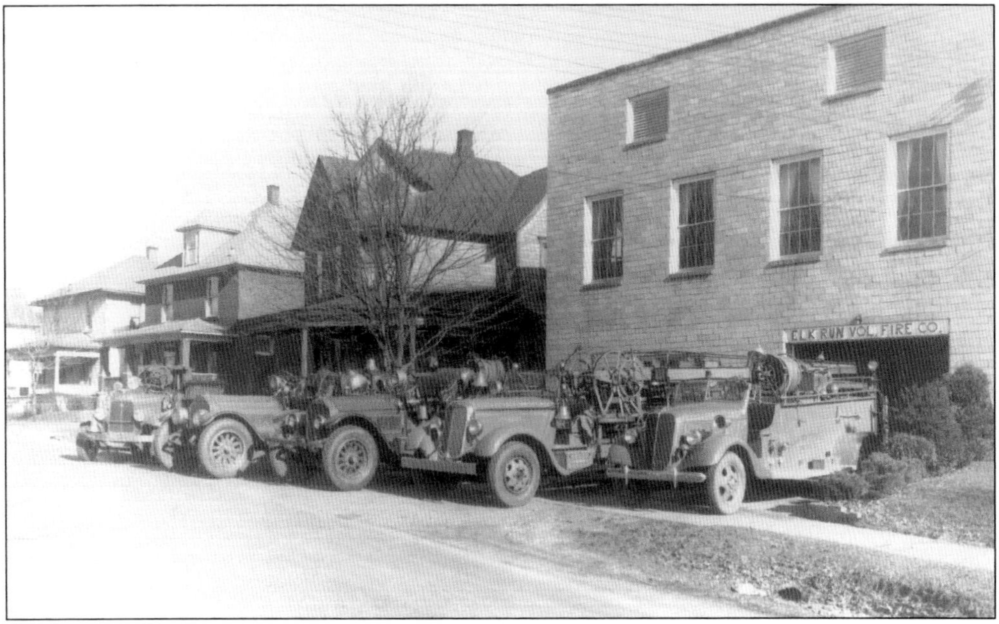

Elk Run fire trucks are lined up and ready for action in 1945. Citizens of the Second Ward formed this company in January 1922 with James Padden as the first president. The company purchased a site on Elk Run Road, but it was two years before a building could be constructed to house the equipment. The one-story building of that era was adequate to accommodate the company's International chemical truck.

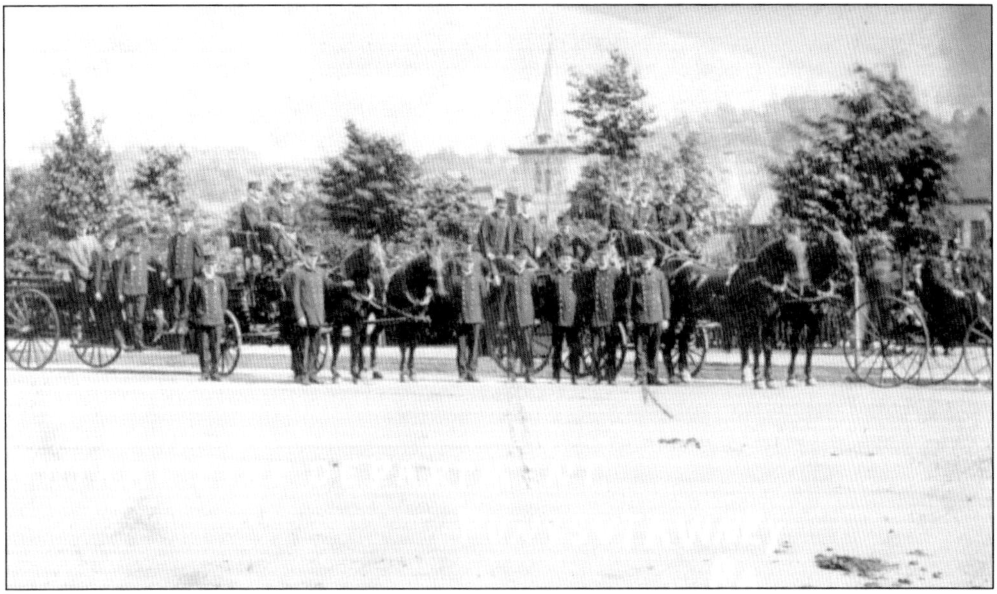

The Punxsutawney Fire Department was formed following a huge fire in 1879. It was known as the Central Fire Department, with William Torrence serving as its first chief. A Babcot chemical extinguisher was among the early equipment. Ordinances provided for the organization and government of the department. Amendments to the original ordinance were included through the years. One such mandate in 1919 stated that "a salary of fifty cents per hour be given to each foreman for his services."

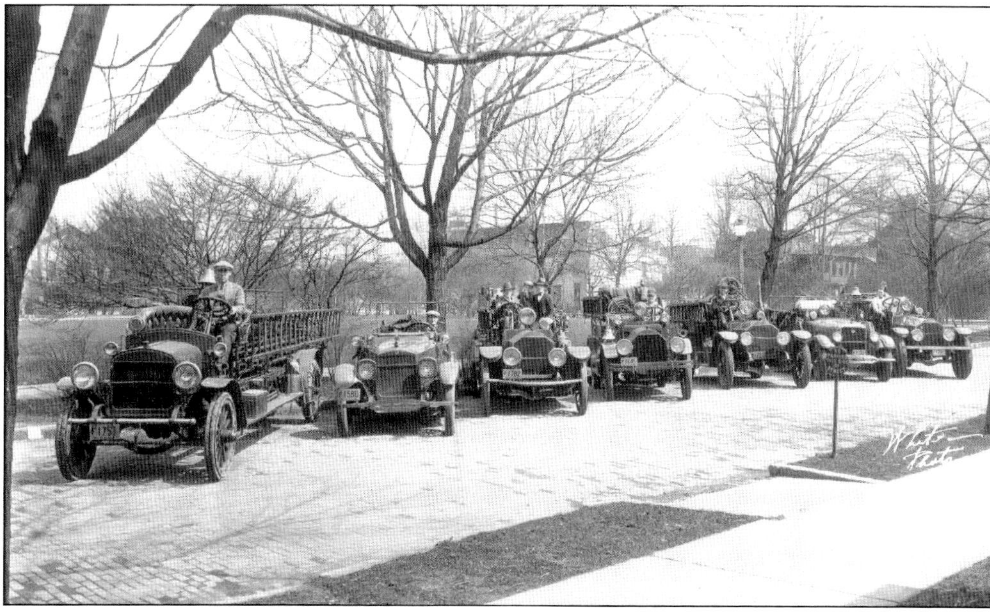

Punxsutawney's Central Fire Department trucks are now vintage early-20th-century vehicles. Note the visible spokes on the wheels, the running boards, the fenders, and the bumpers of a bygone era. These were all part of vehicles during the first decades of their existence.

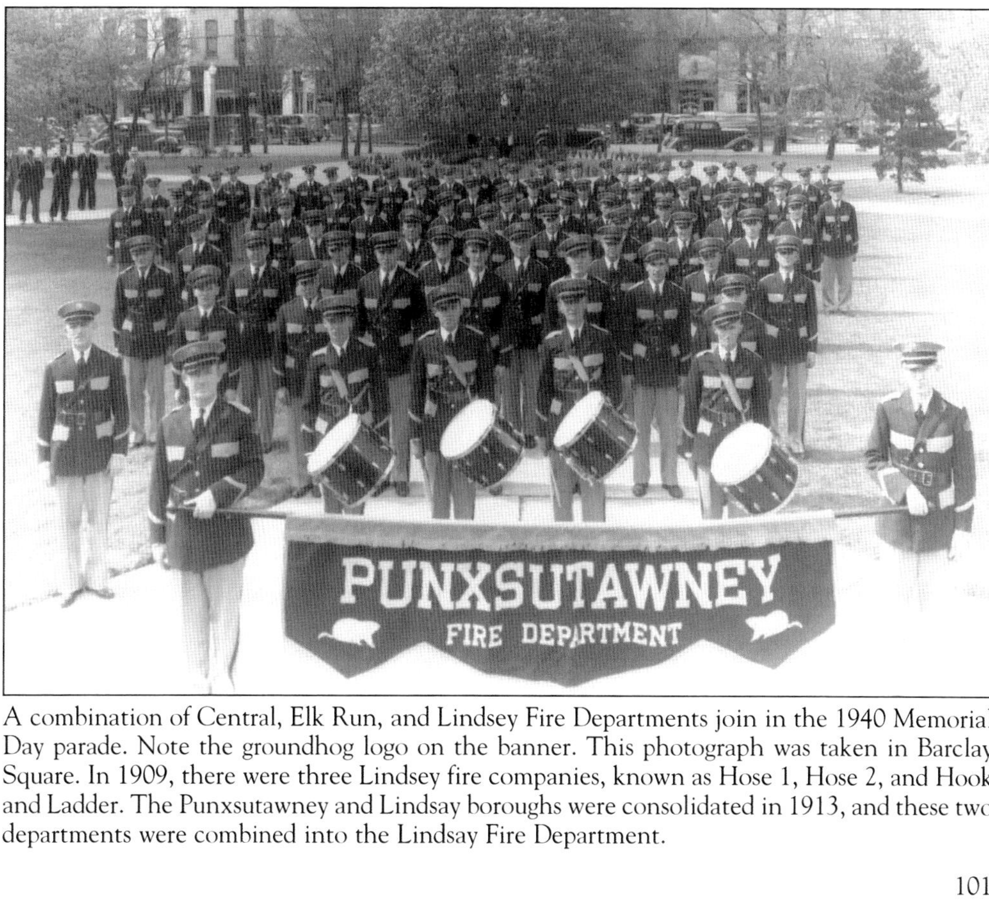

A combination of Central, Elk Run, and Lindsey Fire Departments join in the 1940 Memorial Day parade. Note the groundhog logo on the banner. This photograph was taken in Barclay Square. In 1909, there were three Lindsey fire companies, known as Hose 1, Hose 2, and Hook and Ladder. The Punxsutawney and Lindsay boroughs were consolidated in 1913, and these two departments were combined into the Lindsay Fire Department.

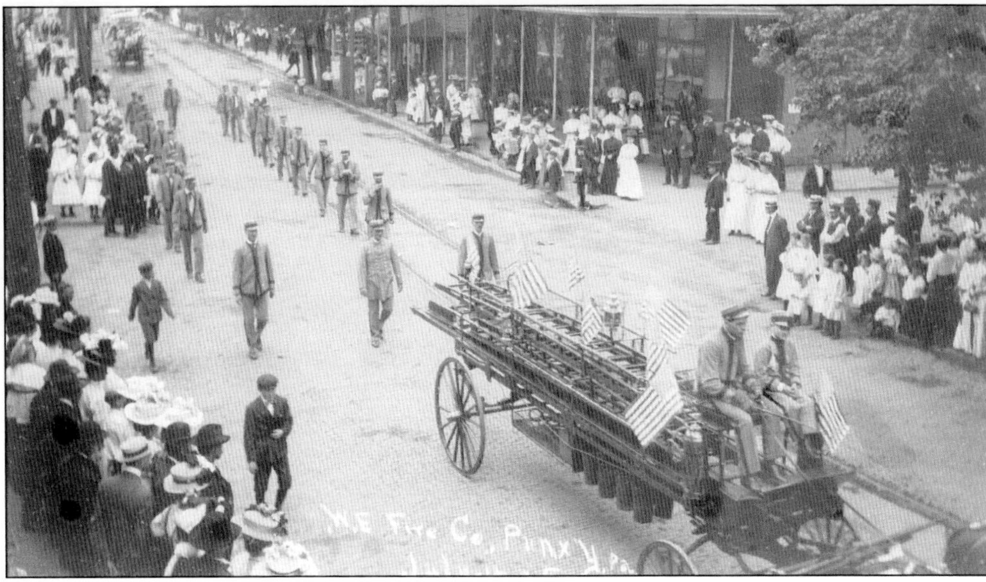

These firemen, with hook and ladder, participate in the Groundhog Festival parade of 1908. J.H. Fink's general store is in the background. Note the trolley tracks along Mahoning Street. The Groundhog Festival pays tribute to Punxsutawney's world-famous citizen, Punxsutawney Phil, who is asleep in his burrow while the festivities continue in his honor.

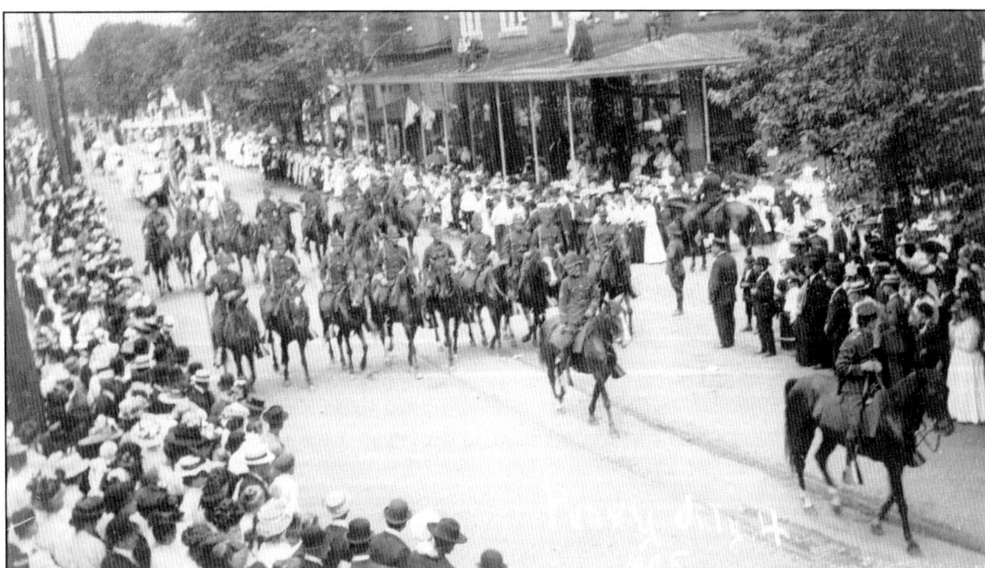

Mounted officers join the parade on July 4, 1908. This parade sets the tone for the annual Groundhog Festival. Groundhog Day is in February, but Punxsutawneyites celebrate their famous weather prophet throughout the year. The Groundhog Festival continues to be celebrated each summer with a wide variety of entertainment for everyone. Note the folks viewing the parade from the roof of J.H. Fink's general store on the corner of Mahoning and Gilpin Streets.

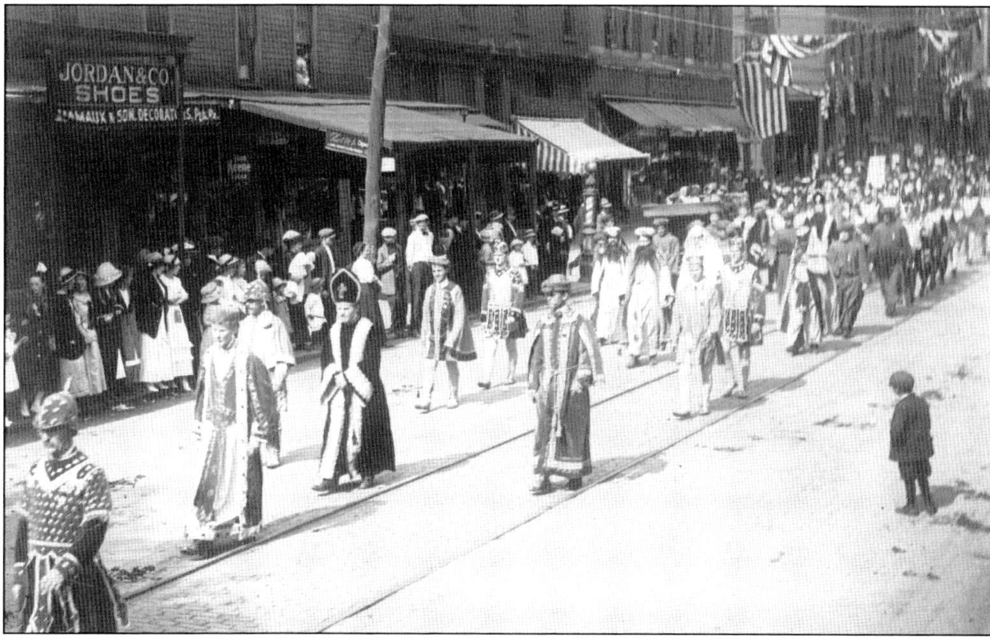

The Knights of Pythias were established in Punxsutawney in 1883. In this early-20th-century view, lodge men in ancient ceremonial robes march the parade route. This fraternal organization is a relief group based on love and mercy. Its chief function is to relieve misery, help the distressed, and minister to anyone in genuine need. A tremendous amount of humanitarian work is carried on quietly by the Knights of Pythias. Members are accepted regardless of race, color, or creed and must pledge to aid humanity.

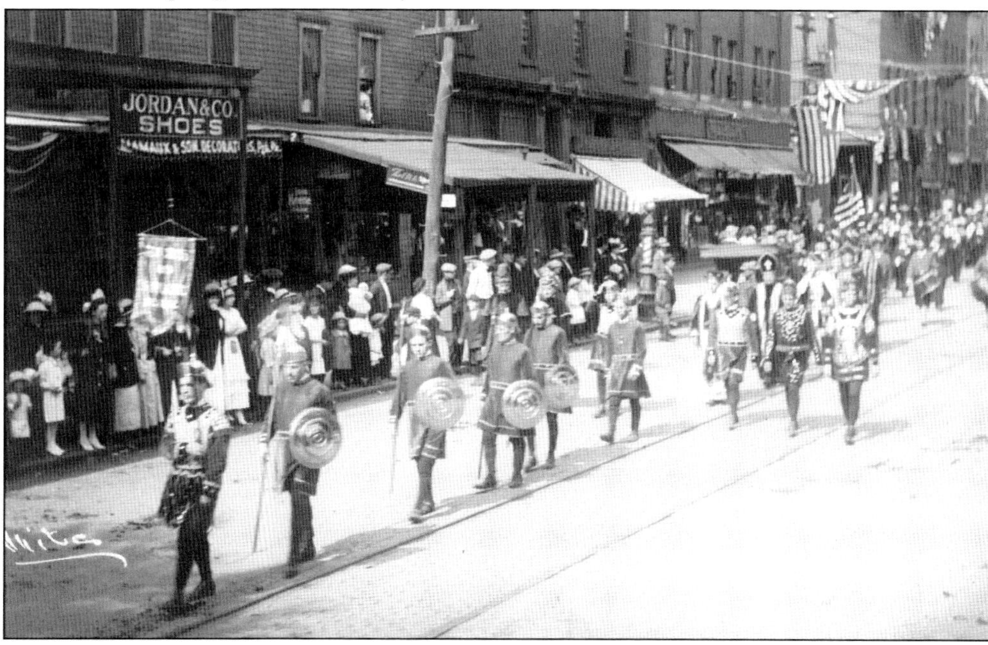

As the parade makes its way east on Mahoning Street, the Knights of Pythias add their pageantry to the festive occasion. Local church programs, craft shows, country singers, rock music, oldies, and fiddle contests are among the activities of the week. There is something for everyone.

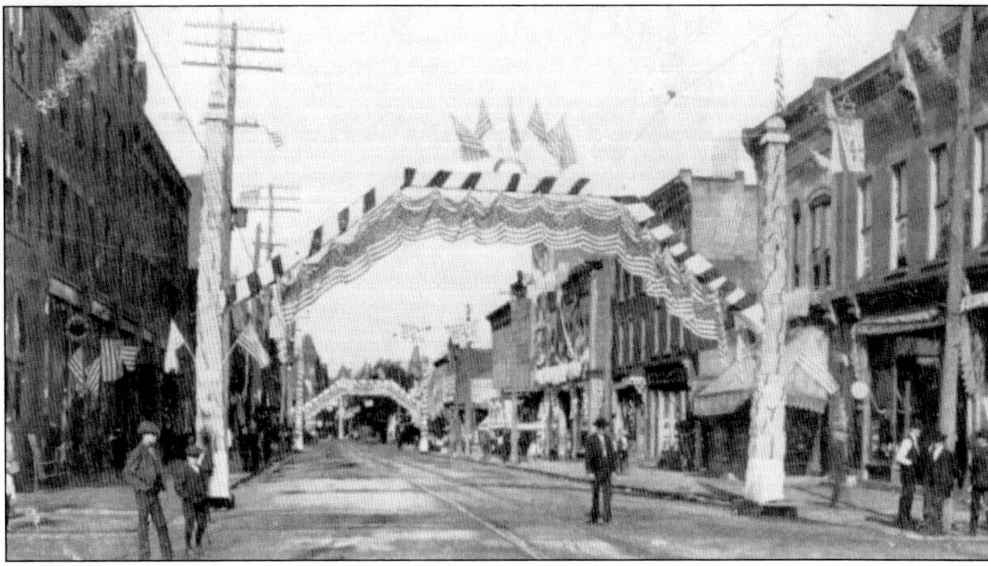

Great decorative arches span Mahoning Street in preparation for the historic parade in 1909. It was the first official Old Home Week parade. The buildings sport their festive finest, and a lively hometown spirit of gaiety, fun, and frolic prevails. The parade and festival have created a spirit of cooperation within the community. Thirty thousand residents and visitors viewed the parade, which was more than a mile long.

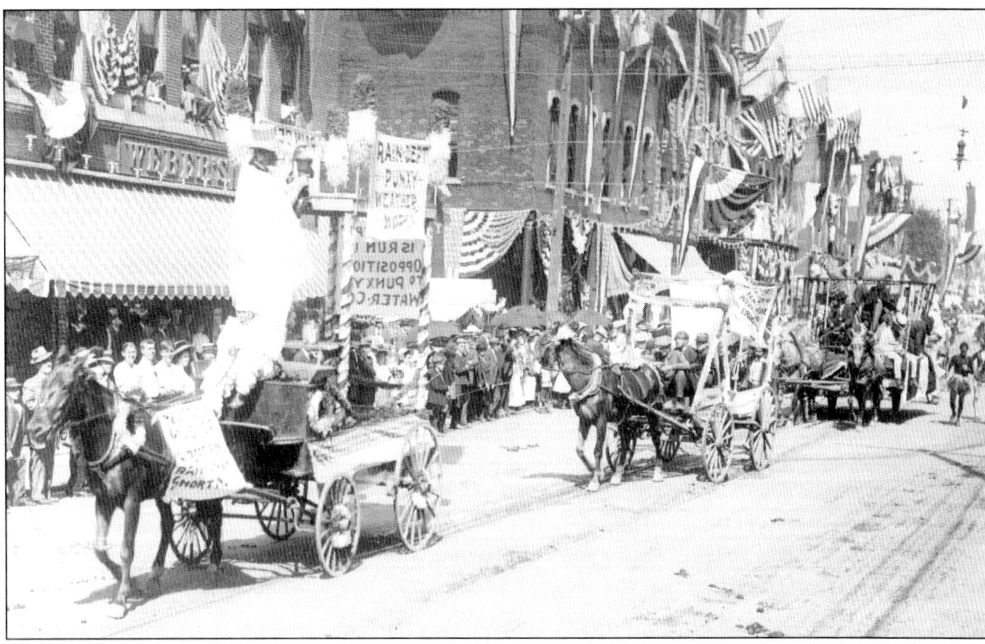

A patriotic buckboard float represents the "Rain Dept. Punxy Weather Works." It passes the Weber Department Store on Mahoning Street. Note the gentleman in a white coat and high silk hat holding a torch. The week-long festivities took place at the armory grounds on north Findley Street. This special event has been kept alive and marches right into the 21st century.

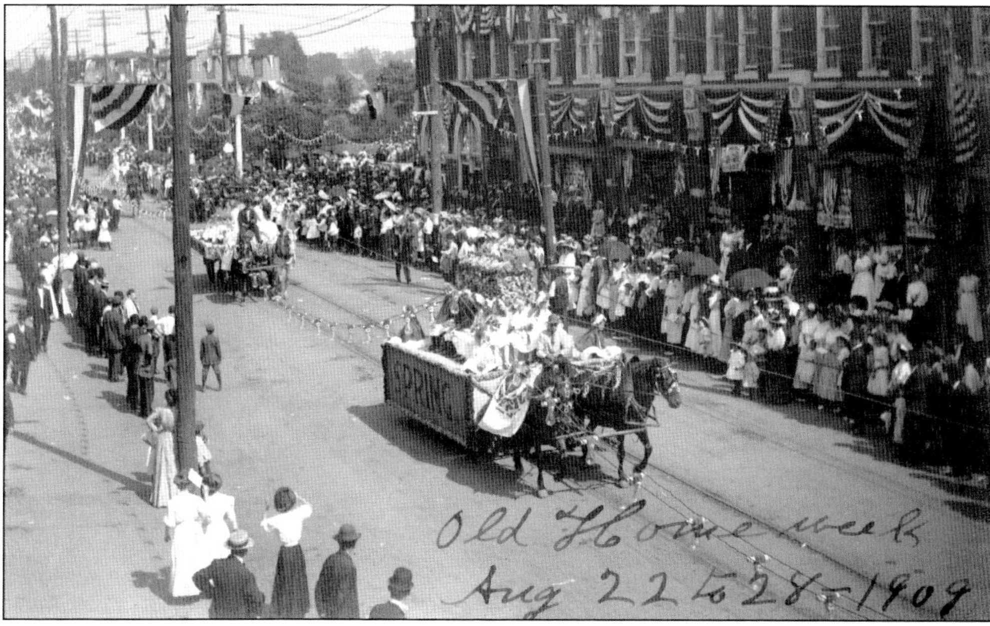

"Spring" is painted in big, bold letters on the side of the float as the 1909 Old Home Week parade proceeds along Mahoning Street. Nearly everyone in Punxsutawney and surrounding areas joins in the festivities. The annual event offers a break from their everyday chores. The floats represent the seasons. The parade and festivities create a carnival spirit in town that has lasted for more than a century.

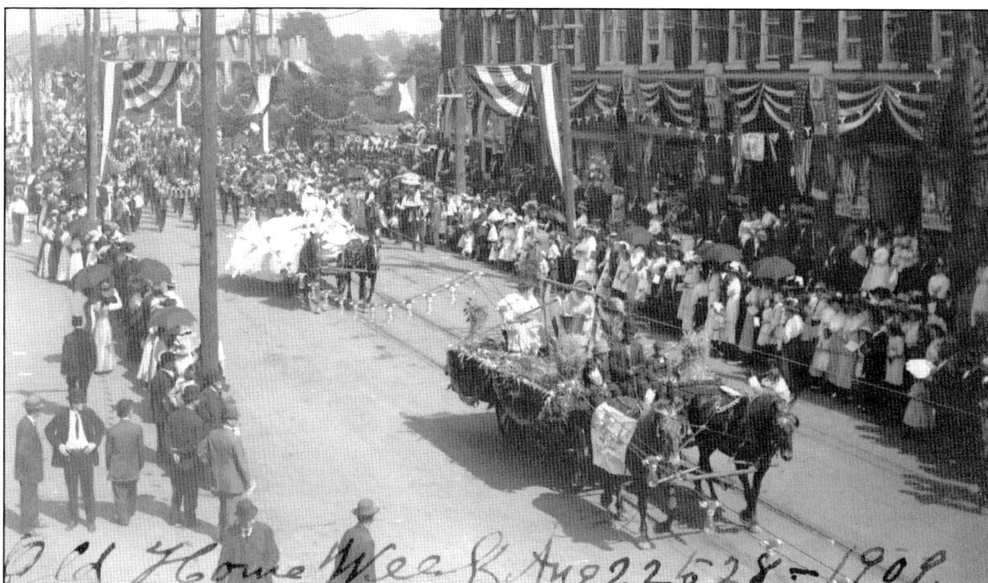

A float representing harvest time is complete with straw. It makes its way along Mahoning Street in the Old Home Week parade. The colors for the present Punxsutawney High School, red and white, were chosen as preparations were underway for the parade. Initially, lapel buttons were made showing the groundhog surrounded by the lettering, in red on white. The dates August 22 to August 28, 1909, indicate that this is the first Old Home Week parade. Citizens were requested to wear red and white.

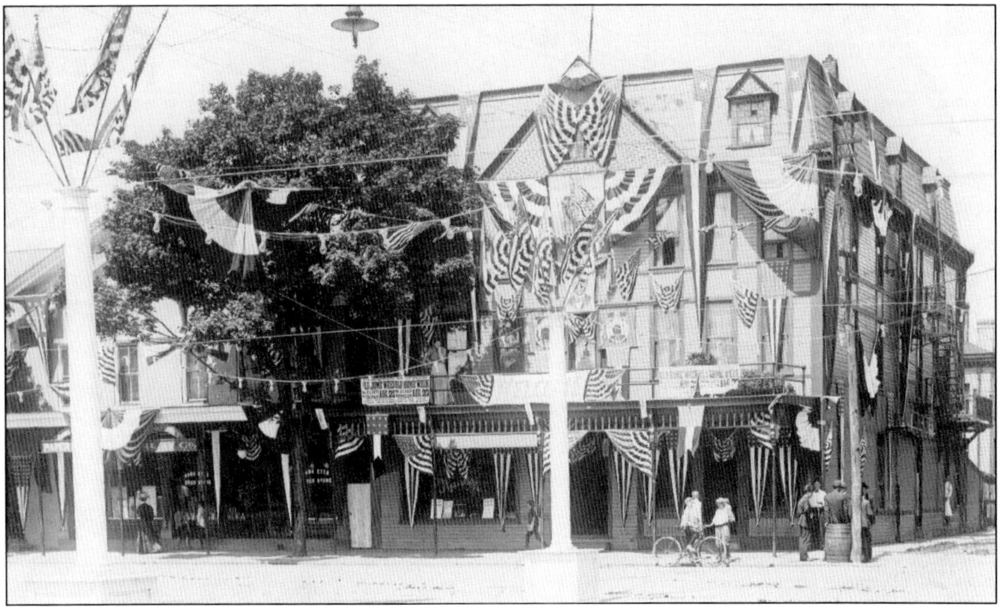

The people of Punxsutawney not only turn out in style, but also decorate the parade route in celebration. Punxsutawneyites love ceremony and ritual. They have long maintained a spirit of cooperation among themselves. Note the headline on the upper porch and the welcome sign in the center. Spectators from the surrounding hamlets come to join in the activities or just to watch the parade.

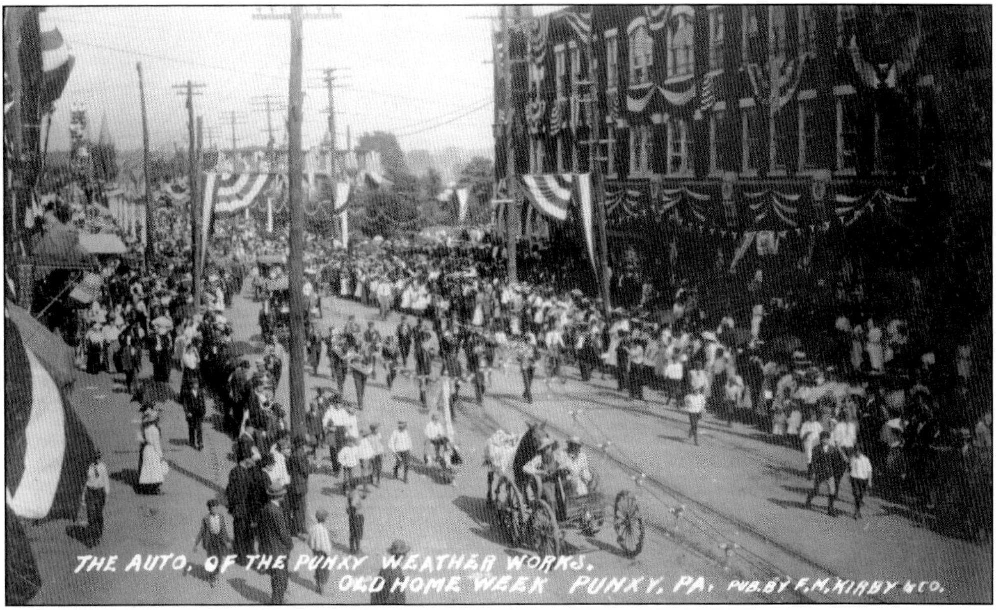

The automobile of the "Punxy Weather Works" was considered by some a "new noisy novelty." Old Home Week is sponsored by the fire department to serve a dual purpose. It provides entertainment for the community and raises funds for much needed firefighting equipment. Old Home Week continues to be celebrated into the new millennium. The Central, Elk Run, and Lindsey Fire Departments organize the week-long event that is highlighted by a carnival.

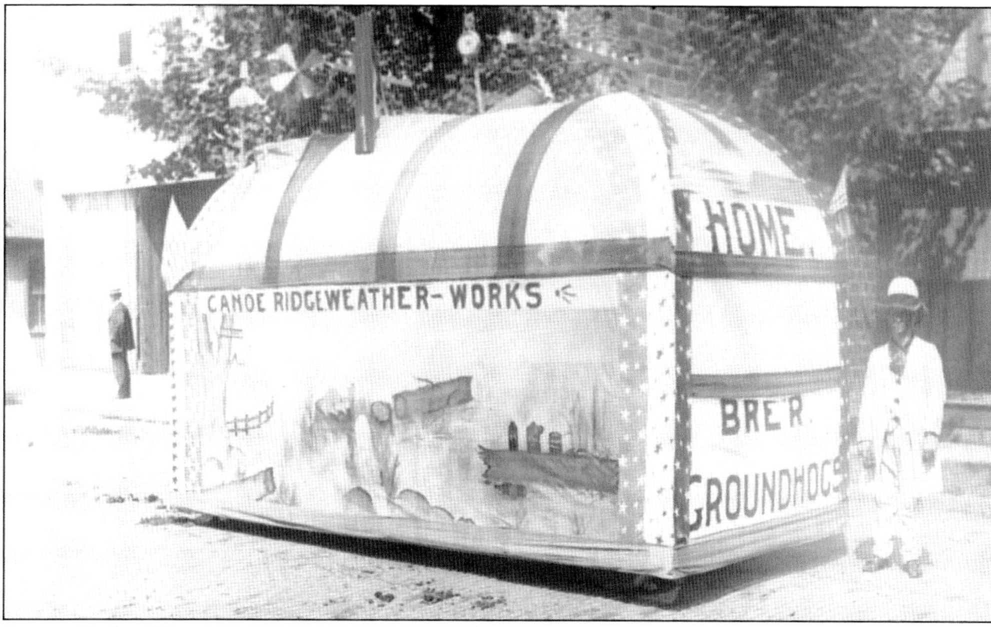

Canoe Ridge Weather Works was the lead float in the 1909 Old Home Week parade. It was an ingenious satire on the government weather observatory. Canoe Ridge was the allegorical home of Phil. Dressed in white, it represented a specific section of Canoe Ridge. The famous groundhog was housed in various places before the days of Groundhog Zoo. In 1905, Gobbler's Knob became the designated site of his annual appearance, and in 1962 Groundhog Zoo became his permanent home.

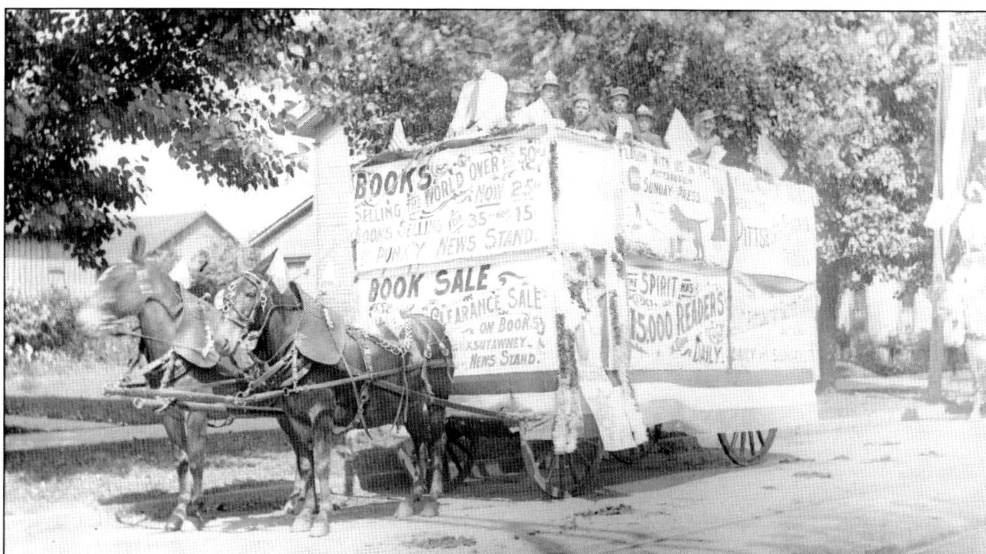

A billboard on wheels makes its way along Mahoning Street in the Old Home Week parade in August 1909. It was an era when libraries were scarce and reading was a chief method of entertainment. Among the advertisements early in the century are, "The *Spirit* has 15,000 readers," "Read the *Pittsburgh Chronicle*," and "Laugh with us in the *Pittsburgh Sunday Press*." The book advertisement was meaningful to those without television, radio, or even the luxury of sharing news and stories with neighbors because of distance.

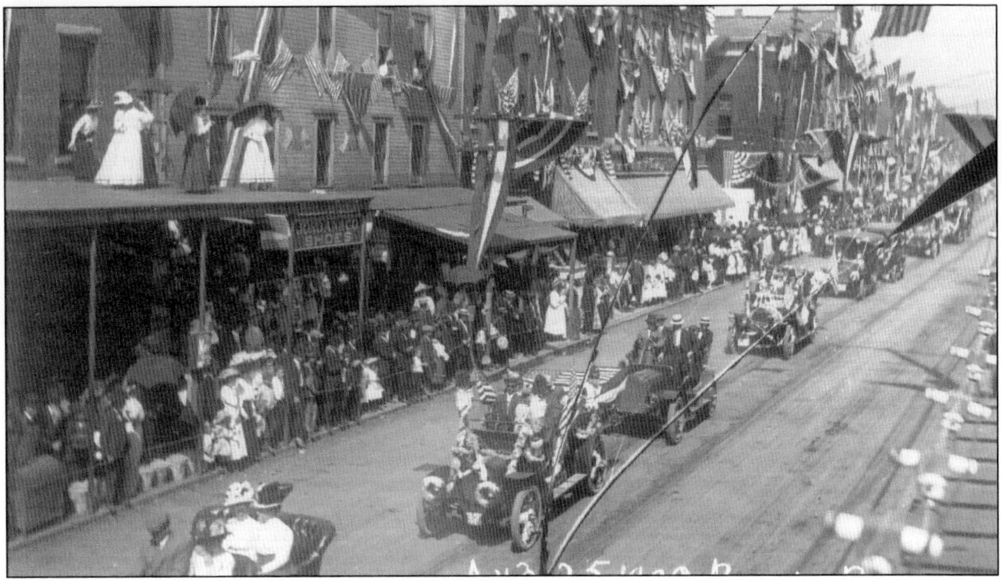

Cars were taken in both the Old Home Week and Groundhog Festival parades. They were an innovation and a new fad. Citizens reasoned that they may have far-reaching effects someday when the noise was eliminated. The townsfolk had an opportunity to see, for the first time, the new noisy machine. The celebrations surrounding Old Home Week included airship flights. Just before flight time, a whistle blew so people could go to the baseball field and watch the airship take off.

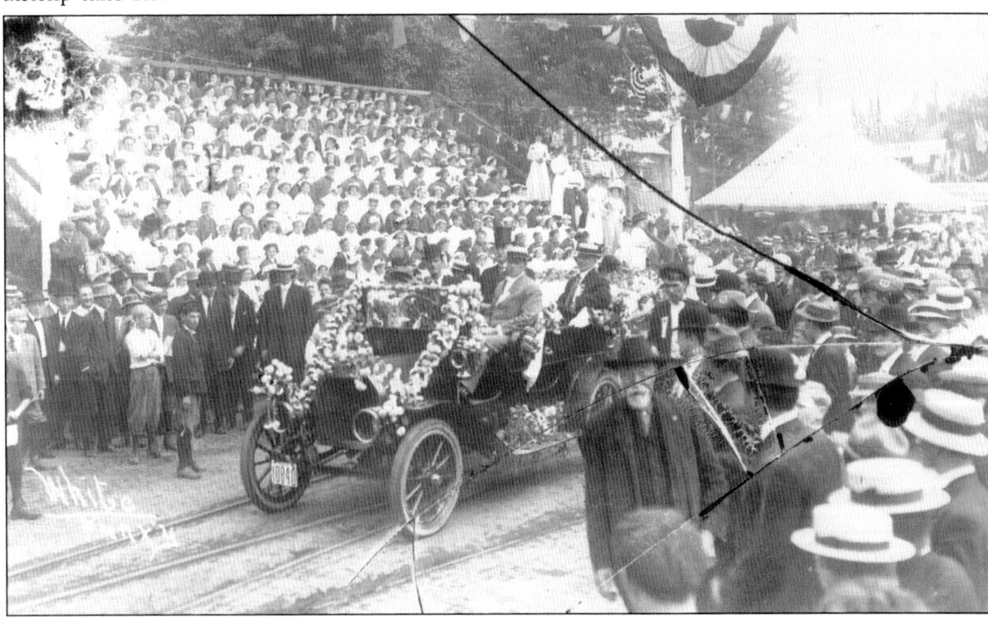

Governor of Pennsylvania Edwin Stuart was guest of honor at the initial Old Home Week festivities. He addressed the people and was impressed by the 400 girls who made up the living flag. He rode with Burgess Philip Freas, an Elks charter member who led the automobile parade. The original wooden bandstand, built on Barclay Square, is in the right background. Folks in the bleachers are enjoying the revelry and the presence of a dignitary in the parade. The governor wears the top hat.

Seven

MEET PUNXSUTAWNEY PHIL

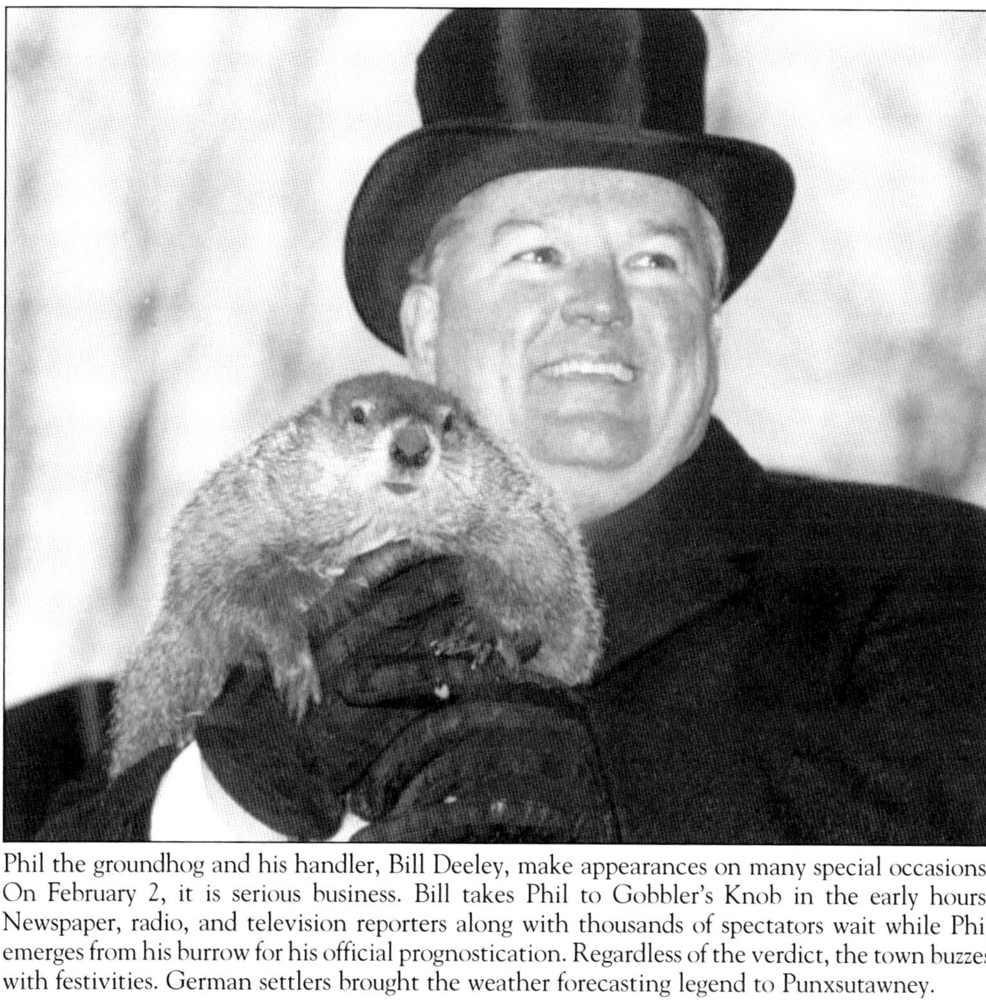

Phil the groundhog and his handler, Bill Deeley, make appearances on many special occasions. On February 2, it is serious business. Bill takes Phil to Gobbler's Knob in the early hours. Newspaper, radio, and television reporters along with thousands of spectators wait while Phil emerges from his burrow for his official prognostication. Regardless of the verdict, the town buzzes with festivities. German settlers brought the weather forecasting legend to Punxsutawney.

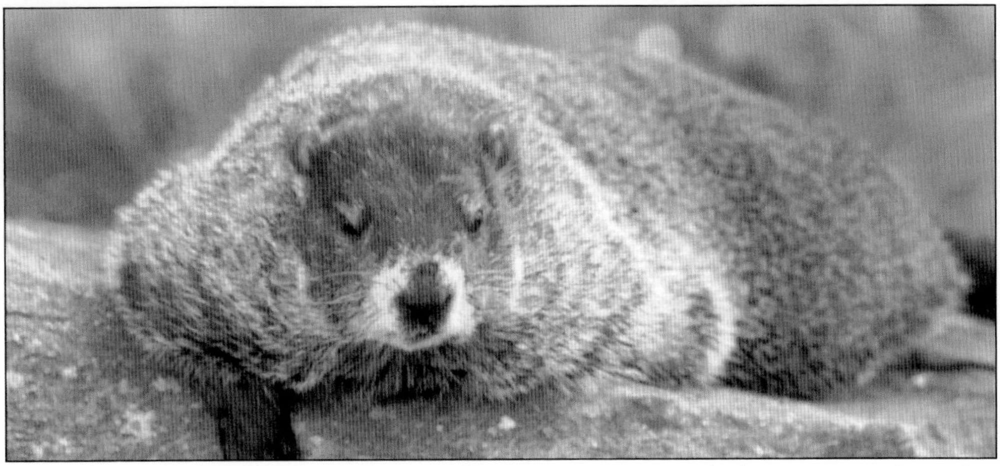

Groundhog Day originated in Europe. The Germans initiated this version of weather forecasting. Candlemas Day followed the new year and signaled an end to winter. An old English song declared, "If Candlemas Day is bright and clear there'll be two winters in the year." They chose a hedgehog as a weather indicator because hedgehogs were prevalent in Europe. A hedgehog is an old-world, nocturnal, insectivorous mammal that has hair and a spine. It resembles the groundhog.

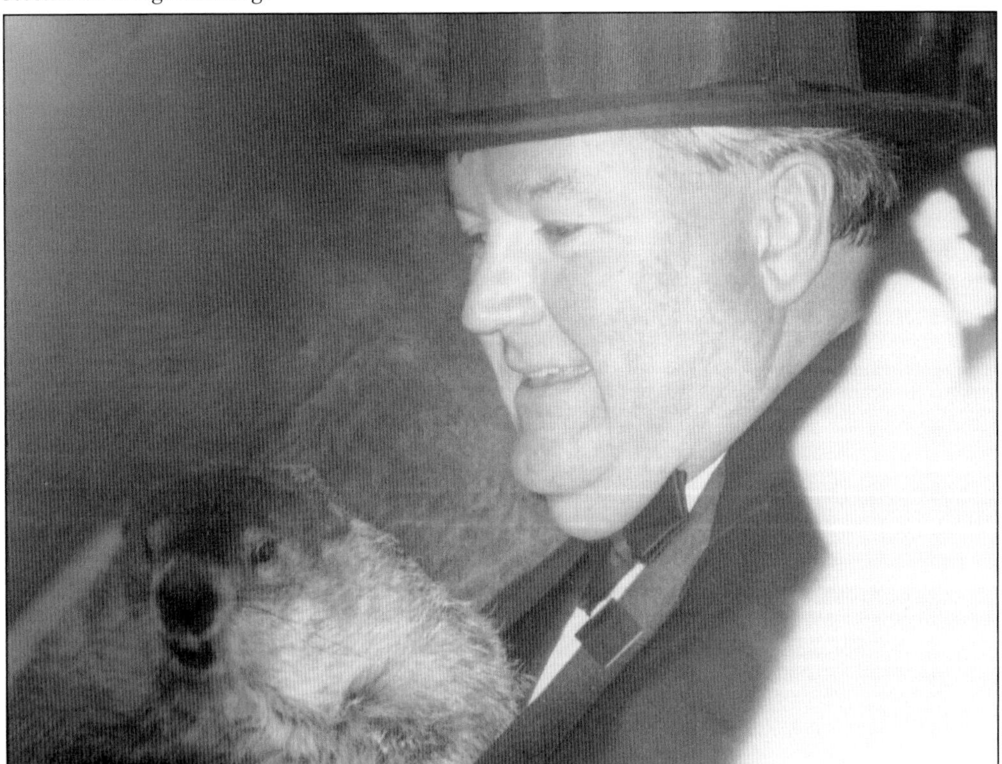

The Europeans reasoned that if the hedgehog came out of burrowed hibernation and saw its shadow, there would be six more weeks of winter. If the German hedgehog did not see his shadow on this quick visit from its burrow, then spring was dawning. Groundhogs were plentiful in the United States and became the unanimous choice as the weather forecaster.

Groundhog meat was a delicacy early in the 19th century. It was a social custom to hunt the groundhog and then feast on it. Late in the 1880s, Harry E. Beatty, an original "groundhogger," introduced groundhog meat to his fellow Elks at their annual banquet of the newly formed Punxsutawney chapter. These dinners are the forerunners of the Groundhog Banquet held every year by locals, citizens, and distinguished guests who visit Punxsutawney each year on Groundhog Day.

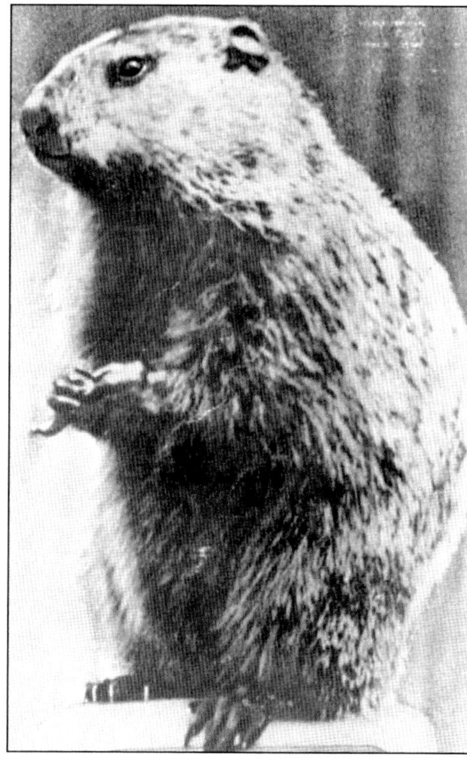

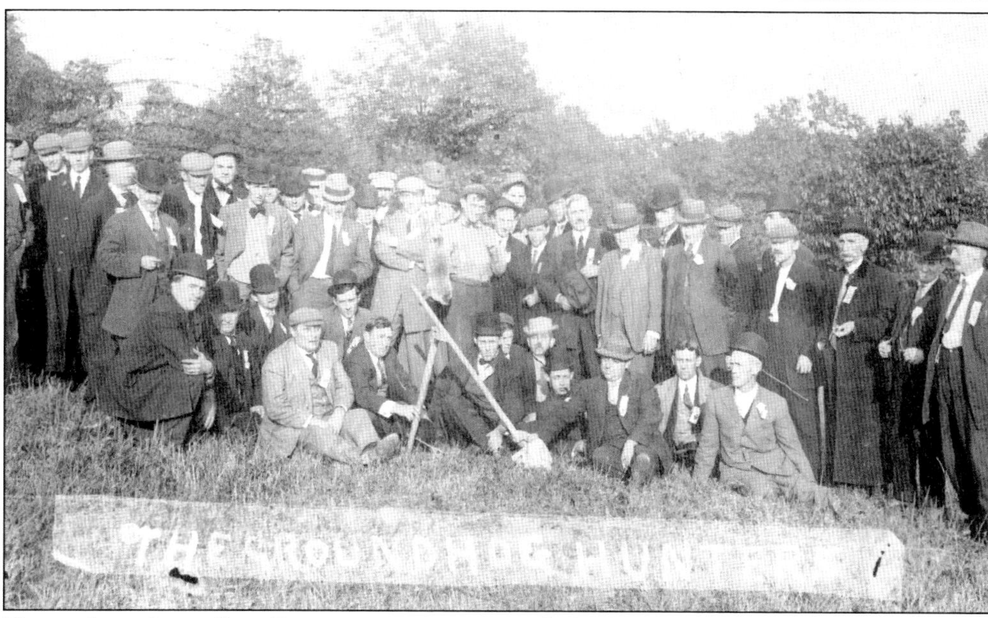

The earliest Groundhog Banquets were comprised chiefly of Elks. Philip Freas ignited the spark that evolved into today's famous Groundhog Club. Freas was a charter member of the Elks and owned an electric shop. He introduced his brother, Clymer, into membership. It was Clymer who led the groundhog to national prominence. This savvy, 19th-century *Spirit* editor established an official Groundhog Day. Harry E. Beatty prepared the first banquet and the succeeding 21 feasts for the club.

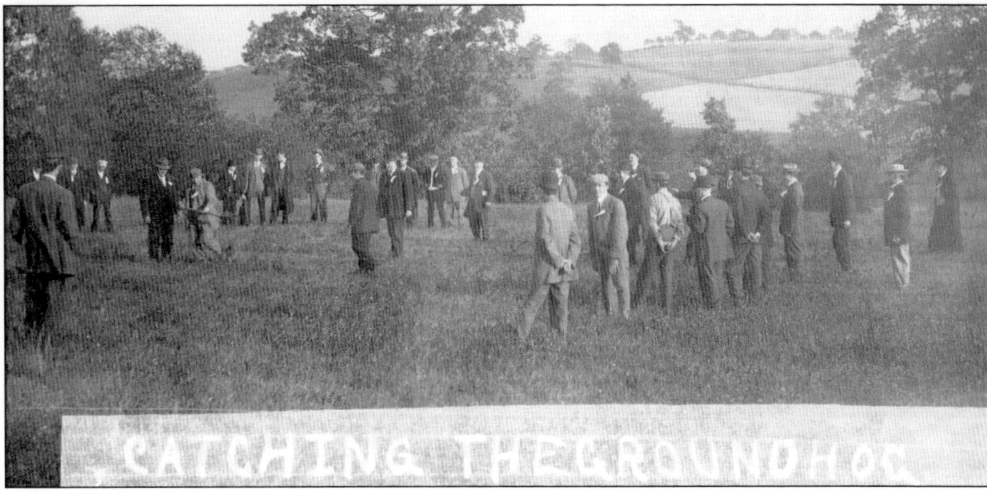

One evening in the fall of 1899, a half dozen gentlemen gathered on a breezy little knob south of town for an afternoon of fun. Armed with excavating tools and an adequate supply of groundhog punch, these picnickers captured and fricasseed a few groundhogs and then partied the evening away. The phenomena of Phil the groundhog is maintained by the Inner Circle, 15 top-hatted, bow-tied businessmen of the area whose earlier personifications were groundhog hunters.

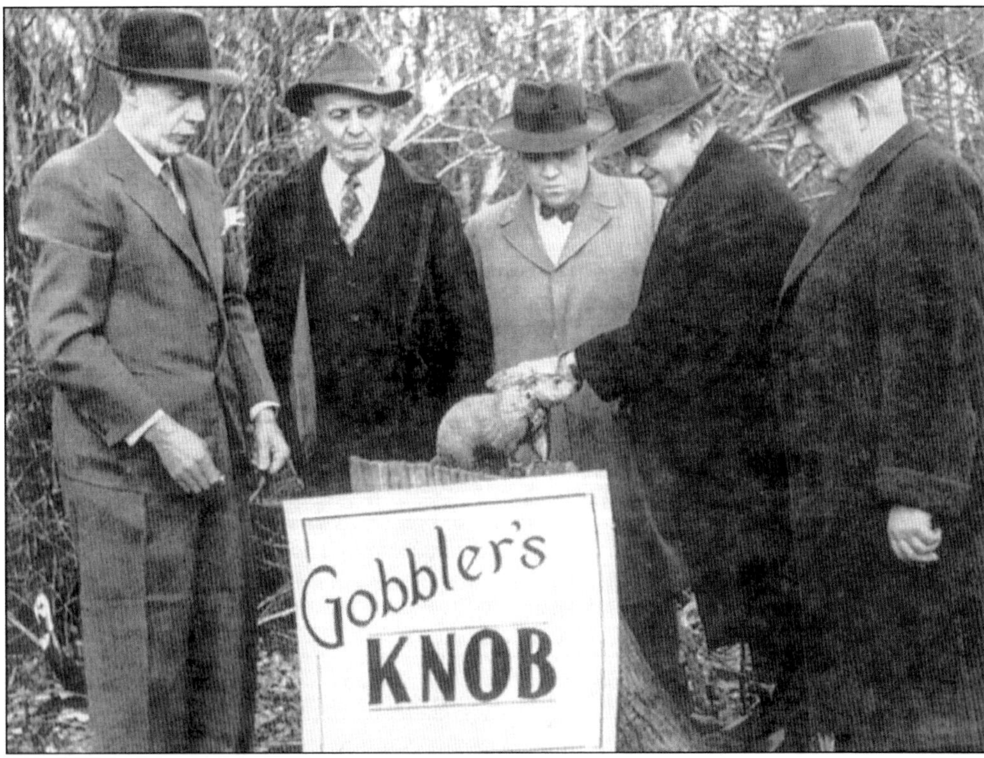

Five members of the Groundhog Club gather on Gobbler's Knob near the Canoe Ridge Mountain with Phil the groundhog in 1947. The trek includes, from left to right, Mike Donnelly, Otto Phillips, Robert S. Philliber (vice president of the club), Dr. Francis Lorenzo (president), and Roy Shirley (secretary). These were the days before top hats and tuxedos became part of the pageantry.

Clymer H. Freas was editor of the *Punxsutawney Spirit* in 1899. A group of local hunters held a groundhog hunt and then celebrated by barbecuing their game. They washed it down with home-brewed beer. Freas dubbed the picnickers the Punxsutawney Groundhog Club. Freas was a progressive citizen who, with his typewriter and position as secretary of the *Spirit*, propelled Phil to national prominence. He coined "Home of the Groundhog" and sited Gobbler's Nob as the original location of the weather works.

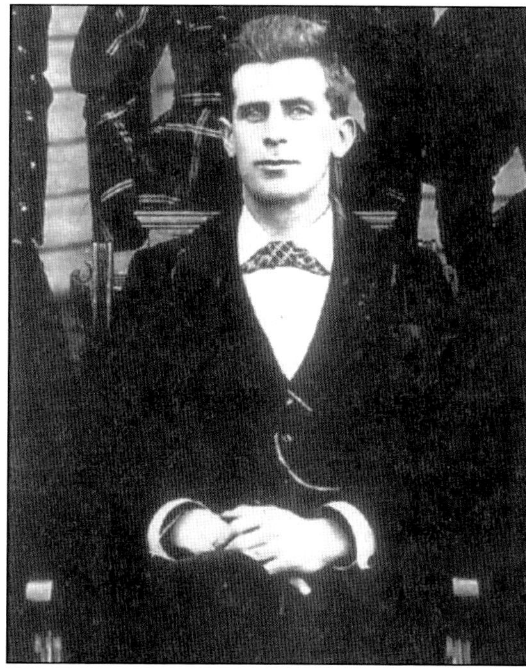

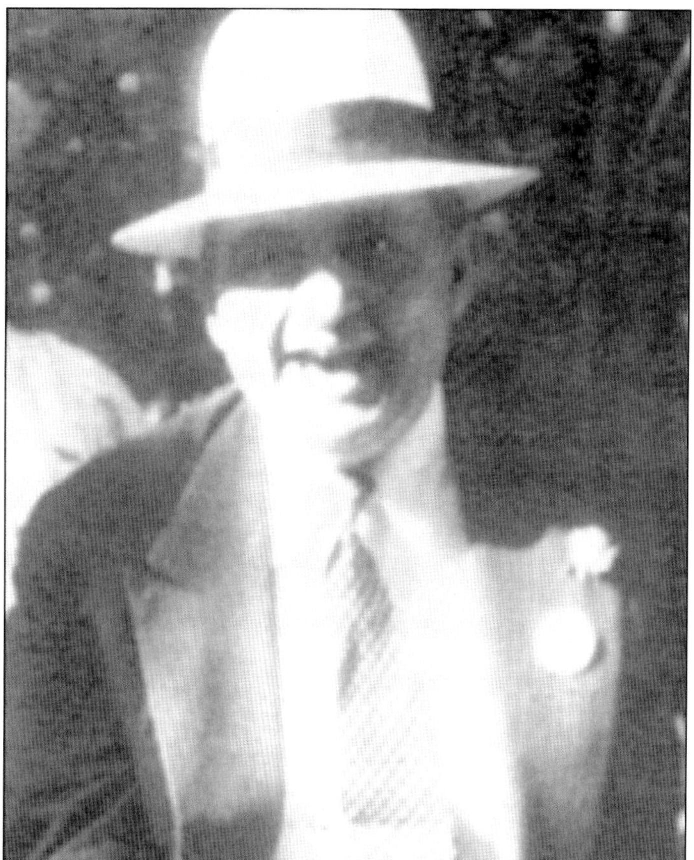

Dr. Francis Lorenzo made the Punxy groundhog known throughout the world and kept the legend alive. Lorenzo had a reputation as an outstanding physician, a surgeon, a gourmet chef, a coal operator, an inventor, and a sportsman. He always found time to promote the groundhog tradition. Lorenzo entertained lavishly, traveled extensively, and made contacts from coast to coast regarding the weather forecaster. On Groundhog Day, he arranged trains to be sent from Pittsburgh bringing newsmen, politicians, and reporters. Guests were invited from Boston, Philadelphia, and New York.

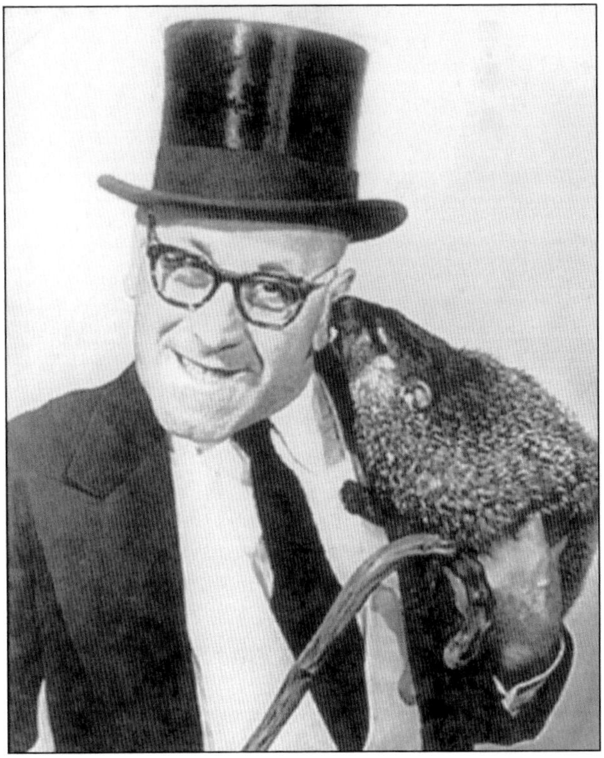

Samuel Light listens to Phil's secret. Light brought formality and pageantry to the midwinter saga when he became president in 1952. Light introduced the Inner Circle with its formal dress code. Here, the honor guard or executive branch of the club conducts the annual weather forecasting at Gobbler's Knob. A tall silk hat and tuxedo is the traditional dress for dignitaries greeting VIPs. The Inner Circle plays that role on Groundhog Day; therefore, it is fitting that these dignitaries dress accordingly.

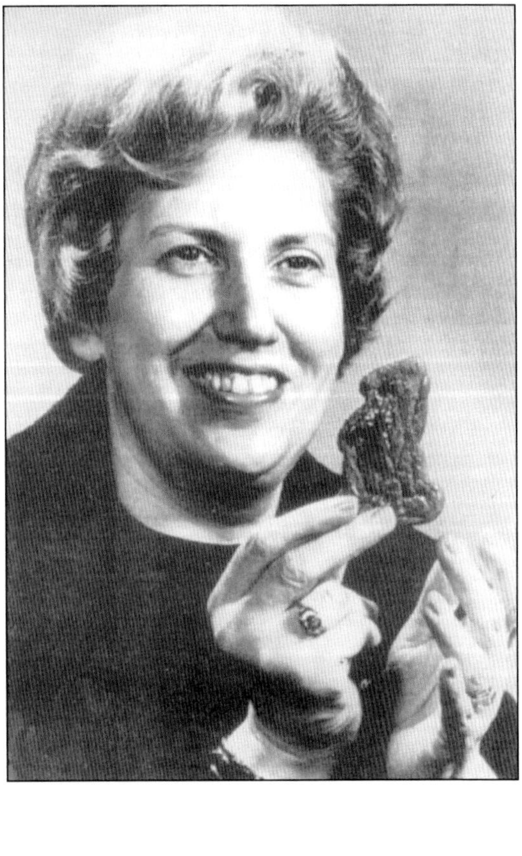

Elaine Light was a Pittsburgh reporter. While covering the story of Hollywood's Colleen Townsend in 1955, she met Punxy's most eligible bachelor, Samuel Light. She had been the first woman hired by the Associated Press and the first to report from Pitt Stadium as a sports editor. Sam Light and she were married a few months later. Impressed by home cooking and ethnic cookbooks, Elaine designed the groundhog cookie cutter. She published two cookbooks: *Cooking with the Groundhog* and *Gourmet and Groundhogs*.

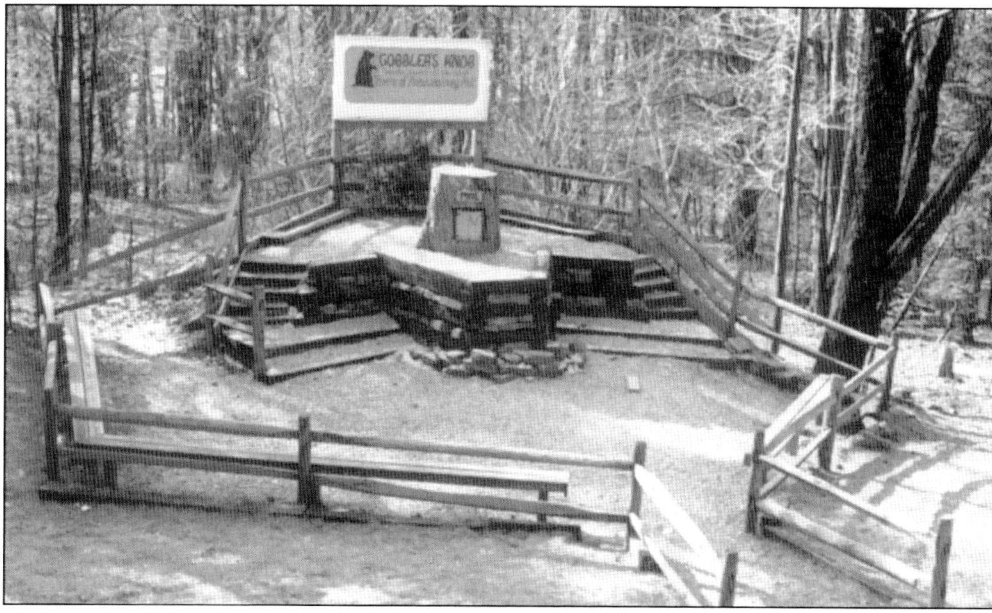

Punxy Phil first witnessed Gobbler's Knob in 1905. For several decades, he struggled to gain recognition and notoriety. Fall hunts and feasts continued to grow more popular each year. Phil's fame reached national proportions when Dr. Francis Lorenzo spread word of Phil across the land. Groundhog Day became a popular midwinter holiday. Television, radio, and the press flooded to Gobbler's Knob for his prognostications. All eyes are on Gobbler's Knob on February 2.

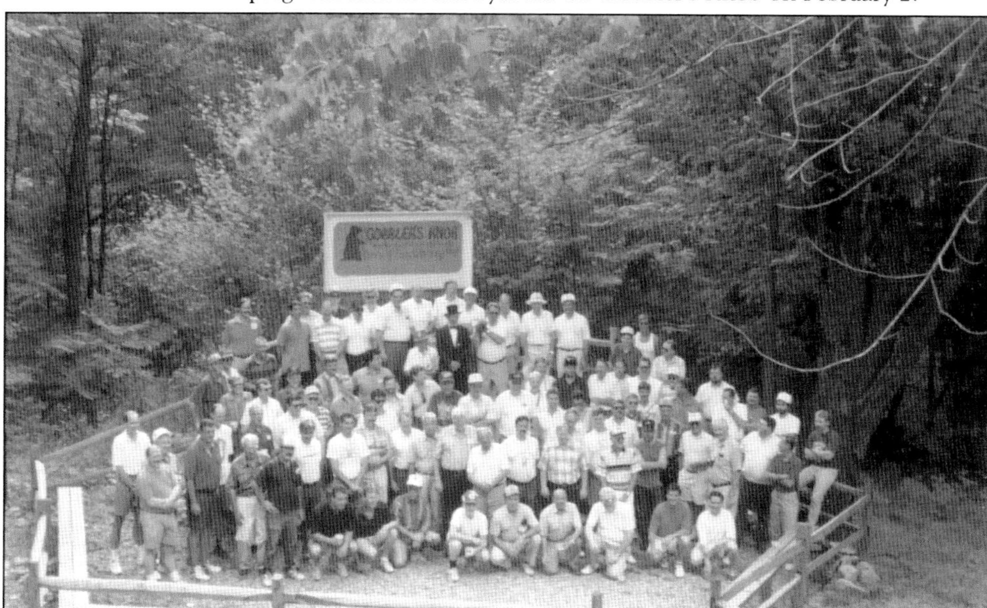

Groundhog Club members gather on Gobbler's Knob for the great annual hunt. The weather in this valley community hovers near zero all winter. Groundhog Day is a midwinter holiday when everyone celebrates regardless of the frost, sleet, snow, or frigid temperatures. There are also warm weather activities when groundhog celebrations are in order. The town hosts Groundhog Festival and Old Home Week every summer, along with parades and parish festivals.

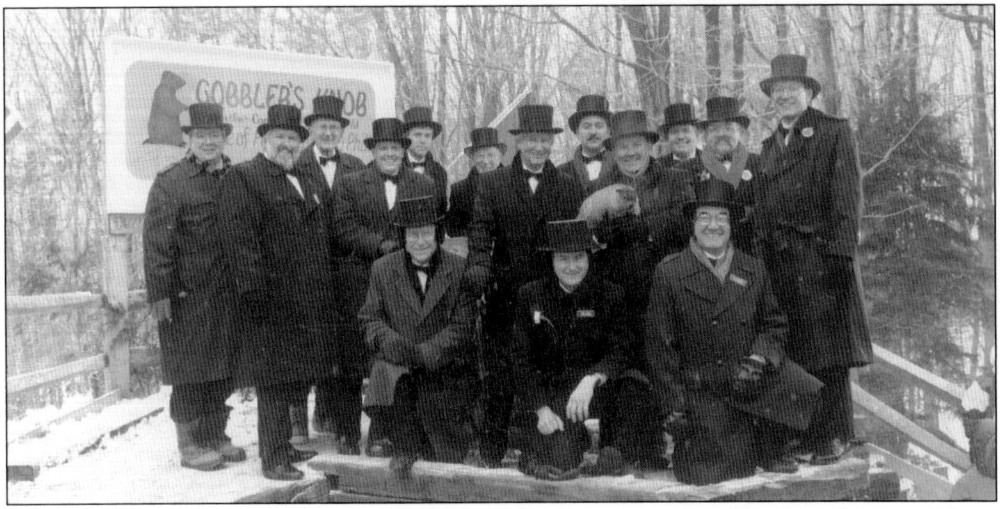

Groundhog Day is a day of diversion and festivity in Punxsutawney. The formal attire of these Inner Circle gentlemen set the stage for an intermingling of fantasy, drama, and legend. The members assume individual titles. Among these are Cold and Fair Weathermen, Sage, Stump and Wind Wardens, Weatherman, Cloud Builder, Iceman, Protector, Handler, Sleet Master, Hail Maker, Burrow Master, Proclaimer, Dew Dropper, Storm Chaser, and Big Flake Maker. These men represent all professions.

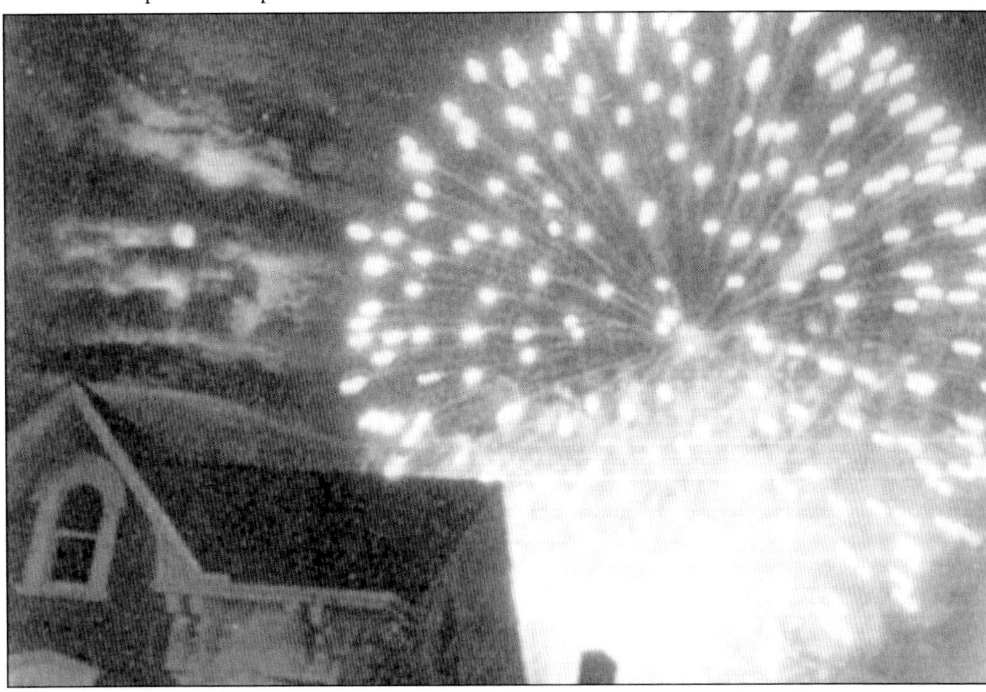

Fireworks over Gobbler's Knob are part of the entertainment preceding the magic moment. This period of anticipation takes many forms. Multicostumed performers appear and bands play as predawn fireworks light up the winter sky. There are songfests, ice sculptures, games, and activities relating to the groundhog. In the very early hours, Bill carries Phil the 1.5 miles from his home in the Groundhog Zoo to Gobbler's Knob and places him in a heated burrow. Inner Circle members spend the night at Gobbler's Knob.

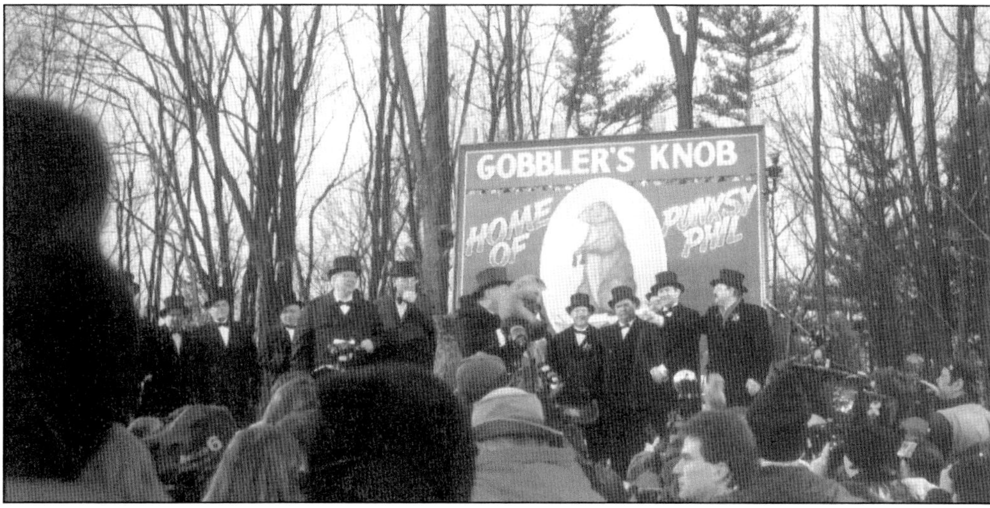

Just before the great drama, Inner Circle members are individually introduced to the crowd. "The Star-Spangled Banner" is played. The pageantry and festivities at Gobbler's Knob compensate for any chill in the winter air. The enthusiasm of the crowds creates a warm glow in the freezing atmosphere. At the appointed hour, Phil's burrow door is tapped three times with a cane and then opened. His handler, Bill Deely, then reaches in and presents Phil to the cheering throng.

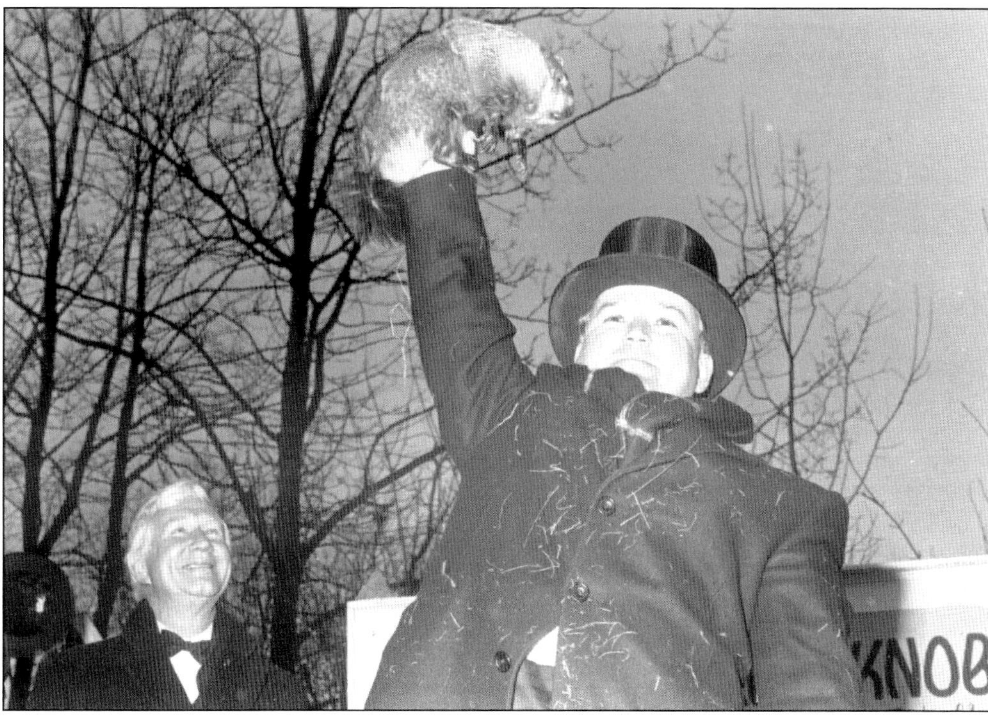

Phil makes his formal appearance as he is lifted high in the hands of Bill Deeley. Cameras flash in Phil's face and throngs converge upon him, but he takes it all in stride. He is very good about making formal appearances. Punxsutawney stages a successful production starring its perennial prognosticator. Gobbler's Knob becomes an outdoor theater and witnesses the climax of the drama. Here, Bud Dunkel looks on.

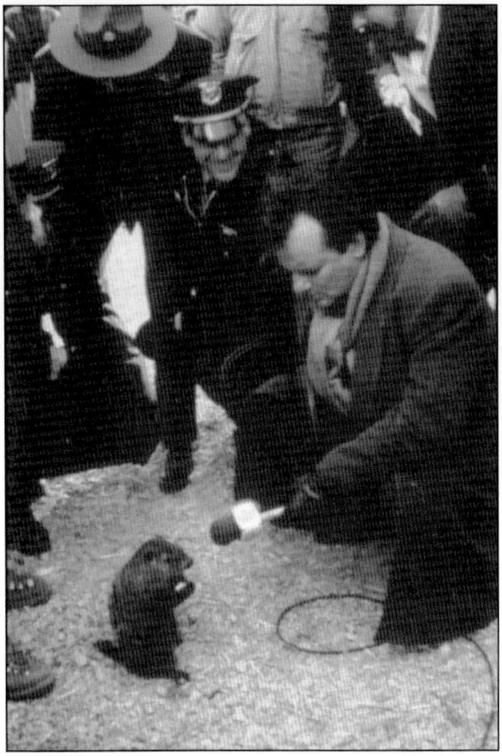

Actor Bill Murray gives Phil, the celebrity, a chance to say a few words. Murray was in town before starring in *Groundhog Day*, which was produced in Virginia. During the Groundhog Day ceremonies, Phil's words are deciphered and the proclamation is read from one of two scrolls: one saying that he has seen his shadow and the other that he has not seen it. This proclamation goes out over national television and around the world.

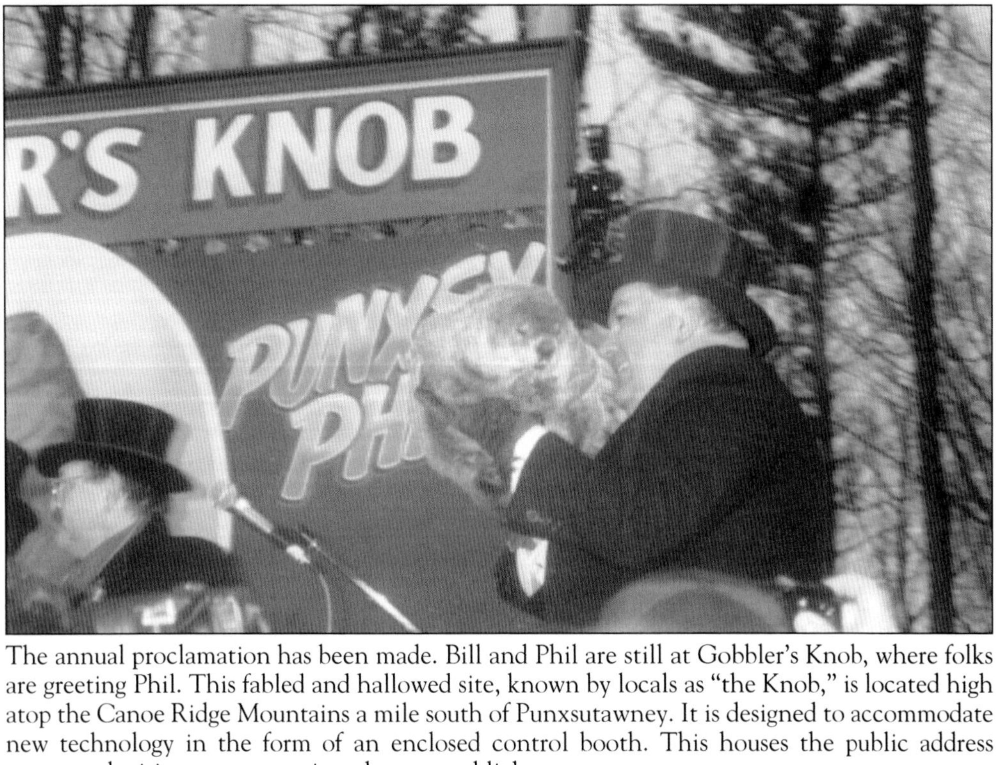

The annual proclamation has been made. Bill and Phil are still at Gobbler's Knob, where folks are greeting Phil. This fabled and hallowed site, known by locals as "the Knob," is located high atop the Canoe Ridge Mountains a mile south of Punxsutawney. It is designed to accommodate new technology in the form of an enclosed control booth. This houses the public address system, television cameras, microphones, and lights.

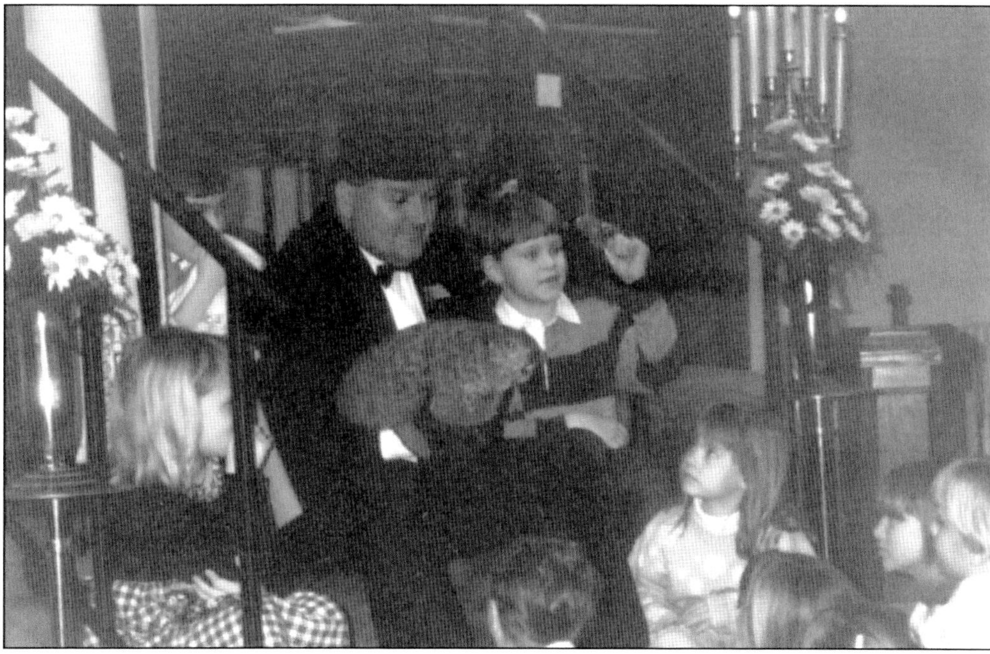

Phil has many engagements throughout the year. He travels to schools, nursing homes, and wherever he is invited. Here, Phil visits the children of the Presbyterian Church in Punxsutawney. Bill and Phil cannot respond to all such invitations because Phil becomes restless and nippy and lets his handler know when he has had enough.

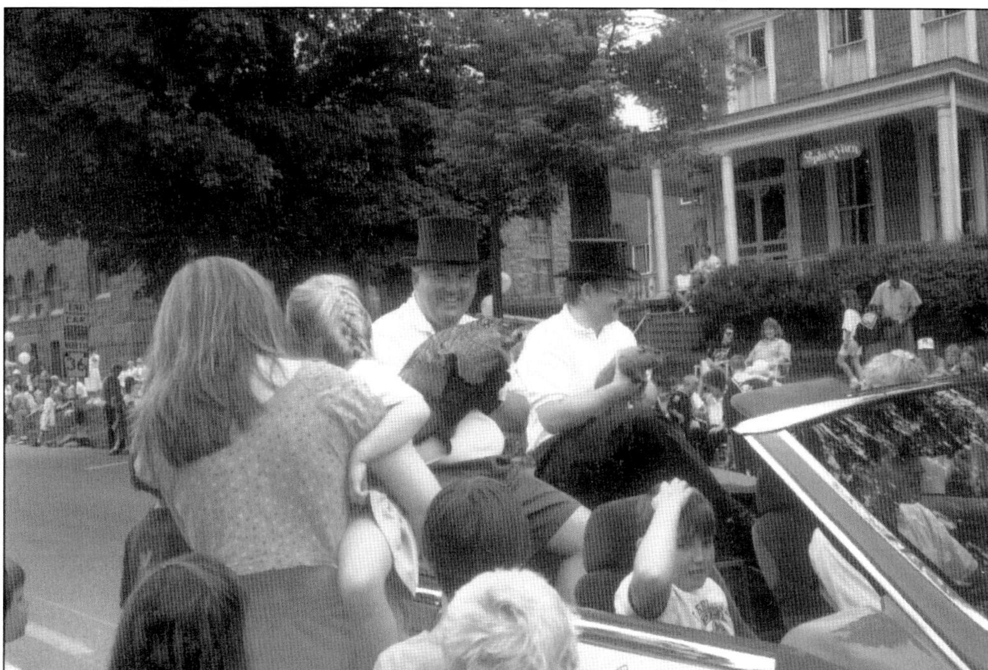

Phil takes part in many parades, placidly watching all his admirers along the parade route. On his 100th birthday in 1986, Phil visited Pres. Ronald Regan in the Oval Office. This publicity brought commercial endorsements and crowds numbering 30,000 to Gobbler's Knob.

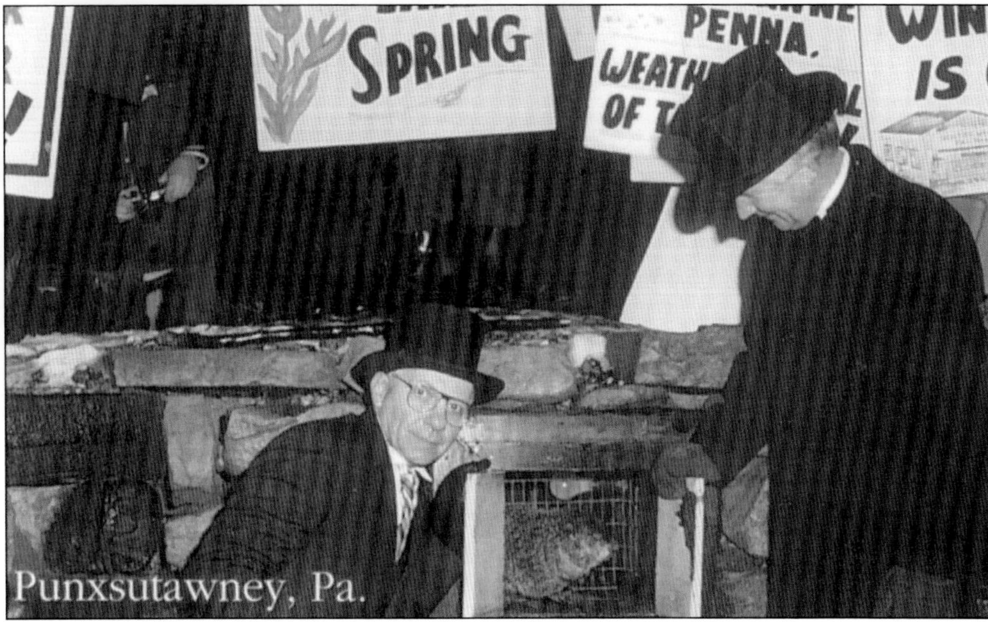

Phil enjoys his cage because he feels safe there. Jim Means and Bud Dunkel, both members of the Inner Circle, place him in the cage. Phil has never known the wild as his cousins of the woodlands have. He has been sheltered since infancy and knows only his zoo home. These mammals must be trained from very early in their lives or they would be too wild to perform on the distinguished stage of Gobbler's Knob.

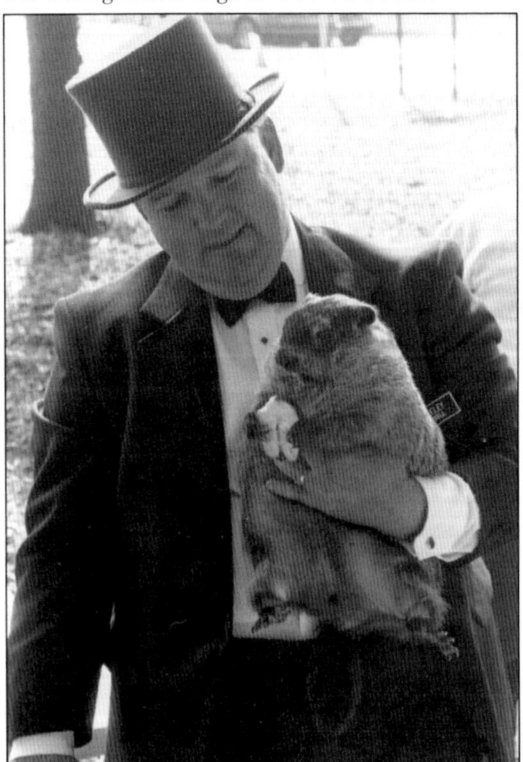

The groundhog must be procured as a tiny baby, before its eyes are opened. Farmers bring groundhogs to Bill Deeley when they find nests on their farms. Deeley trains and raises them. The baby groundhogs are fed evaporated milk with a medicine syringe. A groundhog is a North American woodchuck. It is a stout, heavy-bodied, short-legged burrowing rodent with a short bushy tail, coarse brown fur, very small ears, and sharp claws.

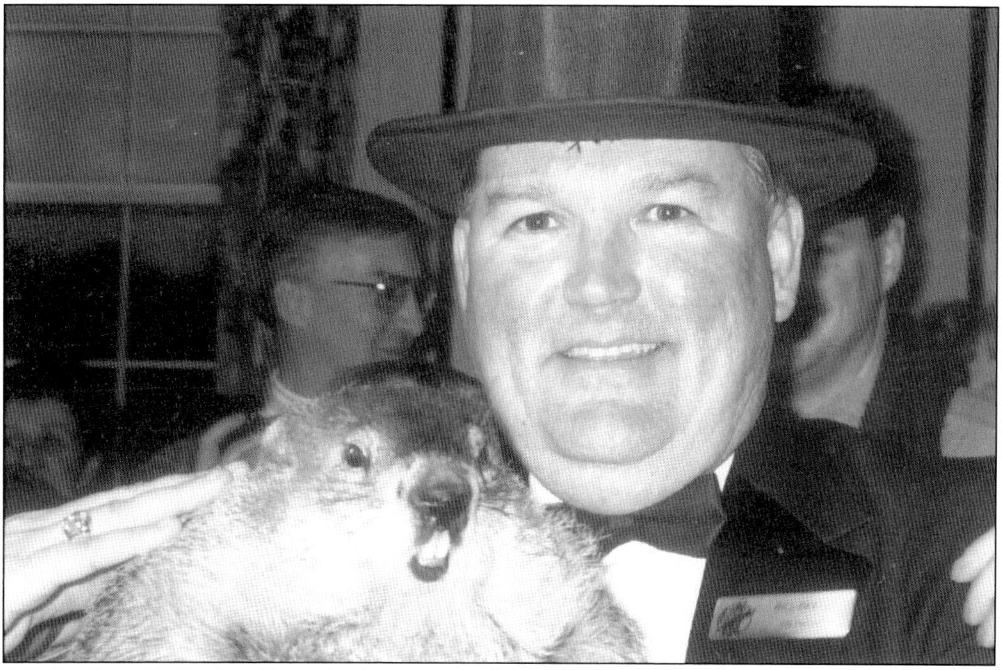

Bill Deeley, Phil's handler, checks on and feeds Phil and his companions regularly. The woodchucks are happy to see Bill come to their habitat in the library of the civic center. Phil's eating and sleeping habits change with the seasons. In spring and summer, he eats well. After the first frost, he winds down to half of what he ate in the summer. He enjoys dining on dry dog food along with apples, bananas, greens, and anything with a sweet, fruity taste.

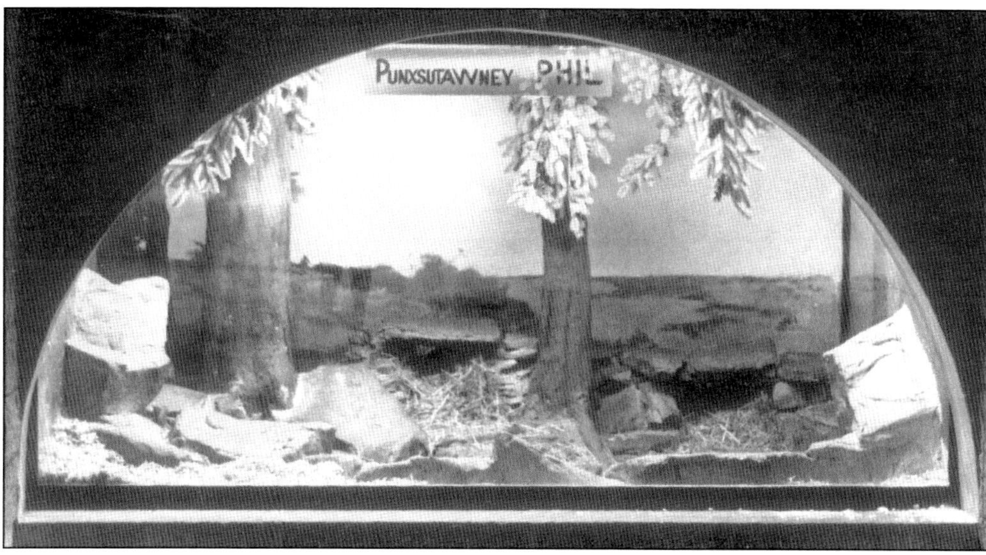

Phil lives in Punxsutawney's Groundhog Zoo at the library of the East Mahoning Civic Center. Visitors enjoy his antics through windows both inside and out. Punxy Phil's companions are Phyllis and several small groundhogs who share the zoo with him. The light and heat of his state-of-the-art quarters prevent him from going into true hibernation. Phil and companions took up residence in their new zoo on September 22, 1974. Phil is plumper and more luxuriant than his roadside cousins. He enjoys first-class accommodations in the zoo.

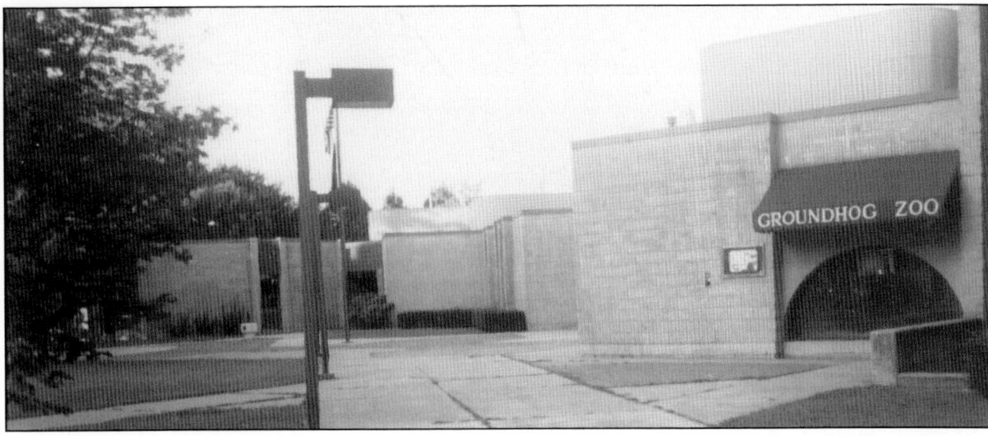

Groundhog Zoo in Barclay Square is a natural habitat for its distinguished dweller. Situated in the library of the civic center, Groundhog Zoo attracts thousands of visitors year round. Large windows afford a glimpse of the famous weather forecaster. Curators from the Pittsburgh Zoo were instrumental in designing the interior. Phil has a comfortable home befitting a famous groundhog.

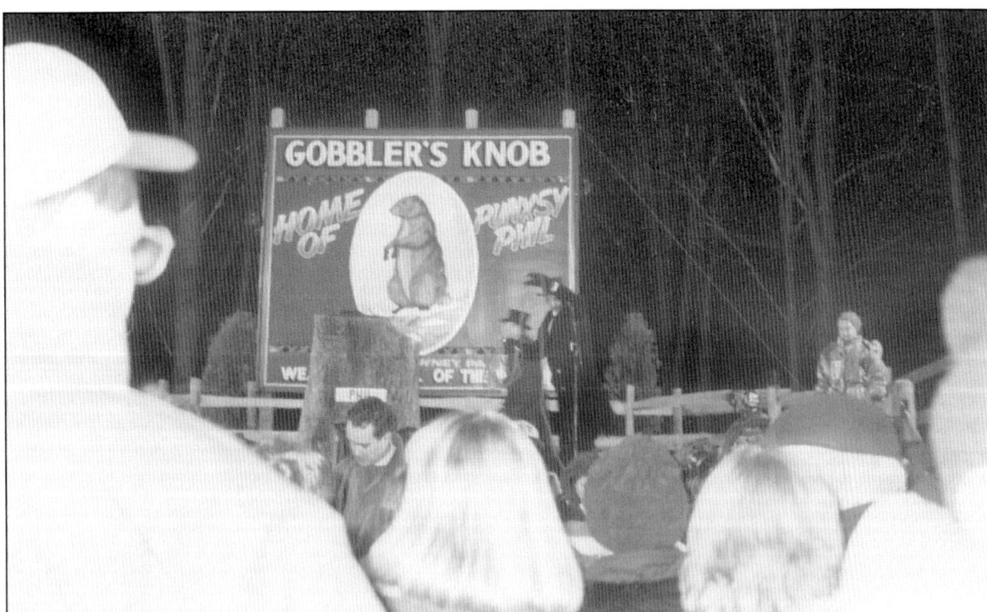

Some 30,000 people gather each February 2 from around the world. Many return annually, but many are seeing the spectacle for the first time. Although the mercury hardly reaches above freezing, the crowds cheer on. The frigid morning air is often enhanced by the windchill. This is a holiday in one small town of western Pennsylvania where children will grow into an awareness of its notable place in history. Punxsutawney schools are closed in honor of Phil.

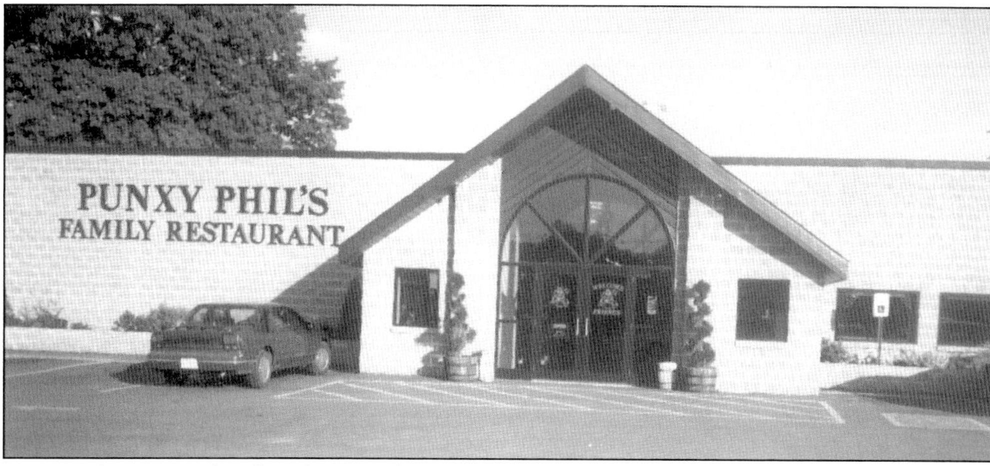

Punxy Plaza was the first home of Punxsy Phil's Family Restaurant. Established in the bicentennial year, it maintained a distinguished career on west Mahoning Street. Two decades later, the restaurant owners, Dean and Diane HeLal, relocated to a newly constructed site on Indiana Street and operate a first-class restaurant. This is another accolade in a town that reveres its claim to fame.

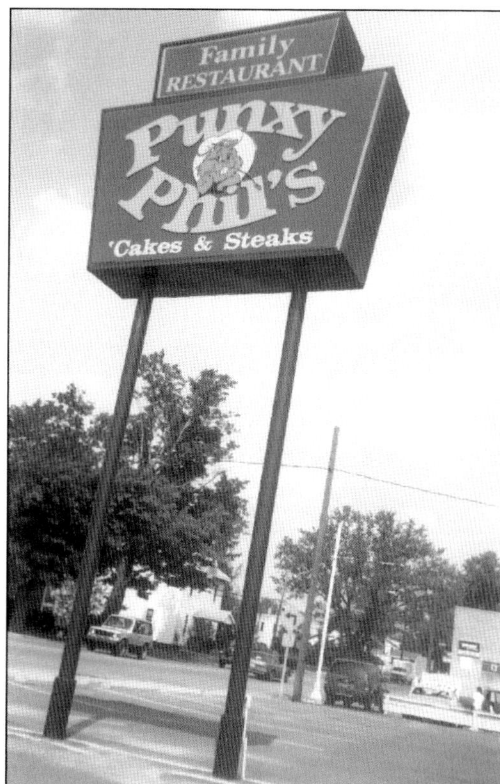

This sign indicates one of the many businesses in town that keep the groundhog in mind. Among others, there are Groundhog Auto Parts, Groundhog Instant Lube and Oil, and Groundhog Bowling Lanes. Groundhog coverage in newspapers, radio, and on national television reaches peak proportions on Groundhog Day. Phil's prognostications are recorded in the Congressional Record.

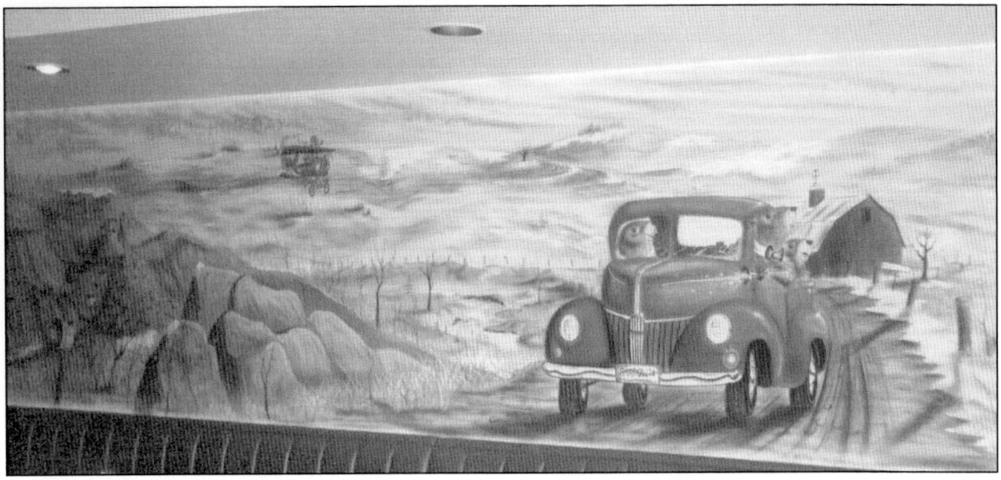

A mural on the back wall of the Punxy Phil Restaurant reminds folks they are in groundhog country. A fiery red Volkswagen bearing the license plate "Shadow #1" is depicted in this outstanding mural, painted by Robert Harrison. It is a clear indication of how this industrialized town reveres its famous resident.

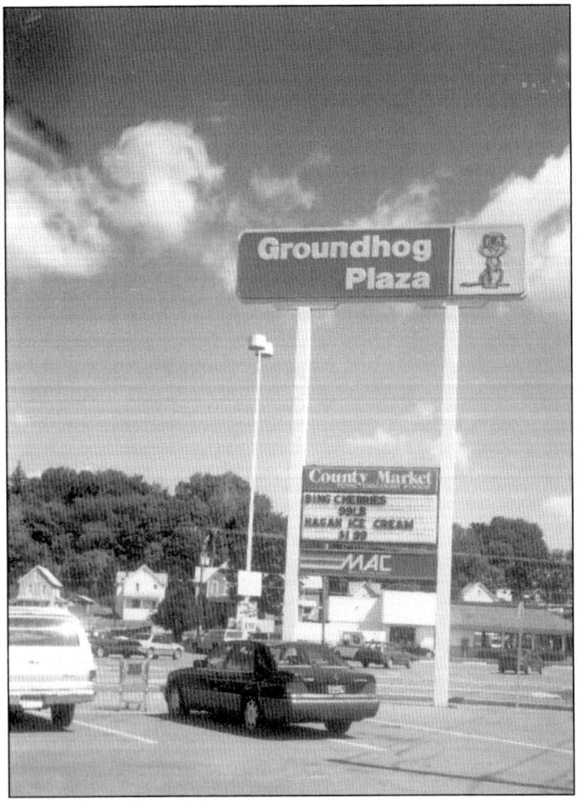

Groundhog Plaza, across from Barclay Square, is another site that features the famous groundhog. Situated at the hub of activity just north of East Mahoning Street, the plaza contains a line of businesses. Television has added much publicity and pageantry to the world-famous Punxsutawney groundhog.

Bill and Phil celebrate Groundhog Day in style. It becomes a genuine winterfest. Celebrations begin the evening before and continue throughout the night and into the day. Following Phil's prognostication, the Groundhog Club sponsors a breakfast. Indiana University culinary students demonstrate ice carving. Two high school seniors are crowned king and queen. They become guests of honor at the Groundhog Banquet. There is a woodchuck whittle carving show at the community center and a dance known as the Shadow Swing.

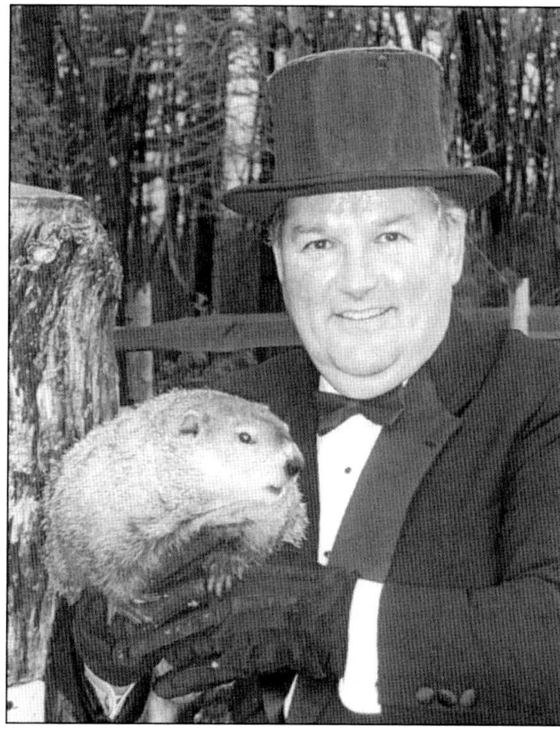

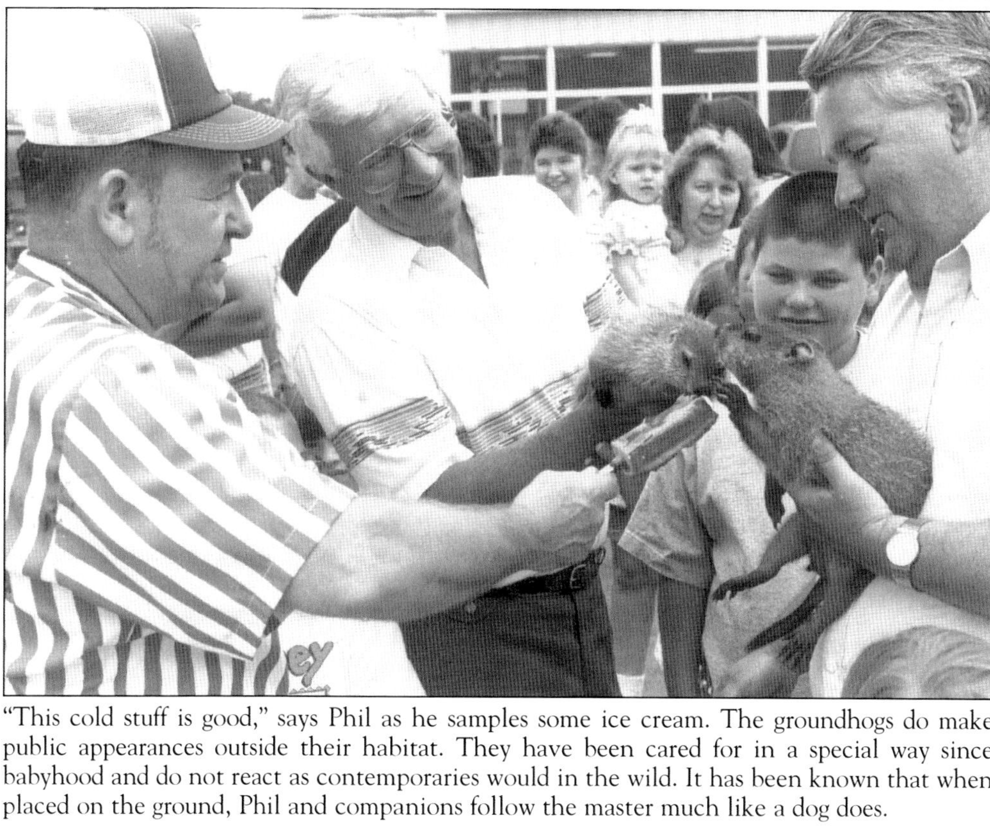

"This cold stuff is good," says Phil as he samples some ice cream. The groundhogs do make public appearances outside their habitat. They have been cared for in a special way since babyhood and do not react as contemporaries would in the wild. It has been known that when placed on the ground, Phil and companions follow the master much like a dog does.

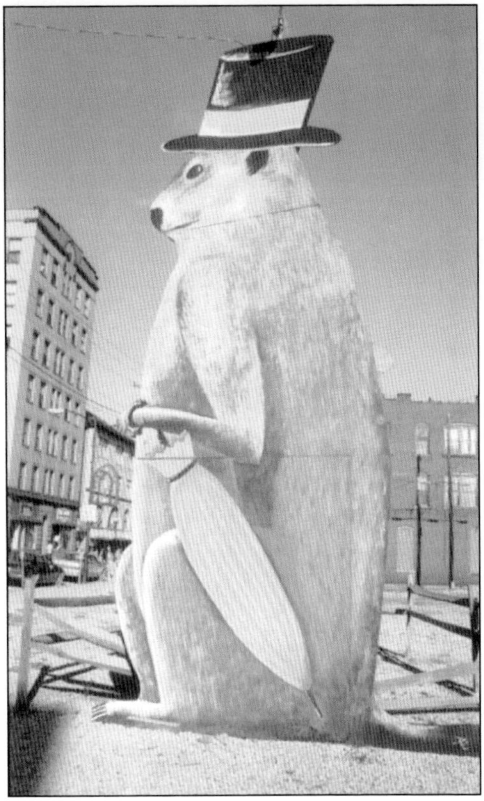

This three-story wooden likeness of Phil was painted by Carl Eichom and Joe Elliot in 1991. It is the world's largest tribute to Punxsutawney Phil and is located in downtown Punxy. The project, made of plywood, is the most recognizable landmark in the town. It was recently relocated across the bridge. It greets folks as they drive across the bridge.

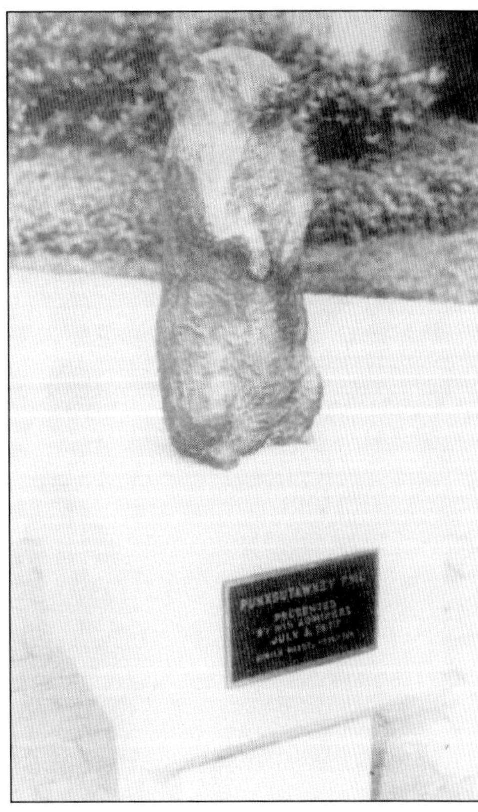

This life-sized, bronze statue of Phil was unveiled near Groundhog Zoo on July 11, 1977. An entourage of town, county, and state officials was present for the ceremony outside the municipal civic complex. The president of the Groundhog Club, Charles Erhart, called the dedication a symbol of the fidelity of the people who have been unwavering in their loyalty to the tradition. Jimilu Mason was captivated by the idea of a Groundhog Grove and designed Phil on his haunches.

This eight-foot statue of the famous weather forecaster was carved from a Norwegian maple tree that had been damaged in Barclay Square. The carving was done with a chain saw by Sam Clapoole in 1992. The statue of the groundhog remains attached to its roots. It is a special attraction in the center of Barclay Square.

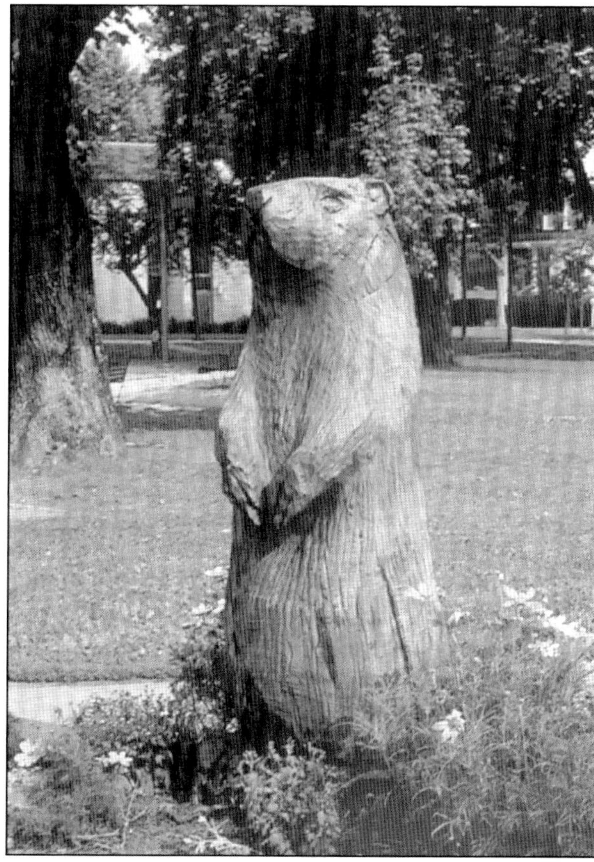

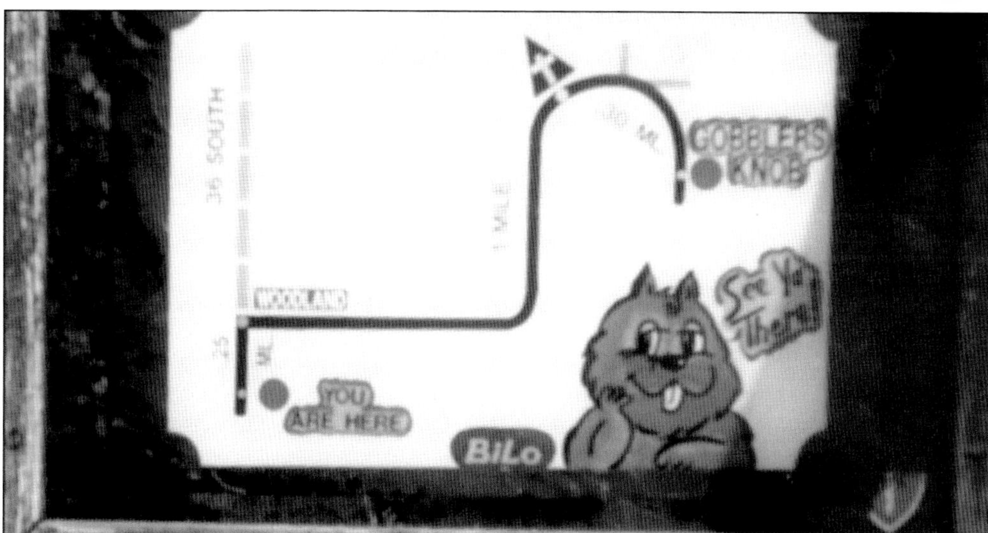

This sign embedded in the wall of the civic center indicates that Gobbler's Knob is located just 1.5 miles from Groundhog Zoo. A little button in the wall on the right, along with a quarter, will give one a short television show about Phil. A television camera has been installed in Groundhog Zoo.

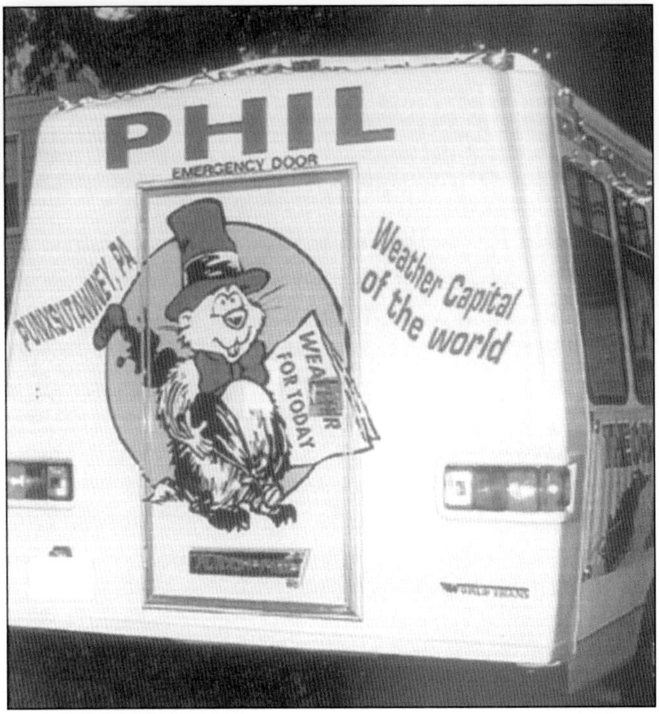

A new Philmobile was recently acquired by the Inner Circle. It made its debut at the sesquicentennial celebrations in 2000. Large enough for the Inner Circle members, the once airport shuttle bus becomes a rolling billboard to promote Phil. The Philmobile includes a special place for Phil's cage. Club members Barney Stockdale and Steve Means aided in the rehabilitation of the Philmobile.

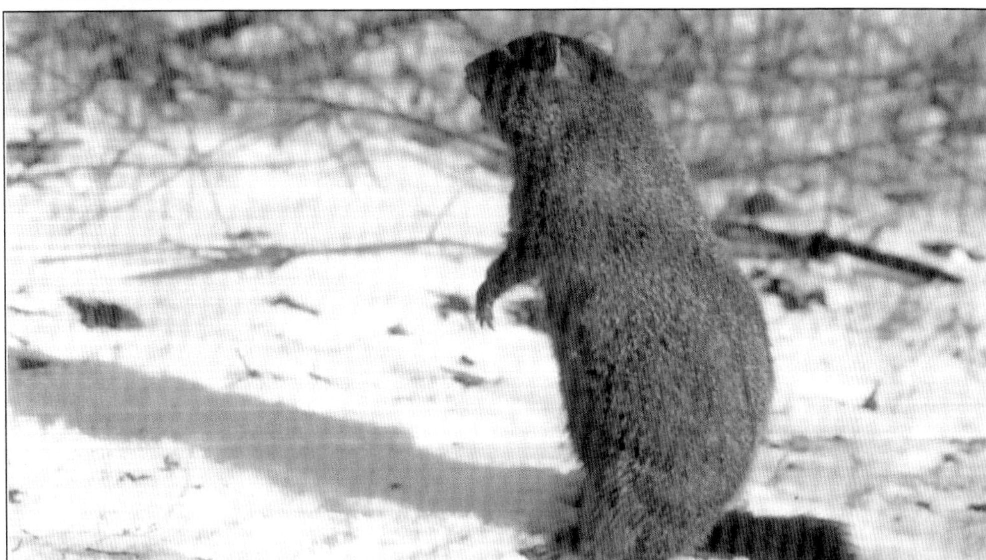

Were you looking for me? I am usually at home in my Groundhog Zoo at the Punxsutawney Library. Sometimes I'm out visiting, entertaining, or socializing. I make appearances at schools and nursing homes. I ride in cars, on fire trucks, and in airplanes. In 1995, I flew to Chicago and appeared on the Oprah Winfrey talk show. I really enjoy riding in my new Philmobile, where I have been given a place of honor with all my Inner Circle buddies. I always welcome visitors. Come see me any time.

Best Regards,
Phil